Bridging Relational and NoSQL Databases

Drazena Gaspar
University of Mostar, Bosnia and Herzegovina

Ivica Coric
Hera Software Company, Bosnia and Herzegovina

A volume in the Advances in Data
Mining and Database Management
(ADMDM) Book Series

Published in the United States of America by
IGI Global
Information Science Reference (an imprint of IGI Global)
701 E. Chocolate Avenue
Hershey PA, USA 17033
Tel: 717-533-8845
Fax: 717-533-8661
E-mail: cust@igi-global.com
Web site: http://www.igi-global.com

Library of Congress Cataloging-in-Publication Data

Names: Gaspar, Drazena, 1960- author. | Coric, Ivica, 1968- author.
Title: Bridging relational and NoSQL databases / by Drazena Gaspar and Ivica
   Coric.
Description: Hershey, PA : Information Science Reference, 2017. | Includes
   bibliographical references and index.
Identifiers: LCCN 2017016124| ISBN 9781522533856 (hardcover) | ISBN
   9781522533863 (ebook)
Subjects: LCSH: File conversion (Computer science) | Non-relational
   databases. | Relational databases.
Classification: LCC QA76.9.F48 G37 2017 | DDC 005.7/2--dc23 LC record available at https://
lccn.loc.gov/2017016124

This book is published in the IGI Global book series Advances in Data Mining and Database
Management (ADMDM) (ISSN: 2327-1981; eISSN: 2327-199X)

British Cataloguing in Publication Data
A Cataloguing in Publication record for this book is available from the British Library.

All work contributed to this book is new, previously-unpublished material.
The views expressed in this book are those of the authors, but not necessarily of the publisher.

For electronic access to this publication, please contact: eresources@igi-global.com.

Advances in Data Mining and Database Management (ADMDM) Book Series

ISSN:2327-1981
EISSN:2327-199X

Editor-in-Chief: David Taniar, Monash University, Australia

MISSION

With the large amounts of information available to organizations in today's digital world, there is a need for continual research surrounding emerging methods and tools for collecting, analyzing, and storing data.

The **Advances in Data Mining & Database Management (ADMDM)** series aims to bring together research in information retrieval, data analysis, data warehousing, and related areas in order to become an ideal resource for those working and studying in these fields. IT professionals, software engineers, academicians and upper-level students will find titles within the ADMDM book series particularly useful for staying up-to-date on emerging research, theories, and applications in the fields of data mining and database management.

COVERAGE

- Educational Data Mining
- Factor Analysis
- Heterogeneous and Distributed Databases
- Web mining
- Information Extraction
- Data Mining
- Text mining
- Decision Support Systems
- Cluster Analysis
- Data quality

IGI Global is currently accepting manuscripts for publication within this series. To submit a proposal for a volume in this series, please contact our Acquisition Editors at Acquisitions@igi-global.com or visit: http://www.igi-global.com/publish/.

Titles in this Series

For a list of additional titles in this series, please visit:
https://www.igi-global.com/book-series/advances-data-mining-database-management/37146

Deep Learning Innovations and Their Convergence Wit Big Data
S. Karthik (SNS College of Technology, Anna University, India) Anand Paul (Kyungpook National University, South Korea) and N. Karthikeyan (Mizan-Tepi University, Ethiopia)
Information Science Reference • ©2018 • 265pp • H/C (ISBN: 9781522530152) • US $205.00

Modern Technologies for Big Data Classification and lustering
Hari Seetha (Vellore Institute of Technology-Andhra Pradesh, India) M. Narasimha Murty (Indian Institute of Science, India) and B. K. Tripathy (VIT University, India)
Information Science Reference • ©2018 • 360pp • H/C (ISBN: 9781522528050) • US $215.00

Data Visualization and Statistical Literacy for Open and Big Data
Theodosia Prodromou (University of New England, Australia)
Information Science Reference • ©2017 • 365pp • H/C (ISBN: 9781522525127) • US $205.00

Web Semantics for Textual and Visual Information Retrieval
Aarti Singh (Guru Nanak Girls College, Yamuna Nagar, India) Nilanjan Dey (Techno India College of Technology, India) Amira S. Ashour (Tanta University, Egypt & Taif University, Saudi Arabia) and V. Santhi (VIT University, India)
Information Science Reference • ©2017 • 290pp • H/C (ISBN: 9781522524830) • US $185.00

Advancing Cloud Database Systems and Capacity Planning With Dynamic Applications
Narendra Kumar Kamila (C.V. Raman College of Engineering, India)
Information Science Reference • ©2017 • 430pp • H/C (ISBN: 9781522520139) • US $210.00

Web Data Mining and the Development of Knowledge-Based Decision Support Systems
G. Sreedhar (Rashtriya Sanskrit Vidyapeetha (Deemed University), India)
Information Science Reference • ©2017 • 409pp • H/C (ISBN: 9781522518778) • US $165.00

For an enitre list of titles in this series, please visit:
https://www.igi-global.com/book-series/advances-data-mining-database-management/37146

701 East Chocolate Avenue, Hershey, PA 17033, USA
Tel: 717-533-8845 x100 • Fax: 717-533-8661
E-Mail: cust@igi-global.com • www.igi-global.com

Table of Contents

Chapter 8

Preface

Relational databases have been the predominant database model for the last forty years. Since 1970, when E.F. Codd, from the IBM Research Laboratory, published his famous paper "A Relational Model for Large Shared Data" (Codd, 1970), the world of databases changed significantly. Codd established the theoretical ground of relational databases that ensured the independence of data presentation (data model) with regard to physical data storage implementation. Relational databases share a common architecture, based on three pillars: relational model, ACID (atomicity, consistency, isolation, durability) transactions, and SQL (structured query language).

The relational databases experienced the first shake in the mid-1990s when object-oriented programming became the dominant programming paradigm. As opposed to traditional procedural programming languages, which separate data and application logic, object-oriented programming combines attributes and behaviors into a single object, meaning that all the details necessary to a logical unit of work are stored within the one class or directly linked to that class. At the beginning, the change of programming paradigm was not followed by the changes in relational databases. As a result, it was not strange that object-oriented developers were frustrated by what they saw as an impedance mismatch between the object-oriented representations of their data within their programs and the relational representation within the database (Harrison, 2015). However, relational databases found a way, through constant innovations and implementation of object-oriented features, to respond to object-oriented requests. Mainstream database vendors, including Oracle and Informix, had successfully implemented many object-oriented database system (OODBMS) features, but even these features were rarely used (Harrison, 2015). Very soon, the development of object-relational mapping (ORM) frameworks, which automated the most tedious aspects of the object-relational mapping, were quiet opponents of relational databases.

Relational databases remained unchallenged until the latter half of the 2000s and no significant new databases were introduced. The development of Web 2.0 applications, social networks, Big Data, cloud computing, and Internet of Things caused the second big shake of relational databases. Big Data players, such as Google, Amazon, Facebook, and Twitter, were first faced with the limitations of relational databases in solving their requests, and they have become pioneers in developing and implementing different NoSQL databases.

NoSQL databases emerged as an answer to challenges related to a huge quantity, velocity, and variety of data that have to be managed, searched, and stored by modern database systems. The first use of the term NoSQL in the present sense of the word was registered in 2009 as the name of a meetup which was organized by Johan Oskarsson. Oskarsson was inspired by the Hadoop summit in San Francisco. Although the term NoSQL has become generally accepted, no universally-adopted definition exists for it. Some IT experts believe that the term is misleading because it suggests that NoSQL databases do not use SQL at all, which, in the case of some NoSQL databases, does not correspond to facts (for example Cassandra's CQL). Most agree that "no" stands for "not only." They believe that it emphasizes that NoSQL databases aim to overcome the technical limitations of relational databases, rather than abandon SQL.

First, NoSQL databases were promoted as databases developed for coders, with one of the primary goals to avoid the eternal impedance mismatch between object-oriented approach to programming and relational databases. This is why SQL was avoided and the focus was on the development of specific APIs and programming languages. However, such an approach soon turned out to be a limiting factor of wider implementation of NoSQL databases because it lacked the critical mass of well-trained developers, while a plethora of different APIs and programming languages was not beneficial for their faster training.

However, NoSQL is an umbrella term related to numerous databases. Each NoSQL database has different architecture and purpose. NoSQL supporters believe that a universal solution which could be applicable to all data types, volumes, and objectives does not exist. Accordingly, NoSQL database can be classified into four basic categories, each resolving a different type of big data problems:

- Key-Value.
- Column-Family (BigTable).
- Document.

- Graph.

The key-value type of NoSQL databases uses a key to locate a value (e.g., traditional data, BLOBs – Binary Large OBjects, files) in simple, standalone tables, known as hash tables. In this case, searches are performing against keys, not values, and they are restricted to exact matches.

Column-family (Bigtable) or column-oriented NoSQL databases have been named for their design with data stored in columns. In contrast, a row-oriented database (such as RDBMS) keeps information about a row together.

Document NoSQL stores have been designed to store and manage documents. The documents are encoded in standard data exchange formats, including XML, JSON (JavaScript Object Notation), and BSON (Binary JSON).

Graph NoSQL databases excel at dealing with highly interconnected data. They focus on relationships, rather than data. A graph store consists of nodes and relationships between nodes. Both nodes and relationships have properties (or key-value pairs) to store data.

After 10 years of development and use of NoSQL databases, it is clear that neither everything was good in NoSQL nor everything was so bad in relational databases. Practice shows that transaction-oriented requirements can be better solved using relational databases, while NoSQL databases are better suited to specific Big Data demands. However, these problems are not always clearly separated, and in everyday life they are often intertwined. Database users are generally not concerned with details about how data is stored: they want to have the possibility to view and analyze data together, regardless of whether the data is stored in relational or NoSQL databases. Therefore, vendors of relational databases have been forced, partly for the sake of solving customers' requirements, partly for the sake of keeping market share, to look for solutions within relational databases that would allow them to work with data stored in NoSQL databases as well.

All these changes on the both sides, relational and NoSQL, have been leading to the process of convergence between these two groups of databases. Today, this process is in full swing. Their convergence is the most visible among the approaches to consistency, schema development, and database language (SQL). The result of this process can lead to the development of the next database generations, with configurability as a main feature. Although relational databases are still committed to strict consistency, even for distributed transactions, there are signs of changes, because some vendors offer the possibility to run transactions under various conditions, including

ACID (IBM's CICS [Customer Information Control System]). The changes are visible on the sides of NoSQL databases that primarily offer eventual consistency. Today, most of them also offer strict consistency, at least at the level of the single-object transaction. Some of NoSQL databases, such as MongoDB and Cassandra, offer a tunable consistency model that allows the administrator or developer to choose the level of consistency based on the application requirements. This approach merits full attention, especially from the perspective of relational database vendors.

The schemaless approach proved to be one of the main weaknesses of NoSQL databases in the context of support for business intelligence (BI) applications. Users' requirements related to data analysis through BI tools showed that the need for a comprehensible and unambiguous data model that can be used for BI is even more important in the world of Big Data than it was in the relational era (Harrison, 2015, p. 197). It is not strange that data modeling in NoSQL world has attracted more and more advocates every day. Some of them have proposed new modeling notations for presenting everything from the real-world objects and concepts to a functional database running by either a NoSQL or a SQL database. Both relational and NoSQL databases offer support for JSON, meaning that hybrid solutions, in the context of the schema, are already at the stage.

Most of NoSQL vendors have recognized the necessity to provide support for SQL, in order to attract more experienced developers and users, to enhance usability and programmer efficiency, and to provide easier integration with BI and analytical tools. Some of the SQL-like languages which are used in NoSQL databases are HQL (Hive Query Language), CQL (Cassandra Query Language), N1QL(non-first normal form query language), and Cypher.

The future development of relational and NoSQL databases will show if the process of convergence will shape the main features of next database generation.

THE CHALLENGES

The challenges related to Big Data support have been the main driving force behind NoSQL database development. The spectrum of big data problems is broad and diverse. It is related to extensive requests for the storage and management of complex, dynamic, evolving, distributed, and heterogeneous data from different sources and platforms. In resolving Big Data issues, organizations are faced with challenges, including:

- Rapid data growth.
- Numerous and diverse data sources.
- Data heterogeneity.
- Data incompleteness.
- Diverse and immature technology solutions.
- Shortage of big data experts.
- Data availability.
- Data quality.
- Data security.
- Legal issues.
- Readiness to change.

From the very beginning, NoSQL databases promoted themselves as efficient in resolving Big Data challenges. However, the development of NoSQL databases has shown that they really resolve some open issues, especially those related to data distribution and Big Data. Unfortunately, NoSQL databases have generated new problems, this time related to their features. Data modeling is one of the big challenges. NoSQL databases are recognized as schemaless, that is they enable developers to start storing data right away, without losing time on schema creation. However, the time savings at the beginning of the project are usually the cause of many problems later, both in the data storage itself and in the efficiency of their maintenance and query performance. This is usually manifested when handling large amounts of data, which requires data reorganization to speed up the access and update times and find the appropriate balance between consistency, availability, and access speed. However, if the amount of data is large, their reorganization can be expensive, both in terms of time and the space necessary for temporary storage, all of which can cause reduced availability of data for users. If the database is implemented without previously creating a model (schemaless), the only way to understand the data after the implementation is to speak with the developer or to analyze the code. The user's dependence on developers to understand the code significantly reduces his/her possibility of proposing changes and expansions of data and may create additional pressure on developers.

The integration of relational and NoSQL databases is one of the possible ways of bridging them. This approach is also generating specific challenges, including the following:

- Increased responsibility of developers in the optimization of database processes, which means that additional programming and time are necessary for completing this task.
- Difficulties in finding developers with good knowledge of NoSQL databases, while finding developers with knowledge about both worlds, relational and NoSQL, is still equal to a jackpot.
- Finding an appropriate driver or tool for a particular problem is a time-consuming and exhaustive process because the market is full of many different drivers and tools offered by third vendors.

As a result, big database vendors (Oracle, Microsoft, and IBM) are oriented toward NoSQL databases, with the main aim of offering the best from both worlds in one database management system to their users.

SEARCHING FOR A SOLUTION

The very first motif behind the development of NoSQL databases is to find solutions for the abovementioned Big Data challenges. The solutions have been searched in innovative NoSQL features, including a distributed storage architecture that comprises: distributed, cluster-oriented, and horizontally scalable features; a consistency model that refers to CAP (consistency, availability, partitioning) and BASE (basically available, soft-state, eventually consistent) features; a query execution that refers to the schemaless feature.

Data distribution and use of clusters are natural features of NoSQL databases. The ability of NoSQL databases to run on a large cluster is the feature that has drawn attention to this type of databases.

One of the pillars of relational databases is the ACID transaction approach. The implementation of ACID transaction properties ensures efficient concurrency control and recovery process in case of limited scale-up and shared-something environments, which are natural environments for relational databases. Nevertheless, with the emergence of the Big Data phenomenon and the urgent need for storing an enormous quantity of data across multiple database servers, the ACID approach has become a serious limitation. The result has been the development of the BASE approach, which has become popular, especially with the development of NoSQL databases. These databases, which are distributed naturally, have been designed to avoid the restrictions of strict ACID consistency and to be promoted as databases that do not support the ACID transaction approach. This often leads to the misconception that NoSQL databases provide only a weak or, at best, eventual consistency, and that their consistency implementation mechanisms are very simple. However, NoSQL databases offer different consistency guarantees, including strict consistency, even if only at the level of an individual object. Also, owing to their departure from strict and predictable rules of ACID models, most NoSQL databases have developed complex mechanisms for establishing acceptable levels of consistency.

The increasing number of NoSQL database applications has brought about a growing awareness of the need for data modeling in these systems, too. Hence, efforts are made to find a solution that will enable modeling both relational and NoSQL databases. Wang (2016) proposes the use of unified data modeling (UML) techniques that support features like the document schema of NoSQL databases, reverse engineering of data from an existing database, and visual refactoring of existing databases.

Also, Hills (2016) proceeds from the idea that a single model can be used for both relational and NoSQL databases at the logical level, whereas on the physical side multiple models can be considered. This is why Hills's (2016) concept and object modeling notation (COMN) was designed to enable data modeling in both relational and NoSQL databases. The basic idea of COMN notation is to integrate real objects, data, and implementation to allow all operations and functions, from user requests to logical models, to functional databases, to be represented in a single model, regardless of whether it is executed in a relational or NoSQL database management system.

The integration of relational and NoSQL databases is one of the possible solutions of bridging them. Three approaches to integration are discussed: native, hybrid, and reduction to one solution, either relational or NoSQL.

A native solution involves the use of standard drivers and ways in which the business layer communicates with a particular database. Since a part of the data is in NoSQL and the other part in the relational database, it is necessary to collate data. This is implemented in the business layer. When data is extracted from a database, they are linked and converted into a format which is suitable for use in the user layer. When data is stored in a database, the business layer is programmed to prepare data for storage and pass them on to the particular database.

A hybrid solution introduces an additional layer, which provides SQL communication between the business layer and the data layer. Developers continue to use familiar SQL programming patterns in the business layer, and employ a new layer to translate these patterns into the NoSQL programming interface for communication with the NoSQL database.

Reducing to one option, either relational or NoSQL, refers to vendors' efforts in adding the functionalities of the "counterpart" option, to convince the developer community that their solution is sufficient.

The development of databases showed that NoSQL was moved away from relational databases because of the structural relational constraints it imposed, especially related to the ACID transactions which became a serious limitation to scaling and dealing with large data sets. Although the umbrella name for the new generation of databases is NoSQL, their recent development is showing that they are not necessarily opposed to SQL, i.e. that NoSQL means not just SQL. Today, a generally accepted view is that the aim of NoSQL databases is not to abandon SQL, but to find solutions to overcome the technical limitations of relational databases, especially when it comes to working with Big Data. One of the reasons for the shift to SQL probably lies in the fact that, when it comes to data manipulation and search, the requirements of NoSQL databases are almost identical to those of relational databases. Namely, both the databases must allow entering, updating, deleting, and searching data, except that all this has already been solved long ago in SQL, the query language that has been associated mainly with relational databases until now. After the initial enthusiasm regarding various NoSQL programming languages and APIs, SQL turned out to have important advantages. It is a language with a high-level abstraction that simplifies access and manipulation of data. Besides, it is a language in which literally millions of database users are conversant, and hundreds of popular BI and analytic tools use it under the hood as the means for getting at data (Harrison, 2015).

While vendors of NoSQL databases are oriented toward SQL, the vendors of relational databases, at least the leading three (i.e., Oracle, Microsoft, and IBM) are working on extending their databases in order to include NoSQL capabilities. They realized that NoSQL databases bring some innovative and good solutions to the problems they had been facing for years (e.g., Big Data, data distribution, and high availability). The three largest DBMS vendors have innovated and expanded their relational databases and, thus, they brought them closer to NoSQL databases. These expansions primarily involve manipulating unstructured data (e.g., JSON documents), providing sharding, improved possibilities of SQL, and high availability.

Database vendors, at least the biggest ones, are fully aware of their responsibilities, not just in ensuring storage of vast amounts of quality data, but also in providing solid data foundation, which is crucial for the development and successful implementation of many other technologies (e.g., IoT [Internet of Things], AI [Artificial Intelligence], predictive analytics, cloud, DBaaS [Database as a Service], and blockchain).

Database evolution could take place by bridging the gap between relational and NoSQL databases. Indeed, this would meet different and often opposite users' requirements, by enabling combinations of both approach and tunable and configurable capabilities.

ORGANIZATION OF THE BOOK

The book is organized into eight chapters and divided into two main sections:

- **Section 1:** The Birth of NoSQL Databases
- **Section 2:** Bringing Together Relational and NoSQL Databases

The first section of the book describes the reasons behind the appearance of NoSQL databases, their main characteristics, and their classification.

Chapter 1 is an introductory chapter that gives an overview of the three main stages of database development: Hierarchical and network database models, relational database model, and NoSQL databases. It gives an overview of the pillars of relational databases: Relational data model, ACID transaction, and SQL language. Also, the concepts that make the base for NoSQL database development are explained, including the CAP theorem, the BASE approach, and the sharding phenomenon. At last, the limitations of relational databases which led to the development of NoSQL databases are discussed.

Chapter 2 sustains that NoSQL databases emerged as an attempt for resolving the limitations of relational databases in coping with Big Data. The issue of Big Data is related to extensive requests for the storage and management of complex, dynamic, evolving, distributed, and heterogeneous data from different sources and platforms. The chapter provides an overview of the technologies, including Google File System (GFS), MapReduce, Hadoop, and Hadoop Distributed File System (HDFS), which were the first responses to Big Data challenges and main driving forces for the development of NoSQL databases. Also, the chapter asserts that NoSQL is an umbrella term related to numerous databases with different architectures and purposes, which can be classified in four basic categories: Key-value, column-family, document, and graph stores. This chapter discusses the general features of NoSQL databases, as well as the specific features of each of the four basic categories of NoSQL databases.

Chapter 3 discusses the necessity for data modeling in NoSQL world. Namely, relational databases are generally based on the entity-relationship (ER) logical model, opposite to NoSQL databases. Indeed, one of the main features of NoSQL databases is that they are schema-free, that is they allow data manipulation without the need for the previous modeling or developing an ER or similar model. Although the absence of a schema can be an advantage in some situations, with the increase in the number of NoSQL database implementations, it appears that the absence of a conceptual model can be a source of certain problems. This is why this chapter emphasizes the need for data modeling with NoSQL databases as well. In order to better understand the need for data modeling in NoSQL databases, first the basic structure of an ER model and an analysis of its limitations are summarized, especially in terms of application in NoSQL databases. Hill's COMN model is then presented as one of the possible solutions for data modeling in NoSQL databases. The COMN model is designed to allow to present the real world, or its objects and concepts—data about the real world—but also objects in a computer's memory, or to present everything from the naming of requirements to a functional database running by either a NoSQL or a SQL database management system.

Chapter 4 explains how NoSQL databases work. Since different NoSQL databases are classified into four categories (key-value, column-family, document, and graph stores), three main features of NoSQL databases are chosen, and their practical implementation is explained using examples of one or two typical NoSQL databases from each NoSQL database category. The three chosen features are: Distributed storage architecture that comprises the distributed, cluster-oriented, and horizontally scalable features; consistency model that refers to the CAP and BASE features; query execution that refers to the schemaless feature. These features are chosen because, through them, it is possible to describe most of the new and innovative approaches that NoSQL databases bring to the database world.

The second section of the book shows the necessity and possible ways of integration the two, at the beginning very opposite worlds: Relational and NoSQL databases. Also, the convergence processes from relational to NoSQL and from NoSQL to relational databases are analyzed, as well as the features of next database generation.

Chapter 5 discusses the fact that the development and use of NoSQL databases showed that neither everything was good in NoSQL nor everything was so bad in relational databases. Namely, when operating with data, NoSQL databases have identical requirements for entering, updating, deleting or searching data, or for the data manipulation that SQL already resolved long ago. Therefore, it is not surprising that further development of many NoSQL databases shifted towards supporting SQL, which is one of the topics of this chapter. First, NoSQL databases were promoted as databases which were developed for coders. One of their primary goals was to avoid the eternal impedance mismatch between the object-oriented approach to programming and relational databases which lead to SQL avoidance and the focus on the development of specific APIs and programming languages. However, such an approach soon turned out to be a limiting factor of wider implementation of NoSQL databases, because it lacked the critical mass of well-trained developers. On the other hand, database users are generally not concerned with details about how data is stored. Rather, they want to have the possibility to view and analyze data together, regardless of whether the data is stored in relational or NoSQL databases. Therefore, producers of relational databases were forced, partly for the sake of solving customers' requirements and partly for the sake of keeping market share, to look for solutions within relational databases that would allow them to work with data stored in NoSQL databases as well. This chapter describes how this was accomplished by three largest database producers: Oracle, Microsoft, and IBM.

Chapter 6 proposes three ways of integration of the two different worlds of relational and NoSQL databases: Native, hybrid, and reducing to one option, either relational or NoSQL. The native solution includes using vendors' standard APIs and integration on the business layer. In a relational environment, APIs are based on SQL standards, while the NoSQL world has its own, unstandardized solutions. The native solution for integrating these two environments is to use the APIs of the individual systems that need to be connected, leaving to the business-layer coding the task of linking and separating data in extraction and storage operations. A hybrid solution introduces an additional layer that provides SQL communication between the business layer and the data layer. Developers continue to use familiar SQL programming patterns in the business layer, and employ a new layer to translate these patterns into the NoSQL programming interface for communication with the NoSQL database. The third integration solution includes vendors' effort to foresee functionalities of "opposite" side, thus convincing developers' community that their solution is sufficient.

Chapter 7 presents a real case study of the integration of relational and NoSQL databases. The example of a real project related to vehicle registration, particularly to testing vehicles for compliance with environmental standards, explains how this two worlds can be integrated. Oracle database is used as a relational database, while MongoDB is used as NoSQL database. The chapter sustains that the COMN notation can be successfully used in the process of modeling both relational and nonrelational data. All three ways of integration of relational and NoSQL databases, which are explained in chapter 6, are tested. The native solution was tested by using of native drivers for communication with Oracle and MongoDB databases. The hybrid solution (i.e., development of an additional level of communication between the business and the data layer) used a Unity product. The reducing-to-one option, in this case SQL, was tested on Oracle database. The capabilities of Oracle 12c database to work both with relational and nonrelational data by using SQL were tested.

Chapter 8 concludes the story about bridging relational and NoSQL worlds. It presents how relational databases answer to typical NoSQL features, and, vice versa, how NoSQL databases answer to typical relational features. Open issues related to the integration of relational and NoSQL databases, as well as next database generation features are discussed. The big relational database vendors (Oracle, Microsoft, and IBM) have continuously worked to incorporate NoSQL features into their databases, as well as NoSQL vendors are trying to make their products more like relational databases. The convergence of these two groups of databases has been a driving force in the evolution of database market, in establishing a new level of focus to resolving big data requirements, and in enabling users to fully use data potential, wherever data is stored, in relational or NoSQL databases. In turn, the database of choice in the future will likely be one that provides the best of both worlds: a flexible data model, high availability, and enterprise reliability.

REFERENCES

Codd, E. F. (1970). A relational model of data for large shared data banks. *Communications of the ACM, 13*(6), 377–387. doi:10.1145/362384.362685

Harrison, G. (2015). *Next generation databases: NoSQL, NewSQL, and big data*. Apress. doi:10.1007/978-1-4842-1329-2

Hills, T. (2016). *NoSQLand SQL data modeling – Bringing together data, semantics, and software* (1st ed.). Technics Publications.

Wang, A. (2016). *Unified data modeling for relational and NoSQL databases*. Retrieved January 16, 2017 from https://www.infoq.com/articles/unified-data-modeling-for-relational-and-nosql-databases

Section 1
The Birth of NoSQL Databases

Chapter 1
The End of Relational Databases Domination

ABSTRACT

The chapter gives an overview of the three main stages of database development: hierarchical and network database models, relational database model, and NoSQL databases. It gives a short overview of the pillars of relational databases: relational data model, ACID (atomicity, consistency, isolation, and durability) properties of a transaction, and SQL (structured query language). Also, the concepts that make the base for NoSQL database development are explained, including the CAP (Consistency, Availability, Partitioning) theorem, the BASE (Basically Available, Soft-state, Eventually consistent) approach, and the sharding phenomenon. At last, the limitations of relational databases which led to the development of NoSQL databases are discussed.

INTRODUCTION

Relational databases have been the predominant database model for the last forty years. Since 1970, when E.F. Codd from the IBM Research Laboratory published his famous paper *A relational model for large shared data* (Codd, 1970) the world of databases changed significantly. Codd established the theoretical ground of relational databases that ensured the independence of data presentation (data model) with regard to physical data storage implementation. Relational databases share a common architecture based on three pillars: relational model, ACID (atomicity, consistency, isolation,

DOI: 10.4018/978-1-5225-3385-6.ch001

durability) transactions, and SQL (structured query language) language. Relational databases even found a way, through constant innovations and implementation of object-oriented features, to respond to object-oriented requests, but the era of massive Web-scale applications created completely different pressures on the relational database, which could not be easily resolved through incremental innovation.

In order to support readers in more easily understanding further chapters and the book as a whole, this chapter gives an overview of the three main stages in database development. In short, this chapter explains the pillars of relational databases, CAP (consistency, availability, partitioning) theorem, BASE (basically available, soft-state, eventually consistent) approach, and limitations of relational databases which led to the development of NoSQL databases.

THREE STAGES IN DATABASE DEVELOPMENT

The very first attempt of the manual filing system digitalization was related to the file-based approach (Figure 1). The file-based approach translated manual file organization (labeled files stored in cabinets) into digital files (Figure 1). However, this approach had two main drawbacks:

- Data definition was inseparable from application programs.
- Data could be accessed and manipulated only through application programs.

The consequences were:

- Any change of file structure forced modifications in all the programs that used that file and resulted with additional programming time and effort.
- Difficulties in combining data from multiple sources caused a high level of redundancy in the file based approach, so the same data was stored in different location (poor data security and consistency).
- Files which were created using one programming language could not be accessed by any other programming language.

It became obvious that inseparability of data and application programs caused huge maintenance problems in file-based systems. Thus, a new

Figure 1. File-based vs. database approach

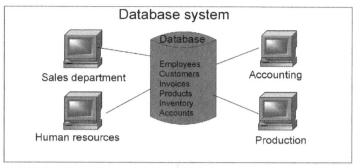

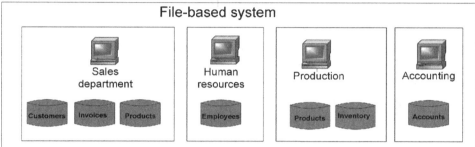

database approach was based on the separation of data from the application programs. The result was the possibility of data abstraction (e.g., the possibility to present a logical view of data without knowing its physical structure). This means that, if data structures are changed, through adding new elements or modifying existing components, the application programs that do not directly work with changed data stay unaffected. Since databases enabled the organization and integration of data independently of application programs, they allowed different applications and programming languages to work with the same data.

A database can be defined as a shared, integrated computer structure that stores a collection of data and metadata of interest to the end user, through which the user data is integrated and managed (Coronel, Morris & Rob, 2011).

Database development can be analyzed through three main stages:

Stage One: Hierarchical and network database models (1968–1971).
Stage Two: Relational database model started in 1970 with Edgar Codd's paper (Codd, 1970).

Stage Three: NoSQL databases started in 2005 with Hadoop's project (Harrison, 2015).

Hierarchical and Network Database Models

Historically, hierarchical databases were the first databases which had been ever developed. IBM IMS (information system management) database was the first hierarchical database. Nevertheless, some authors (Connolly & Begg, 2005) think that the roots of database development were inseparable from the USA Apollo Moon-Landing Project, in the 1960s. Since this project generated a huge amount of data, it was necessary that the system could handle and manage those data. As a result, the North American Aviation (NAA), as project contractor, developed the GUAM (generalized update access method) system. The idea behind GUAM was that smaller components should be kept together as a part of larger ones, and the whole could be presented as a tree structure, also known as a hierarchical structure. A few years later, in the mid-1960s, IBM joined NAA in the further development of GUAM and finally transformed it into the well-known IMS database. The main reason why IBM was stuck to the hierarchical structure was the necessity to use serial storage devices, such as magnetic tapes, which were prevailing storage devices in that time.

At the same time, in the mid-1960s, Charles Bachmann, from General Electrics, started with the development of IDS (integrated data store), the first network database. Network databases were developed as an answer to the limitation of hierarchical databases in representing more complex data relationships than hierarchical structures. The process of database standardization started with the development of network databases. For this purpose, the Conference on Data Systems Languages (CODASYL), comprising representatives of the US government and the business, formed a List Processing Task Force in 1965. In 1967 it was renamed into the Data Base Task Group (DBTG). Although the report was not formally adopted by the American National Standards Institute (ANSI), a number of systems were subsequently developed following the DBTG proposal. These systems are now known as CODASYL or DBTG systems (Connolly & Begg, 2005).

Both hierarchical and network databases were based on a schema, which represented a definition of the data structure, and an access path, which represented navigation from one record to another. Figure 2 provides a graphical presentation of these data structures. These early databases are "navigational"

Figure 2. Hierarchical and network models
Harrison, 2015.

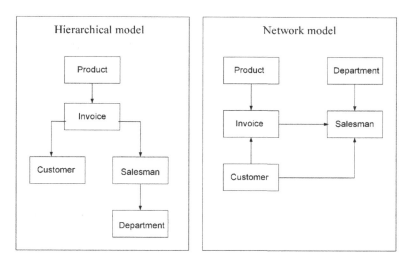

by their nature because they used pointers or links for navigation from one object to another. Hierarchical and network database systems dominated during the era of mainframe computing up until the late 1970s.

The main limitations of hierarchical and network databases are:

- All queries are performed on predefined and precisely specified paths.
- All relations between objects must be precisely defined in advance.
- Optimization is performed manually–the programmer optimizes the code and defines the method to be used in communication between the application and the database.
- Network and hierarchical databases are not grounded in formal theory.
- Existing databases were too hard to use. Databases could only be accessed by people with specialized programming skills. Existing databases lacked a theoretical foundation.
- Existing databases used arbitrary representations that did not ensure logical consistency or provide the ability to deal with missing information (Harrison, 2015).
- Existing databases mixed logical and physical implementations. The representation of data in existing databases matched the format of the physical storage in the database, rather than a logical representation of the data that could be comprehended by a nontechnical user (Harrison, 2015).

5

Relational Database Model

The development of relational databases was initiated by the limitations of hierarchical and network databases which arose in their practical use (see "Hierarchical and Network Database Models"). The creator of relational databases, E.F. Codd, was, as a mathematician, fully aware of the lack of theoretical foundation in those databases. Codd (1970) presented the core ideas and defined the formal data structure and logical operators that made the relational database model. The structure of the relational model is made of two-dimensional tables, called relations, a row of a table is called tuple, a column header is an attribute, while a domain is a set of possible values that can appear in each column (Elmasri & Navathe, 2011).

However, the first response to the relational ideas was far away from ecstatic. Database vendors had high reservations to relational databases, especially related to their performance because they propagated that data representation should be directly linked with physical access mechanisms. Despite high disbelief, in 1974 IBM launched the development of System R, the first prototype of a relational database. System R denied existing doubts and showed that relational databases are capable to ensure satisfying performances. Almost at the same time, Stonebraker at Berkeley started to work on a database system that was later called INGRES (Harrison, 2015). In 1977 Larry Ellison, together with Bob Miner and Ed Oates, founded the company Software Development Laboratories, which changed the name to Oracle Systems in 1982. In 1979, Oracle Version 2, the first commercial SQL relational database management system, was released (Oracle, 2007).

In the 1980s, the domination of relational databases began, and in the succeeding decades many new databases emerged on the market (e.g., Sybase, Informix, DB2, Microsoft SQL Server).

In order to more easily distinguish relational databases from other database management systems, in 1985 Codd defined the rules that a database system must obey to be considered as "fully relational" (Codd, 1985a; Codd, 1985b). He defined the following twelve rules, along with a fundamental, overarching rule that he called Rule Zero (Codd, 1985a, Codd, 1985b):

- **Rule Zero:** A relational database management system must manage its stored data using only its relational capabilities. This is the fundamental principle upon which the remaining 12 rules are based.

- **Rule 1-Information Representation:** All information must be represented, at the logical level, only as values in tables.
- **Rule 2-Guaranteed Access:** It must be possible to access any data item in the database by giving its table name, column name, and primary key value.
- **Rule 3-Representation of Null Values:** The system must be able to represent null values in a systematic way, regardless of the data type of the item. Null values must be distinct from zero or any other number, and from empty strings.
- **Rule 4-Relational Catalog:** The system catalog which contains the logical description of the database must be represented the same way as ordinary data.
- **Rule 5-Comprehensive Data Sublanguage:** Regardless of the number of other languages it supports, the database must include one language that allows statements expressed as character strings to support data definition, the definition of views, data manipulation, integrity rules, user authorization, and a method of identifying units for recovery.
- **Rule 6-Updating Views:** Any view that is theoretically updatable can actually be updated by the system.
- **Rule 7-Insert, Delete and Update Operations:** Any relation that can be handled as a single operand for retrieval can also be handled that way for insertion, deletion, and update operations.
- **Rule 8-Physical Data Independence:** The application programs are immune to changes made to storage representations or access methods.
- **Rule 9-Logical Data Independence:** Changes made to the logical level, such as splitting tables or combining tables that do not affect the information content at the logical level, do not require modification of applications.
- **Rule 10-Integrity Rules:** Integrity constraints, such as entity integrity and referential integrity, must be specifiable in the data sublanguage and stored in the catalog. Application program statements should not be used to express these constraints.
- **Rule 11-Distribution Independence:** The data sublanguage should be such that, if the database is distributed, the applications programs and users' commands need not be changed.
- **Rule 12-Nonsubversion:** If the system allows a language that supports record-at-a-time access, any program using this type of access cannot bypass the integrity constraints expressed in the higher-level language.

These rules represent the relational ideal and became guidelines for relational database management system development, but it is hard to expect that any commercial relational database can completely fulfill all 12 rules. From today's perspective, it is clear that the relational databases are grounded on three pillars: Codd's relational model, ACID transactions, and SQL language.

NoSQL Database Model

NoSQL databases emerged as an answer to challenges related to a huge quantity, velocity, and variety of data that have to be managed, searched, and stored by modern database systems. Different concepts and technologies form a foundation for NoSQL database appearance and further development (Harrison, 2015):

- **Google File System (GFS):** A distributed cluster file system that allows all of the disks within the Google data center to be accessed as one massive, distributed, and redundant file system.
- **MapReduce:** A distributed processing framework for parallelizing algorithms across large numbers of potentially unreliable servers and being capable of dealing with massive datasets.
- **BigTable:** A nonrelational database system that uses the Google File System for storage.
- **Sharding:** Partitioning the data across multiple databases based on a key attribute, such as the customer identifier. The operational costs of sharding, together with the loss of relational features, made many seek alternatives to the relational database management system (RDBMS).
- **AJAX (Asynchronous JavaScript and XML):** Programming style that offers far more interactivity to Web sites through direct browser communication with a backend by transferring XML messages. XML was soon superseded by JavaScript Object Notation (JSON), which is a self-describing format similar to XML, but it is more compact and tightly integrated into the JavaScript language. JSON became the de facto format for storing and serializing objects to disk.

Additionally, the environment in which NoSQL databases have arisen and developed is characterized by cloud deployment, mobile applications, social networking, and the Internet of Things. The developers of NoSQL databases have understood from the very beginning that in this new, distributed environment integrity and consistency of data based on ACID transactions represent a big problem.

In the short period (2008–2009), dozens of new database systems emerged. Many of these disappeared as soon as they appeared, but today some of them, such as MongoDB, Cassandra, and HBase, have a place at database market.

In the beginning, these new types of databases lacked a common name. The name Distributed Non-Relational Database Management System (DNRDBMS) was proposed, but, obviously, it was too long and technical to capture anybody's imagination. As a result, at the end of 2009, the new term NoSQL quickly became popular as shorthand for any databases that broke with traditional relational databases based on SQL. Although many objections arose, especially because the term NoSQL defines what a database is not rather than what it is (Harrison, 2015), it was generally accepted in the very short time period. Reasons for this probably lay in the fact that the term NoSQL is very short and easy to memorize, and that it highlights the absence of the SQL language, that is one of the most visible properties of NoSQL databases.

RELATIONAL DATABASE PILLARS

The complete explanation of the relational theory is far beyond the scope of this book. In order to better understand the reasons for NoSQL appearance, readers should be familiar with the main concepts of the relational model, ACID transaction, and SQL language.

The Relational Model

The purpose of the relational model is to describe how a given set of data should be presented to the user, rather than how it should be stored on disk or in memory.

According to Codd (Codd, 1970), key concepts of the relational model include (Harrison, 2015):

- Relation.
- Tuples.
- Constraints.
- Operations.

The heart of the relational model is a relation or table. These two terms are used as synonyms in the relational model. Codd defined a relation as a named, two-dimensional table of data. The relation is composed of a set of named columns and an arbitrary number of rows (Figure 3). An attribute is a named column of a relation. The row of a relation is called tuple. Each tuple (row) contains only one value per attribute.

Nonetheless, not all tables are relations in the sense of the relational model. Relations or tables in the relational model must have the following properties (Hoffer, Ramesh, & Topi, 2011):

- Each relation (or table) in a database has a unique name.
- An entry at the intersection of each row and column is atomic (or single valued). Only one value can be associated with each attribute on a specific row of a table; no multivalued attributes are allowed in a relation.
- Each row is unique; no two rows in a relation can be identical.
- Each attribute (or column) within a table has a unique name.
- The order of columns (left to right) is insignificant. The order of the columns in a relation can be changed without changing the meaning or use of the relation.

Figure 3. Structure of the relational model

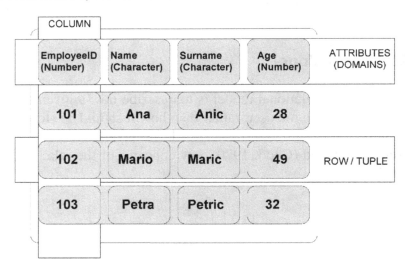

- The order of rows/tuples (top to bottom) is insignificant. As with columns, the order of the rows of a relation may be changed or stored in any sequence.

Constraints in the relational model are rules that limit acceptable values and actions. Their purpose is to facilitate maintenance and to ensure accuracy and integrity of data in the database. The three main types of integrity constraints are: domain constraints, entity integrity, and referential integrity (Hoffer, Ramesh, & Topi, 2011).

A domain is the set of allowable values that may be assigned to an attribute. All of the values that appear in a column of a relation must belong to the same domain (Figure 3).

The entity integrity rule guarantees that the value of the primary key is not null. It is the result of the definition of a primary key, which is an attribute or a set of attributes that uniquely identify tuples within a relation.

The referential integrity rule establishes that the foreign key value must match a candidate key value of some tuple in its home relation or must be null. The candidate key is a superkey such that no proper subset is a superkey within the relation. A superkey is an attribute or a set of attributes that uniquely identifies a tuple within a relation. Therefore, a primary key is the candidate key that is selected to identify tuples uniquely within the relation (Connolly & Begg, 2005).

Codd proposed eight fundamental operations that can be used in the relational model. They are (Connolly & Begg, 2005):

- Union.
- Intersection.
- Set difference.
- Cartesian product.
- Selection.
- Projection.
- Join.
- Division.

Selection and projection operations are unary because they operate on one relation, while other six operations are binary because they operate on two relations.

The union operation as a result has the relation that contains all tuples from both relations, with duplicate tuples being eliminated.

The intersection operation as a result has the relation that consists of the set of tuples that exist in both relations.

The set difference operation as a result has the relation that contains only tuples that exist in one, but not in other relations.

The union, intersection, and set difference operations work only on relations that are union-compatible. The two relations are union-compatible if they both have the same number of attributes where each pair of corresponding attributes is defined on the same domain.

The result of the Cartesian product of two relations is a new relation that consists of all possible combinations of pairs of tuples, where the first tuple is from the first relation and the second tuple is from the second relation.

The selection operation as a result has a relation that contains only those tuples that satisfy the specified condition. The new relation is the horizontal subset of the original relation.

The projection operation as a result has the relation that contains only specified attributes. The new relation is the vertical subset of original relation.

The result of the join operation is a new relation that consists of all combinations of pairs of tuples that satisfy the specified condition. The join operation is the subset of the Cartesian product, which is equivalent to performing a selection operation, using the join predicate as the selection criteria, over the Cartesian product of two relations (Connolly & Begg, 2005).

The division operation can be described by assuming that the relation R1 is defined over the attribute set A and the relation R2 is defined over the attribute set B, so that B is a subset of A and let C=A-B (e.g., C is a set of attributes of R1 that are not attributes of R2). The division operation defines a relation over the attributes C, which consists of the set of tuples from relation R1 that match the combination of every tuple in relation R2 (Connolly & Begg, 2005).

ACID Transactions

A database transaction is any activity run by the application program which reads or updates a database. It is a logical unit of work that must be entirely completed or entirely aborted; no intermediate states are acceptable (Coronel, Morris & Rob, 2011). This means that each transaction can have only one of two outcomes: committed or aborted.

If the transaction is completed successfully, it is committed, and the database reaches a new consistent state. A consistent database state indicates that a database fulfills all the defined rules (i.e. integrity constraints).

The transaction is aborted if it does not execute successfully, meaning that it violates integrity constraints or serializability. If a transaction is aborted, the database must be restored (rolled back) to the consistent state it was in before the transaction started (Connolly & Begg, 2005). Consequently, the important database activities are executing and managing transactions.

The main database transaction properties are atomicity, consistency, isolation, and durability. Jim Gray (1981) defined atomicity, consistency, and durability as the properties of database transactions. Isolation as transaction property was added later. In 1983, Theo Härder and Andreas Reuter (1983) coined the acronym ACID (atomicity, consistency, isolation, and durability), which Connolly and Begg (2005) explained as follows:

- **Atomicity:** It is the all-or-none principle, meaning that, as a transaction is an indivisible unit, either the activity or activities within a transaction are performed or none of them are. If one of the transaction activities fails, the entire transaction fails.
- **Consistency:** The transaction must transform the database from one consistent state to another. This means that each transaction must meet all the rules (constraints) which are defined over the relations. The transaction cannot violate these rules, and the database must remain in a consistent state at the beginning and the end of a transaction. This could happen because the new state of the system is valid or because the system was rolled back to its initial consistent state.
- **Isolation:** Transactions execute independently from one another. This means that the partial effects of incomplete transactions should not be visible to any other transactions. The concurrency control, which is the subsystem of a database management system, is responsible for ensuring isolation.
- **Durability:** The effects of a committed (successfully completed) transaction have to be permanently recorded in the database and must not be lost because of subsequent failure. This means that, once the transaction is complete, it will persist as complete and cannot be undone regardless of system failure, power loss, or other types of system breakdowns. The recovery subsystem of a database management system is responsible for ensuring durability.

The concurrency control mechanism of a database management system is responsible for the coordination of the simultaneous execution of transactions. The concurrency control has to ensure the serializability of transactions in a multiuser database environment. The serializability consists in finding a nonserial schedule that allows transactions to execute concurrently without interfering with one another and leaves the database in the same consistent state that will be produced by a serial execution. A schedule is a sequence of operations by a set of concurrent transactions that preserves the order of each operation in each individual transaction. In a nonserial schedule, the operations from a set of concurrent transactions are interleaved, while in a serial schedule the operations of each transaction are executed consecutively, without any interleaved operation from other transactions (Connolly & Begg, 2005).

Two main approaches to concurrency control are available (Connolly & Begg, 2005):

- **Conservative or Pessimistic:** In the case of potential conflict with another transaction, the transactions are delayed at some time in the future. The main methods are locking and timestamp. When the locking method is applied, the database uses a procedure (lock) to deny access to another transaction and prevent incorrect results. The timestamping protocol orders transactions in such a way that older transactions, with a smaller timestamp, get priority in the event of conflict.
- **Optimistic:** This approach is based on the premise that conflicts are rare, so they allow transactions to proceed unsynchronized and only check for conflicts at the end when the transaction commits.

Structured Query Language

The SQL (Structured Query Language) is the standard language for relational databases. The development of the SQL has begun simultaneously with the beginning of the relational database. In 1974, D. Chamberlin, from the IBM Research Laboratory, defined the Structured English Query Language (SEQUEL). Its revised version, SEQEL/2, was produced in 1976, and its name was later changed into SQL. Even today, many people pronounce SQL as "see-quel," although the official pronunciation is "S-Q-L" (Connolly & Begg, 2005). The first prototype of a relational database, IBM's System R was based on SEQEL/2. However, the real roots of SQL are in the language SQUARE (Specifying Queries As Relational Expressions) which predates the

System R project. SQUARE was designed as a research language to implement relational algebra with English sentences (Connolly & Begg, 2005). The first commercial database system that supported SQL was Oracle, in 1979.

The process of SQL standardization began in 1982, by the American National Standards Institute, while the International Organization for Standardization (ISO) joined in this work in 1983 and the initial ISO standard was published in 1987. The SQL standardization is still lasting. Last ISO version was published in 2013.

The original purposes of the SQL standard were (Hoffer, Ramesh & Topi, 2011):

- Specify the syntax and semantics of SQL data definition and manipulation languages.
- Define the data structures and basic operations for designing, accessing, maintaining, controlling, and protecting an SQL database.
- Provide a vehicle for portability of database definition and application modules between conforming DBMSs.
- Specify both minimal and complete standards, which permit different degrees of adoption in products.
- Provide an initial standard, although incomplete that would be enhanced later to include specifications for handling such topics as referential integrity, transaction management, user-defined functions, join operators beyond the equi join, and national character sets.

The main characteristics of SQL are:

- English as a language. The command structure consists of standard English words such as CREATE, INSERT, SELECT, UPDATE, DELETE, and so on.
- Nonprocedural language. Users specify what information is required, rather than how to get it. The SQL does not require users to specify the access methods to the data.
- The SQL is essentially a free-format language, which means that parts of statements do not have to be typed at particular points on the screen.
- Mostly, it works with a set of records, rather than with one record.
- It ensures commands for different tasks, including:
  ○ Queries over data.
  ○ Insert, update, and delete tuples in relations.
  ○ Create, alter, and drop objects in the database schema.

- ○ Control of access to the database and objects in the database schema.
- ○ Provide the database consistency.

The SQL is a relatively easy language to learn. Its basic command set has a vocabulary of less than 100 words. The query is the heart of the SQL. In the SQL environment, the word query covers both questions and actions. SQL queries are usually used to answer questions like "How many employees have a salary higher than the average salary?". Also, SQL queries are used to perform actions such as adding or deleting table rows or changing attribute values within tables. In short, a query is simply a SQL statement that has to be executed (Hoffer, Ramesh, & Topi, 2011).

BASE APPROACH

The implementation of ACID transaction properties ensured efficient concurrency control and recovery process in case of limited scale-up and shared-something environments. Nevertheless, with the fast development of data warehouses and the urgent need for storing an enormous quantity of data across multiple database servers, a different approach became necessary. Data warehouse vendors were looking for a solution through the implementation of a shared-nothing clustered database environment. In 1986 Stonebraker described the following three common architectures for multiprocessor high transaction rate systems (Stonebraker, 1986):

- **Shared Memory:** Where multiple processors share a common central memory. The sharing memory means that every process is on the same server, so the result is a single-node database architecture.
- **Shared Disk:** Where multiple processors, each with private memory, share a common collection of disks. Database processes exist on separate nodes in the cluster, but each has equal access to disk devices, which are shared across all nodes in the cluster.
- **Shared Nothing or Sharding:** Where neither memory nor peripheral storage is shared among processors. In this architecture, each node in the cluster has access not only to its own memory and CPU but also to dedicated disk devices and its own subset of the database.

The shared-nothing model became an attractive solution for data warehousing workloads because queries can easily be parallelized across the multiple nodes based on the data they wish to access. Databases implementing the shared-nothing model are often referred to as massively parallel processing (MPP) databases. Figure 4 illustrates the shared-nothing database architecture (Harrison, 2015).

The shared-nothing architecture put high pressure on concurrency control and recovery based on ACID transaction properties (see "Sharding Phenomenon"). Since ACID transactions are based on the "all or nothing" principle, it becomes necessary for all nodes in the transaction to coordinate closely on transaction execution. Maintaining ACID transactional integrity across multiple nodes in a distributed relational database became a significant challenge (Harrison, 2015). All these problems led to the development of the new BASE (basically-available, soft state, eventually consistent) approach. The meaning of this acronym is the following (Celko, 2014):

- **Basically Available:** This means the system guarantees the availability of the data as per the CAP theorem. However, the response can be "failure" or "unreliable" because the requested data is in an inconsistent or changing state.
- **Soft State:** The state of the system could change over time, so, even during times without input, changes may occur due to "eventual consistency," thus the system is always assumed to be soft as opposed to hard, where the data is certain.
- **Eventual Consistency:** The system will eventually become consistent once it stops receiving input, meaning that, if no additional updates are made to a data item, all reads to that item will eventually return the same value.

The BASE philosophy prizes data availability over consistency. The BASE approach originated as an alternative for ACID transaction properties, with the main purpose of providing more options to expand distributed systems and simple integration of more hardware to expand data operations. In the BASE approach, elements like consistency and availability are often viewed as resource competitors, where adjusting one can impact another. The idea is that data have the flexibility to be "eventually" updated, resolved, or made consistent, rather than instantly resolved (Techopedia, 2016).

Figure 4. Shared-nothing database architecture
Harrison, 2015.

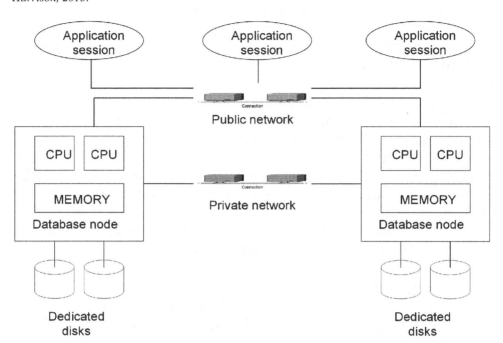

The BASE approach is a relatively weak model. Namely, eventual consistency provides few guarantees. The system can return any data and still be eventually consistent—as it might "converge" at some later point. As a result, the only guarantee is that, at some point in the future, something good will happen (Bailis & Ghodsi, 2013).

The properties of an ACID transaction request that the database is obliged to favor consistency over all other factors. Actually, maintaining ACID transactional integrity across multiple nodes in a distributed relational database is a significant challenge.

Table 1 shows a comparison of ACID and BASE approaches (Vanroose & Thillo, 2014).

The BASE approach has become popular especially with the development of NoSQL databases. Unlike ACID, the BASE approach offers more of a set of programming guidelines (such as the use of partition local transactions) than a set of rigorously specified properties, and its instantiations take a variety of application-specific forms.

Table 1. ACID and BASE approach comparison

ACID (RDBMS)	BASE (NoSQL)
Strong consistency	Weak consistency (=> allow stale data)
Isolation	Last write wins
Transaction	Program managed
Robust database	Simple database
Simple code (SQL)	Complex code
Available and consistent	Available and partition-tolerant
Scale-up (limited)	Scale-out (unlimited)
Shared-something (disk, memory, processes)	Shared-nothing (parallelizable)

Of course, the BASE approach is far away from being an ideal solution. It can be very costly because once a professional gives up ACID guarantees, it is up to developers to explicitly code in their applications the logic necessary to ensure consistency in the presence of concurrency and faults. The complexity of this task has sparked a recent backlash against the early enthusiasm for the BASE (Chao et al., 2014). Some authors stressed that the process of designing applications that should resolve concurrency anomalies in their data could be very apt to errors, time-consuming, and probably not worth the performance gains (Shute et al., 2012).

CAP THEOREM

As Eric Brewer, the creator of the CAP theorem, explained (Brewer, 2012), the theorem first appeared in fall 1998; then, it was published in 1999 (Fox & Brewer, 1999) and in the keynote address at the 2000 Symposium on Principles of Distributed Computing (Brewer, 2001).

The CAP theorem states that any networked shared-data system can have at most two of three desirable properties (Brewer, 2012):

- **Consistency (C):** Enabling a single, up-to-date and readable version of data to all clients. It implies that multiple clients read the same items from replicated partitions and get consistent results.
- **High Availability (A):** The distributed database will always allow database clients to update items without delay. Internal communication failures between replicated data should not prevent updates.

- **Tolerance to Network Partitions (P):** Ability of the system to keep responding to client requests even if a communication failure occurs between database partitions.

Three responses operate on the CAP theorem (Simon, 2012):

1. **Sacrificing Tolerance:** No defined system behavior is foreseen in case of a network partition. A two-phase commit is one of the attempts to fix this issue. It supports temporarily partitions, like node crashes, lost messages, and similar, by waiting until all messages are received.
2. **Sacrificing Consistency:** Partition data can still be used, but, since the nodes cannot communicate with each other, there is no guarantee that the data is consistent. In this case, optimistic locking and inconsistency resolving protocols can be used.
3. **Sacrificing Availability:** Since data can only be used if their consistency is guaranteed, pessimistic locking is implied because it is necessary to lock any updated object until the update has been propagated to all nodes. If a network partition is in question, it might take quite long until the database is in a consistent state again, so the system cannot guarantee high availability anymore.

According to Brewer (2012), one of the purposes of the CAP theorem was to open the designers' minds to a wider range of systems and tradeoffs. The result is that, in the past decade, a lot of new systems appeared, as well as many debates were initiated about consistency, availability, and partitioning. Some researchers sustain that the CAP theorem mentions partition tolerance as a given property, and that, under these conditions, only consistency or availability can be guaranteed. However, even in this case, the correct expression of reference should be a consistency-availability tradeoff, rather than a choice between the two (Simon, 2012).

Even today, partitions are rare. This means that the CAP theorem prohibits only a small area of the design space: perfect availability and consistency in the presence of partitions (Brewer, 2012). Nonetheless, if partitions are present, designers still need to choose between consistency and availability, although a vast range of flexibility exists for handling partitions and recovering from them. According to Brewer (2012), the modern CAP goal should be to maximize combinations of consistency and availability that are aligned with the requirements of a specific application.

The CAP theorem proves that it is not possible to create a distributed database that is consistent, available, and partition tolerant at the same time. Figure 5 shows that during the implementation of databases it is necessary to make a tradeoff between strong consistency, high availability, and partition tolerance.

The CAP theorem offers the following choice: if a distributed system has to be undisturbed by network partitions, then strict consistency between partitions must be sacrificed. When highly available database systems are in question, there are requests for efficient management of multiple copies of data and continuous system operating in the case of node failure.

Today's globally distributed systems are forced to distribute nodes all around the world to reduce latency in various locations. In this case, ensuring strict consistency means ensuring that a database change is propagated to multiple nodes synchronously and immediately. If one of these nodes is on the other side of the world, an unavoidable increase in latency will occur. For some types of applications (i.e., in banking) this latency penalty is unavoidable, but for other applications (i.e., social networks) this global synchronous consistency is unnecessary. Consequently, the concept of eventual consistency has become a key characteristic of many NoSQL databases (Harrison, 2015).

Figure 5. CAP theorem
Harrison, 2015.

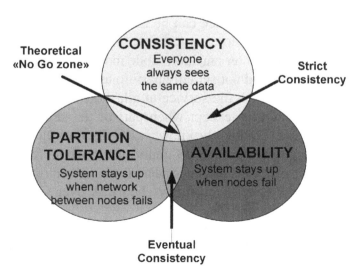

The NoSQL database movement is generally creating choices that focus first on availability and secondly on consistency, while databases which are based on ACID properties do the opposite.

The relationship between CAP and ACID is complex and often misunderstood, partly because the consistency (C) and availability (A) in ACID represent different concepts than the same letters in CAP and partly because choosing availability affects only some of the ACID guarantees (Brewer, 2012).

The original CAP theorem ignores latency, although, in practice, latency and partitions are inseparable. The essence of CAP takes place during a timeout, a period when the program must make a fundamental decision-the partition decision (Brewer, 2012):

- Cancel the operation and thus decrease availability, or
- Proceed with the operation and thus risk inconsistency.

If databases retry communication to achieve consistency (through a two-phase commit), they just delay the decision. Retrying communication indefinitely is, in essence, choosing consistency over availability. As a result, a partition is a time bound on communication. If consistency is not achieved within the time bound, it implies a partition and thus a choice between consistency and availability for this operation. The core design issue with regard to latency is whether to enable these two sides moving forward without communication. The consequence can be that designers are allowed to set time bounds intentionally according to target response times; systems with tighter bounds will likely enter partition mode more often at times when the network is merely slow and not actually partitioned (Brewer, 2012).

When users cannot reach the service at all, there is no choice between consistency and availability, except when part of the service runs on the client. This exception, commonly known as a disconnected operation or offline mode, is becoming increasingly important. Some HTML5 features-in particular, on-client persistent storage-make disconnected operations easier going forward. These systems normally choose A over C and thus must recover from long partitions.

However, instead of choice "two of three," it is better to think about this probabilistically: choosing CA should mean that the probability of a partition is far less than that of other systemic failures, such as disasters or multiple simultaneous faults (Brewer, 2012).

The big challenge for designers is how to mitigate the effects of a partition on consistency and availability. The key idea is to manage partitions very explicitly, including not only detection but also a specific recovery process and a plan for all of the invariants that might be violated during a partition. This management approach has three steps (Brewer, 2012):

- Detect the start of a partition.
- Enter an explicit partition mode that may limit some operations.
- Initiate partition recovery when communication is restored.

The last step aims to restore consistency and compensates for mistakes the program made while the system was partitioned. Once the system enters the partition mode, two strategies are possible. The first is to limit some operations, thereby reducing availability. The second is to record extra information about the operations that will be helpful during partition recovery. Continuing to attempt communication will enable the system to discern when the partition ends.

Over the years, the CAP theorem has constantly been developed and slight adjustments have been made, most prominently by Brewer himself, who amended in a later paper that some of the conclusions, while not wrong, could be misleading (Brewer, 2012). However, the CAP theorem is still one of the most important findings for distributed databases (Simon, 2012).

The CAP theorem asserts that any networked the shared-data system can have only two of three desirable properties. However, by explicitly handling partitions, designers can optimize consistency and availability, thereby achieving some trade-off of all three.

SHARDING PHENOMENON

"BASE APPROACH" explains that shared nothing or sharding is one of three basic architectures for multiprocessor high transaction rate systems. The term sharding was coined by Google engineers and became known thanks to the publication of their works that describe the Big Table architecture (Dean & Ghemawat, 2004; Ghemawat, Gobioff & Leung, 2003;). However, although the term sharding is presently associated with NoSQL databases, the concept of the shared-nothing database partitioning has been referred to in literature since as early as the 1980s (Stonebraker, 1986). Over the past ten years or so, the quantity of data (Big Data) and the number of users who are to be provided with quick and efficient access to the data increased enormously. As a result, the number of implementations of the sharding architecture also increased, especially by the leading Internet companies, such as Google, Amazon, Facebook, eBay, YouTube, Skype, and Wikipedia.

Database sharding is defined as a shared-nothing partitioning scheme for large databases across a number of servers, which allows achieving higher database performance and scalability levels (AgilData, 2016). The term sharding essentially means breaking a database into smaller chunks called "shards" and distributing these across a large number of distributed servers; in other words, sharding allows logical partitioning of a database across a large number of physical servers.

The primary aim of sharding is to provide high database performance and scalability levels, especially when it is necessary to provide the adequate speed of access and operation with huge quantities of data (Big Data). Namely, database management systems are based on the three basic components of a computer: CPU (Central Processing Unit), memory, and disk, which together affect the database performance. Thus, adding new processors to provide improved performance is not enough; it is also necessary to improve memory capacity and performance of the disk management system. Growing demands in terms of quantity of data to be processed by database management systems have posed greater challenges in defining an adequate architecture or finding a proper combination of processing power, memory, and disks, which eventually resulted in sharding.

Sharding provides scalability by using independent servers, each of them with its own CPU, memory, and disk. Sharding is basically very clear and at first sight simple: a large database is split into many smaller databases across servers (Figure 6).

The biggest advantage of sharding is significantly improved scalability, which increases almost linearly with the addition of new servers in the network. Besides, sharding also has other advantages, such as (AgilData, 2016):

- **Easier Management of Smaller Databases:** Database management involves regular backups, optimization, and similar tasks, which, in the case of large databases, can be very complex and time-consuming (routine optimizations of indexes can take hours or even days, which complicates maintenance). In the case of sharding, each shard or smaller database can be maintained independently, and the maintenance is simpler and faster since shards contain smaller amounts of data.

Figure 6. Database sharding

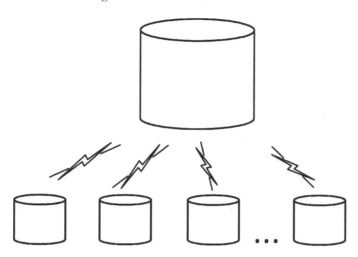

- **Improved Performance Because Smaller Databases are Faster:** As each shard is on its own server, the ratio of memory to the amount of data on disk is significantly improved, which leads to a reduction in disk I/O (Input/Output) operations. The effects of such an architecture are less resource contention, faster index search, and less database locks, which in return improve individual transaction performance.
- **Reduced Costs:** Most sharding implementations are based on open source databases and commodity hardware, which can significantly reduce the database licensing and maintenance costs.

Although sharding seems a simple concept, its practical implementation is very complex, because the applications accessing these databases must include the logic that understands the location of each piece of data as well as the logic that will redirect the request to the appropriate shard. In order to successfully implement sharding, it is necessary to thoroughly analyze many open issues, such as:

- **Ensuring Database Reliability:** Since sharding is based on data distribution and partitioning, the issue of reliability of such a system is critical to its successful implementation. In order to ensure reliability, it is necessary to provide automatic backups of individual shards, redundant copies of shards (at least two), automatic failover, and disaster recovery management.

- **Performing Distributed Queries:** Distributed queries use parallel processing of interim results on shard servers. In order for applications to be able to use this possibility, it is necessary to have a facility that could process a part of the query on each individual shard and then consolidate the results into a single result set for the application.
- **Key Management:** In the case of sharding, it is more complicated to ensure uniqueness of keys because the keys which are located on all shards must be managed in a coordinated manner. In order for the key management to be successful, it is necessary to establish an automated key generation method that is performed on all shards, and that ensures uniqueness of keys across the entire system.
- **Selection of Adequate Shard Scheme:** The possibility of selecting an adequate shard scheme implies the existence of different, flexible shard schemes, each of which is created to address a specific application problem. It is crucial to select the adequate shard scheme because using the wrong scheme can lead to reduced performance. Three basic shard schemes are (AgileData, 2016):
  - **Session-Based Sharding:** Each individual user or process is in interaction with a specific shard during the user or process session.
  - **Transaction-Based Sharding:** A shard is determined based on the first SQL statement in a given transaction, i.e. the "shard key" value used in the statement (e.g., Buyer Code) is evaluated, and then all other statements in the transaction are directed to the same shard.
  - **Statement-Based Sharding:** Each individual SQL statement is evaluated in order to determine the appropriate shard to which the transaction has to be directed.
- **Selecting the Method for Optimum Data Sharding:** This depends on the application type and the selected shard scheme. In order to select the appropriate method, it is important to understand transaction rates, tables sizes, key distribution, and other characteristics of the application. Some of the commonly used methods are (AgileData, 2016):
  - **Shard by a Primary Key on a Table:** It represents the simplest way of mapping to a given application, except that it is efficient only in the case of a relatively good data distribution.
  - **Shard by the Modulus of a Key Value:** It starts from a predetermined number of shards where the modulus function is

distributed to shards on a "round-robin" basis, thereby creating a very even distribution of new key values.

○ **Maintain a Master Shard Index Table:** This means using a single master table that maps different values to specific shards. While this approach is very flexible and suits different application requirements, a big disadvantage is that it typically decreases performance since it requires an additional lookup for each sharded SQL statement.

Sharding is usually associated with rapid growth and provision of increased database performance and scalability. However, although the idea of sharding is very straightforward and logical, implementing sharding can be very complex and cost-intensive because it is necessary to offer solutions for many open issues (see the previous paragraph). In addition, some of the main disadvantages of sharding are (Harrison, 2015):

- **Application Complexity:** The application code must ensure that SQL requests are sent to a particular shard. That is a very challenging task, also in the case of statistically sharded databases and especially in the case of a dynamic shard that is very common in massive Web sites, where shards are added as the Web site grows. A dynamic shard requires a dynamic routing layer or a very complex code that allows dynamic sending of queries to the appropriate shard.
- **Limited SQL:** Sharding does not allow to work with an SQL statement that operates across shards. This means that it is not possible to perform joins across shards or to use grouping (GROUP BY statement) within SQL statements.
- **Loss of Transaction Integrity:** ACID transactions are not possible or, at least, are not practical on multiple shards. Although from a theoretical viewpoint it is possible to implement transactions across databases, and so in the DBMSs that support two-phase commit (2PC), in practice, this causes problems in solving conflicts and can lead to the creation of bottlenecks.
- **Operational Complexity:** Balancing loads across shards represents a big challenge. Further, adding new shards requires very complex data rebalancing, while a change in the database schema requires a rolling operation across all the shards, which leads to transitory inconsistencies in the schema. It follows that the implementation of sharding requires significant operational efforts and well-trained administrators.

Some of the relational database producers, such as Oracle, tried to find a way of implementing relational databases by providing the scalability of sharding, but without impairing the ACID transactions and limiting the use of SQL. This is how Oracle's Real Application Clusters (RAC) was created as the most significant example of a transparently scalable, ACID compliant relational cluster. In Oracle's RAC system, every database node operates with data located on shared storage devices. RAC allows new database nodes to be added without the need for any data balancing, and a form of distributed memory cache is implemented across these database nodes (Harrison, 2015). Although the RAC system appeared promising, it failed to impose itself as an alternative to sharding, primarily because of its high cost, but also because of problems with the scalability necessary for exceptionally large Web sites.

RELATIONAL DATABASES LIMITATIONS

The relational databases experienced the first shake in the mid-1990s when object-oriented programming became the dominant programming paradigm. Namely, at the end of the 1980s and beginning of 1990s, the object-oriented approach was adopted by most programming languages and at the same time emerged new, natively object-oriented languages like Java.

Traditional procedural programming languages separate data and application logic. Programming procedures used data to perform their tasks, but they did not contain the data. As opposed to this traditional approach, object-oriented programming combine attributes and behaviors into a single object, meaning that all the details necessary to a logical unit of work are stored within the one class or directly linked to that class. This representation was inherently nonrelational, and it matched more closely the network databases (Harrison, 2015). In order to store or retrieve an object from a relational database, programmers have to use multiple SQL operations to convert from the object-oriented representation to the relational one. This conversion was not always easy and made a lot of problems to programmers often leading to poor performance or reliability. Figure 7 illustrates this problem.

Generally, object-oriented developers were frustrated by what they saw as an impedance mismatch between the object-oriented representations of their data within their programs and the relational representation within the database (Harrison, 2015).

Figure 7. Storing an object in an RDBMS requires multiple SQL operations

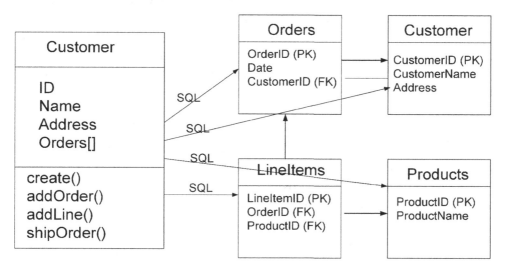

The following weaknesses of relational databases led to the development of object-oriented databases (Connolly and Begg, 2005):

- Poor representation of "real world" entities.
- Semantic overloading.
- Poor support for long lasting transactions.
- Homogeneous data structure.
- Limited operations.
- Difficulty handling recursive queries.
- Impedance mismatch.
- Schema changes.
- Poor navigational access.

Object-oriented databases were founded by the integration of database functionality with the object-oriented approach (object identity, abstract data types, inheritance). Object-oriented databases enable storing program objects directly without normalization and enable applications to load and store their objects easily. In an implementation, object-oriented databases use the navigational model similar to network databases; pointers within one object allow navigation to related objects. Advocates of object-oriented databases saw these structures as logical successors to relational databases. Since then, the leading relational database vendors (Oracle, Informix, Sybase, IBM) did they best to implement object-oriented features within their relational databases as soon as possible. In the same time, some pure object-oriented database management systems were developed and gained initial market share. However, on the surprise of their advocates, by the end of 1995s, object-oriented databases had completely failed to gain any significant market share. Mainstream database vendors, such as Oracle and Informix, had successfully implemented many object-oriented database system (OODBMS) features, but even these features were rarely used (Harrison, 2015). Development of Object-Relational Mapping (ORM) frameworks that automated the most tedious aspects of the object-relational mapping was quiet opponents of relational databases.

Relational databases remained unchallenged until the latter half of the 2000s and no significant new databases were introduced. Considering that this period essentially represents a time when the Internet grew from geeky curiosity to an all-pervasive global network, it is astonishing that no new database architectures emerged during this period and it is a testament to the power of the relational model (Harrison, 2015).

The development of Web 2.0 applications, social networks, Big Data, cloud computing and Internet of Things caused the second big shake of relational databases. Big Data players, such as Google, Amazon, Facebook, and Twitter, were first faced with the limitations of relational databases in solving their requests, and they have become pioneers in developing and implementing different NOSQL databases. Today's applications demand an unparalleled level of scale, availability, and throughput. Advocates of NoSQL databases think that the following limitations of relational databases prevent those databases to adequately respond to modern application demands (Vanroose & Thillo, 2014):

- Convert information from their natural representation into the table(s).
- Have to reconstruct information from tabular representation.
- Data must be modeled (semantics) before storing it.
- A table column can only store similar data ("schema" is fixed).
- Relational systems may not scale well.
- Difficult joins between different systems (different identifiers).
- Complex business rules are not easily expressible in SQL.
- Poor performing approximate terms and fuzzy searches.
- Don't store and validate complex documents efficiently.

These limitations can be good reason to replace relational databases with NoSQL databases when data is not stored in one computer or even one network, when lots of data do not belong to an organization, when data is too big to be put in one place, when data is uncoordinated in time as well as space, and when data is not structured data that SQL was meant to handle (Celko, 2014).

REFERENCES

AgilData. (2016). *Database sharding*. Retrieved July 12, 2017 from http://www.agildata.com/database-sharding/

Bailis, P., & Ghodsi, A. (2013). *Eventual consistency today: Limitations, extensions, and beyond*. Retrieved June 5, 2016, from http://queue.acm.org/detail.cfm?id=2462076

Brewer, E. (2001, July). *Lessons from giant-scale services. IEEE Internet Computing*, 46–55.

Brewer, E. (2012). *CAP twelve years later: How the "rules" have changed*. Retrieved May 11, 2016 from https://www.infoq.com/articles/cap-twelve-years-later-how-the-rules-have-changed

Celko, J. (2014). *Joe Celko's complete guide to NoSQL: What every SQL professional needs to know about non-relational databases*. Elsevier Science.

Chao, X., Chunzhi, S., Kapritsos, M., Wang, Y., Yaghmazadeh, N., Alvisi, L., & Mahajan, P. (2014). Salt: Combining ACID and BASE in a distributed database. *Proceedings of the 11th USENIX Symposium on Operating Systems Design and Implementation*.

Codd, E. F. (1970). A relational model of data for large shared data banks. *Commun. ACM, 13*(6), 377-387. DOI:10.1145/362384.362685

Codd, E. F. (1985a, Oct.). Is your DBMS really relational?. *Computerworld*, 14.

Codd, E. F. (1985b, Oct.). Does your DBMS run by the rules?. *Computerworld*, 21.

Connolly, T., & Begg, C. (2005). *Database systems: A practical approach to design, implementation and management* (4th ed.). Pearson Education Limited.

Coronel, C., Morris, S., & Rob, P. (2011). *Database systems - Design* (9th ed.). Cengage Learning.

Dean, J., & Ghemawat, S. (2004). *MapReduce: Simplified data processing on large clusters*. Retrieved November 20, 2016 from https://static. googleusercontent.com/media/research.google.com/hr// archive/mapreduce-osdi04.pdf

Elmasri, R., & Navathe, S. B. (2011). *Fundamentals of database systems* (6th ed.). Addison-Wesley.

Fox, A., & Brewer, E. (1999). Harvest, yield and scalable tolerant systems. *Proceedings of 7th Workshop Hot Topics in Operating Systems*, 174-178.

Ghemawat, S., Gobioff, H., & Leung, S.-T. (2003). *The Google file system*. Retrieved August 2, 2016 from http://static.googleusercontent.com/media/ research.google.com/hr//archive/gfs-sosp2003.pdf

Gray, J. (1981). The transaction concept: Virtues and limitations. *Proceedings of 7th International Conference on Very Large Data Bases*, 7, 144-154.

Härder, T., & Reuter, A. (1983). Principles of transaction-oriented database recovery. *Journal ACM Computing Surveys*, *15*(4), 287–317. doi:10.1145/289.291

Harrison, G. (2015). *Next generation databases: NoSQL, NewSQL, and big data. Apress*. doi:10.1007/978-1-4842-1329-2

Hoffer, J. A., Ramesh, V., & Topi, H. (2011). *Modern database management* (10th ed.). Pearson Education Limited.

Oracle. (2007). *Defying conventional wisdom*. Retrieved May 27, 2016 from http://www.oracle.com/us/corporate/profit/ p27anniv-timeline-151918.pdf

Shute, J., Oancea, M., Ellner, S., Handy, B., Rollins, E., Samwel, B., & Tong, P. et al. (2012). F1- The fault-tolerant distributed RDBMS supporting Google's ad business. *Proceedings of the 2012 ACM SIGMOD International Conference on Management of Data*, 777–778. doi:10.1145/2213836.2213954

Simon, S. (2012). *Brewer's CAP theorem*. Paper presented at the Symposium on Principles of Distributed Computing (PODC) 2000, Basel, Switzerland.

Stonebraker, M. (1986). *The case of shared nothing.* Retrieved June 7, 2016 from http://citeseerx.ist.psu.edu/viewdoc/download?doi=10.1.1.58.5370&rep=rep1&type=pdf

Techopedia. (2016). *Basically available, soft state, eventual consistency (BASE).* Retrieved April 22, 2016 from https://www.techopedia.com/definition/29164/basically-available-soft-state-eventual-consistency-base

Vanroose, P., & Thillo, K. V. (2014). *ACID or BASE? The case of NoSQL, GSE DB2 Belgium joint user group meeting IBM, Brussels, 12 June, "what's next?".* Retrieved May 20, 2016 from http://www.abis.be/resources/presentations/gsebedb220140612nosql.pdf

Chapter 2
NoSQL Database Phenomenon

ABSTRACT

The chapter explains that NoSQL databases emerged as an attempt for resolving the limitations of relational databases in coping with Big Data. The issue of Big Data is related to extensive requests for the storage and management of complex, dynamic, evolving, distributed, and heterogeneous data from different sources and platforms. The chapter provides an overview of the technologies, including Google File System (GFS), MapReduce, Hadoop, and Hadoop Distributed File System (HDFS), which were the first responses to Big Data challenges and main driving forces for the development of NoSQL databases. Also, the chapter asserts that NoSQL is an umbrella term related to numerous databases with different architectures and purposes, which can be classified in four basic categories: key-value, column-family, document, and graph stores. The chapter discusses the general features of NoSQL databases, as well as the specific features of each of the four basic categories of NoSQL databases.

INTRODUCTION

The growth of NoSQL databases is inseparable from the Big Data phenomenon. This is related to extensive requests for the storage and management of complex, dynamic, evolving, distributed, and heterogeneous data from different sources and platforms. In turn, all that brought relational databases to their breaking

DOI: 10.4018/978-1-5225-3385-6.ch002

points. As described in the first chapter, NoSQL databases emerged to resolve relational database limitations in coping with Big Data. To better understand the NoSQL database phenomenon, this chapter will review the concepts and technologies preceding its occurrence. These include: Big Data; Big Data challenges; MapReduce and a Hadoop distributed file system. It will also discuss the main features and types of NoSQL databases.

BIG DATA CHALLENGES

Since 2012, the term *Big Data* has become increasingly mainstream. However, many different (and sometimes unclear) definitions exist. According to Wu, Buyya, and Ramamohanarao (2016), Big Data definitions can be grouped based on:

- **Domains (Vs):** One of the earliest definitions was based on 3Vs: (1) volume; (2) velocity; and (3) variety (Lanely, 2001). The volume represents continuous and cumulative data growth. Velocity is the speed of data transfer from one point to another (real time data streaming, YouTube uploads, social media posts, e-mail, etc.). Variety refers to different types of data formats. IBM (2016) added a fourth domain, veracity, to refer to data uncertainty (e.g., trustworthy and quality data). Microsoft (2016) added variability and visibility, which extended the number of domains to six. Variability relates to data complexity (e.g., the huge number of data attributes). Visibility refers to the required existence of a complete data picture in the decision-making process. The number of domains (Vs) has grown to as many as 11 (Elliott, 2013).
- **Technology:** This type of definition focuses on technological support to Big Data (Hadoop, MapReduce, Spark, etc.).
- **Application:** Applications based on Big Data is the focus of this definition, including machine learning, data mining, social media analytics, etc.).
- **Signals:** Signal definitions relate to application definitions. However, signals focus on timing and finding new signal patterns in Big Data sets.

- **Opportunities:** This definition focuses on the potential of Big Data in fields of human work and living, especially as a driving force of developments in new technologies.
- **Metaphor:** Metaphor views Big Data as an extension of the human brain.
- **New Term for Old Stuff:** Big Data as a new term for old stuff views the Big Data phenomenon as a buzz word for existing concepts (i.e., business intelligence, data mining, social media analytics, etc.).

These definitions, however, do not focus on the use of data to resolve business problems. Big Data should be used as a powerful tool in the decision-making process. This requires Big Data to be viewed using the following aspects, i.e., domain knowledge (Wu, Buyya, & Ramamohanarao, 2016):

- *Data domain (searching for patterns)*
- *Business intelligence domain (making predictions)*
- *Statistical domain (making assumptions). (p. 11)*

Wu, Buyya, and Ramamohanarao (2016) provided a Big Data definition graphic (see Figure 1). Their 3^2V's definition represents the semantic meaning

Figure 1. 3^2V's Big Data definition
Wu, Buyya, & Ramamohanarao, 2016.

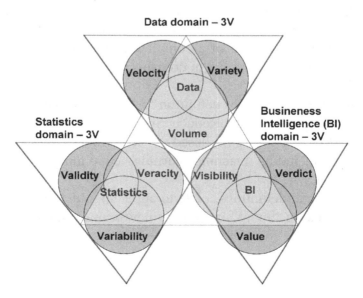

(e.g., the relationship of data, business intelligence, and statistics). The root of this definition is machine learning. Without the machine (computer), it would be impossible to learn from Big Data (Wu, Buyya, & Ramamohanarao, 2016).

Considering all Big Data attributes from different aspects, Figure 1 highlights the main purpose of Big Data. The purpose is to gain hindsight (i.e., metadata patterns from historical data), insight (i.e., a deep understanding of issues or problems), and foresight (i.e., more accurate predictions in the near future) in a cost-effective manner (Wu, Buyya, & Ramamohanarao, 2016).

The spectrum of Big Data problems is broad and diverse. It can be classified as shown in Figure 2. To resolve Big Data problems, organizations are faced with challenges, including:

- Rapid data growth
- Numerous and diverse data sources
- Data heterogeneity
- Data incompleteness
- Diverse and immature technology solutions
- Shortage of Big Data experts
- Data availability
- Data quality

Figure 2. Classification of Big Data problems
McCreary & Kelly, 2014.

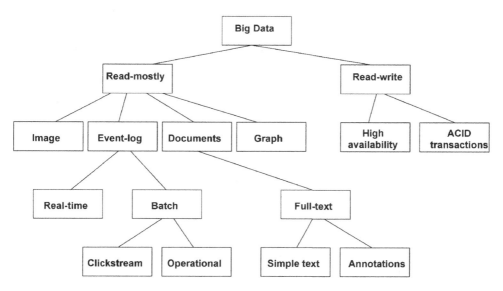

- Data security
- Legal issues
- Readiness to change

Rapid Data Growth

The quantity of data stored in a digital format is rapidly expanding. Main drivers of this data growth include: the transition from analog to digital technologies in almost every aspect of human life; the increase of computer power and data storage capabilities; and the rapid growth of social media users, as well as its generated data.

Hilbert and Lopez (2011) focused on the world's technological capacity to handle information, including worldwide estimates of 60 categories (21 analog and 39 digital) in the period between 1986 and 2007. Their research showed that the total amount of information grew from 2.6 optimally compressed exabytes (1986) to 15.8 (1993). In 2000, there were more than 54.5. In 2007, there were 295 optimally compressed exabytes.

The data contained in storage and communication hardware capacity were converted into bits by normalizing on compression rates. The redundancy of the source was determined by the content in question (text, images, audio, or video). Depending on the type of content, information was measured as if all redundancy were removed with the most efficient compression algorithms available in 2007. This level of compression was called "optimally compressed" (Hilbert & Lopez, 2011).

If CD-ROM with a capacity of 730 MB was used as a measure unit, the quantity of information was less than one 730 MB CD-ROM per person (539 MB per person) in 1986. This was approximately 4 CD-ROM per person in 1993, 12 CD-ROM per person in 2000, and 61 CD-ROM per person in 2007 (Hilbert & Lopez, 2011).

Figure 3 shows that the prevailing quantity of information was stored in analog video tapes, like VHS cassettes, before the emergence of the digital revolution. In 1986, information was also stored on vinyl long play records (14%), analog audio cassettes (12%), and photography (5% and 8%). In 2000, digital data storage became significant (25% of stored data). By 2007, approximately 94% of data was stored digitally (Price, 2015). In 2007, hard disks made up 52% of total storage, optical storage contributed 28%, and digital tapes made up 11% (Hilbert & Lopez, 2011).

Figure 3. Quantity of information stored in analog video tapes
Hilbert & Lopez, 2011.

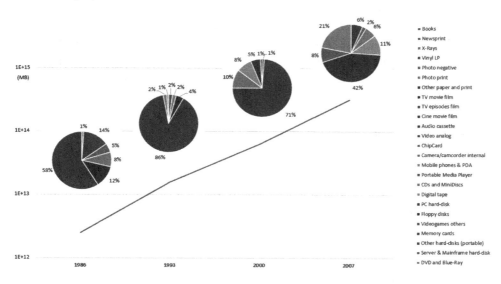

Table 1. Internet data generated on a daily basis (Internetlivestats, 2017)

Internet and Web Services	Numbers
Internet	3,688,480,783 users in the world
E-mails sent today	212,705,854,655 emails
Google searches today	4,705,188,235 searches
Facebook	1,839,344,584 active users
Videos viewed on YouTube today	5,456,144,828 videos
Google+	533,861,850 active users
Blog posts written today	4,411,939 blogs
Twitter	308,931,255 active users
Tweets sent today	593,038,754 tweets
Pinterest	256,184,798 active users
Photos uploaded on Instagram today	61,482,385 photos

SINTEF (2013) estimates that 90% of the world's data has been generated in the past two years. An enormous quantity of data is available on the Internet. The growing number of Internet users produce their own data (Table 1). It is obvious that today's world is already the digital universe.

Estimates show that it will grow 40% per year throughout the next decade. This includes an increase in the number of online users (both people and organizations), as well as things, i.e. smart devices connected to the Internet, called Internet of things (IoT). This will unleash a new wave of individual and organizational opportunities around the world. The expectation is that the quantity of data created and copied annually will reach 44 zettabytes or 44 trillion gigabytes by 2020 (IDC, 2014).

Numerous and Diverse Data Sources

Organizations are challenged by the quantity of digital data from numerous and diverse sources. If organizations aim to benefit from data in the decision-making process, it must be integrated and available in real time. However, the process of data integration from different data sources presents unique challenges.

An organization must first define data sources by choosing the most cost-effective and valuable source. Once data sources are defined, the organization must determine how to get data into its system to define schedules for data gathering. This usually differs depending on the source. Synchronization will be a problem if data is gathered in different schedules (time). Data synchronization has different aspects, including: data currency perspective; semantics perspective (commonality of data concepts, definitions, metadata, and similar); and updating perspective (data coming from one source is updated with data coming from another source). Traditional data marts and/or data warehouses have an extraction, transformation, and loading (ETL) phase to address the problem of data integration from different sources, data cleaning, scrubbing, synchronization, and storing. With rapid data growth and the speed at which updates are expected to be made, ensuring the level of governance typically applied for conventional data management environments becomes more difficult.

The inability to ensure synchrony for Big Data poses the risk of analyses that use inconsistent or invalid information. If inconsistent data in a conventional data warehouse poses a risk of forwarding faulty analytical results to downstream information consumers, allowing more rampant inconsistencies and asynchrony in a Big Data environment can have a more disastrous effect (Loshin, 2015).

Data Heterogeneity

Relational databases work most efficiently with structured data types. However, they face problems in coping with dramatic growth and domination of unstructured data, including photos, video, and social media (see Figure 4). Efficient representation, access, and analysis of unstructured data require different approaches from relational data. Unstructured data is less rigid, less ordered, and more interrelated than structured data (CSC, 2012). An influential challenge is how to automatically generate metadata to describe the context of stored data (i.e., identifying the meaning of stored data, data storage, and data measurement).

Figure 4 presents changes in hardware architecture. In addition, it illustrates access changes to records and queries resulting from data heterogeneity and prevalence of unstructured data.

Figure 4. Structured and unstructured data
CSC, 2012.

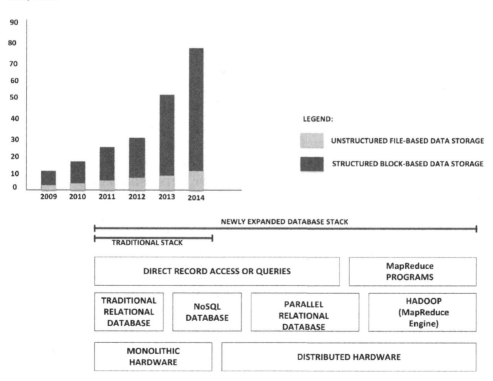

Today, 80% of data generated and/or gathered by organizations is unstructured. This means that data is highly dynamic and without a particular format. Data may exist in the form of e-mail attachments, images, pdf documents, medical records, x-rays, voicemail, graphics, video, audio, etc. It cannot be easily stored in row/column format as structured data. Transforming this data to a format suitable for later analysis is a challenge in Big Data analysis. It is a driving force for adopting new technologies to deal with such data.

Data Incompleteness

In the early 1970s, users recognized a need to handle incomplete data in relational databases. Codd developed what would become null-related features of commercial relational databases (Codd, 1970). He proposed a one-size-fits-all null value propagated through arithmetic and Boolean operations. The use of the three-valued logic for computing with nulls was largely reflected in the SQL standard. It soon became obvious that null feature had several deficiencies. It has become one of the most controversial aspects of SQL design.

Incomplete data is a challenge for Big Data analysis and limits the application of Big Data. For example, mobile phone call detail record (CDR) data records the calling log of phone users throughout a city in a real-time manner and at a low cost. While there is a huge quantity of data in question, the information is incomplete and has a narrow application scope without the socio-economic attribute data of users. Therefore, this type of data cannot reflect differences among respondents or describe residents' behavioral characteristics and other essential information that will interest researchers and readers. A similar situation corresponds to smart card data (Liu, Li, Li, & Wu, 2015).

Incomplete data can cause many problems and create uncertainties during data analysis. Therefore, incomplete data must be managed. Incomplete data refers to a sample's missing data field values. A number of things may cause this, including a malfunctioning sensor node or a systematic policy to intentionally skip values. Most modern data mining algorithms have inbuilt solutions to handle missing values (such as ignoring data fields with missing values). Data imputation, an established research field, seeks to impute missing values to produce improved models (compared to those built from the original data). Many imputation methods exist for this purpose. Major approaches fill the most frequently observed values or build learning models to predict possible values for each data field. These are based on the observed values of a given instance.

Diverse and Immature Technology Solutions

Big Data put IT, especially relational databases and analytical tools, at the edge. Simultaneously, it has become the driving force for the development of new technologies. New technologies provide answers to various issues, including: data integration from different and diverse sources; incompatible standards and data formats; missing data; data availability; data quality; data security; and legal issues.

The development of new technologies for Big Data storing is happening very quickly. Many competing solutions exist within the market (for example, MapReduce, Hadoop, Spark, HBase, MonogDB, and Casandra). In the next chapters, a few of these technologies will be described. However, most of the technologies are relatively new and are not fully confirmed in practice. The solution that is becoming more popular in relation to Big Data storage and management is the NoSQL database approach. This became an answer to meet performance demands for Big Data application (i.e., to ensure managing of huge data quantity and rapid response time).

Shortage of Big Data Experts

Technological development enables the gathering and processing of Big Data. Humans remain irreplaceable in Big Data analysis, interpretation of results, and applying results in daily business activities. New occupations resulted from the development of Big Data technologies. The data scientist is one example. It refers to technical specialists capable of using an array of tools to interrogate data and answer the questions that businesses ask for their data (as well as those questions they did not know they should be asking). Unfortunately, professionals with these skill sets are rare. CrowdFlower's 2016 Data Science Report (CrowdFlower, 2016) found that more than 80% of managers think that there are not enough data scientists. One reason could be that the most recent data storage and processing technologies have been the product of a small group of the best engineering brains. For example, Hadoop is developed by a group of engineers at Google. Yet, it is grown and open-sourced at Yahoo. Another example is Spark, which was developed at UC Berkeley AMPLab. Although these innovations spread like wildfire in the open-source tech community, there is a shortage of talent with the analytical experience to understand and effectively deploy these complex technologies.

The data scientist is expected to know how to use a wide range of tools, including the traditional relational database, in-memory analytics, NoSQL data management frameworks, and the Hadoop ecosystem. The main problem is that most data scientists have gained experience through the implementation of tools (i.e., narrow programming models, somehow forgetting on wider data management aspects). Poor implementation and weak performance can result in a lack of data modeling, data architecture, and data integration.

Currently, the lack of human experts is a pressing issue. In the near future, it may significantly influence the development and implementation of Big Data analytics. By 2018, per McKinsey & Company (Loshin, 2014), the United States will face a shortage of 140,000 to 190,000 people with deep analytical skills. Additionally, it will require 1.5 million managers and analysts with knowledge on how to use the analysis of Big Data to make effective decisions.

The present development and implementation of Big Data show that data scientists (i.e., Big Data experts) require competences and practical experience in different Big Data technologies. These experts should also have the necessary skills and competences related to fundamental data architecture and data management challenges. The lack of these competences may prevent organizations from achieving the advantages of Big Data analytics to ensure competitiveness and sustainable growth.

Data Availability

Big Data supports organizational competitiveness and development by enabling fast analysis on huge amounts of data. However, a larger data set needs a longer amount of time for analysis. Therefore, Big Data environments must develop innovative ways to enable quick access to data.

The scale and variety of data being absorbed into a Big Data environment can also be an intricate issue in data accessibility. In some instances, users of Big Data platforms are unaware of the complexity of facilitating the access, transmission, and delivery of data from the numerous sources and loading various data sets into the Big Data platform.

After data is loaded into the Big Data platform, the next challenge is to catalog the numerous data and ensuring its accessibility, fast browsing, and analysis by different business intelligence tools. These tools must connect to at least one of the Big Data platform. In addition, they must provide transparency to data consumers, reducing or eliminating the need for custom coding.

In the meantime, the number of data consumers will be growing. Therefore, it is necessary to anticipate a need to support an expanding collection of simultaneous user accesses (at different times of the day or in reaction to different aspects of business process cycles). Guaranteeing right-time data availability to data consumers becomes a critical success factor.

Data Quality

Data quality is the precondition for proper data use, independent of purpose and technology used for data analysis. It is a complex issue closely related to a multi-dimensional measurement of the adequacy of certain data sets. Several approaches to data multi-dimensionality exist. The Data Management Association International (DAMA, 2013, p.3) defines the data quality dimension as "… *some thing (data item, record, data set, or database) that can either be measured or assessed in order to understand the quality of data.*"

DAMA defined the six core dimensions of data quality:

1. **Completeness:** The proportion of stored data against the potential of "100% complete" (DAMA, 2013, p.8).
2. **Uniqueness:** No thing will be recorded more than once based on how that thing is identified (DAMA, 2013, p.9).
3. **Timeliness:** The degree to which data represent reality from the required point in time (DAMA, 2013, p.10).
4. **Validity:** Data is valid if it conforms to the syntax (format, type, range) of its definition (DAMA, 2013, p.11).
5. **Accuracy:** The degree to which data correctly describes the "real world" object or event being described (DAMA, 2013, p.12).
6. **Consistency:** The absence of difference, when comparing two or more representations of a thing against a definition (DAMA, 2013, p. 13).

When discussing business needs, data quality presents the measure of trust into data, meaning that data can be used as a basis for making proper business decisions. KPMG third CEO Outlook (study of global CEOs' expectations), after surveying 400 U.S. leaders of companies in a multitude of sectors, stated that "only a third have a high level of trust in the accuracy of their data and analytics, and one out of five have limited trust in nearly every aspect of the way their organization uses data and analytics" (KPMG, 2016, p.20). It is obvious that open issues remain surrounding data quality.

The research was conducted by a team of UALR-IQ and IQ International researchers between February and March 2016. Out of 160 respondents, 46.2% rated the quality of the data in their organization as fair, and 34% rated their data as good. The majority of surveyed participants (68.6%) stated that the data quality in their organization had improved either significantly or very significantly over the last two years (Pierce, Yonke & Youn, 2016).

A November 2015 research study, produced by Loudhouse for Experian Data Quality (2016), had more than 1,400 participants from eight countries around the globe. The research focused on global trends in data quality (Experian, 2016). Results showed that most of the organizations continued to experience problems surrounding a lack of knowledge and skills related to data management. For example, 94% of the companies experienced internal challenges related to data quality. Per Figure 5, the top three challenges are knowledge- and resource-oriented. This means that improvements to internal data quality challenges are limited by the organization's ability to hire the right people and have realistic expectations of data projects (Experian, 2016).

Organizations also face external challenges related to data quality (i.e., data capture and validation; security or governance risk; and data profiling). Figure 6 shows that, apart from data capture and security, approximately one-quarter

Figure 5. Internal challenges to data quality
Experian, 2016.

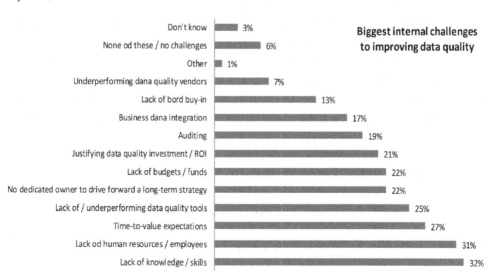

Figure 6. External challenges to data quality
Experian, 2016.

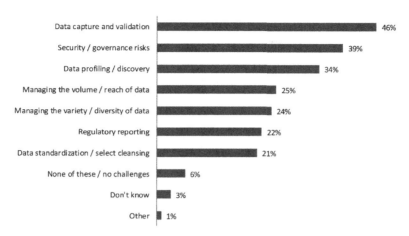

of companies struggle with managing the volume or variety of data collected (Experian, 2016). Unfortunately, the companies can expect an increase of data volume and variety in coming years. Fortunately, developed technologies can help companies respond to challenges. However, the precondition for the proper implementation of these technologies is establishing correct data culture and staffing within a company.

The Experian Data Quality research analyzed how the organizations manage the data quality by using a scale of four levels of data management sophistication: (1) unaware; (2) reactive; (3) proactive; and (4) optimized (see Figure 7). Research showed that most of the U.S. companies (42%) saw themselves as reactive with some sophisticated data management tools. However, they also noted that they have not established specified data-oriented roles or business-wide technological tools. A lesser proportion of businesses (24%) said they are proactive with data quality sponsors in place. They defined success criteria and clear ownership between the business and IT. Only 19% viewed their business approach as optimized (i.e., data quality was monitored as a standard business practice) with a technology platform in place to profile, monitor, and visualize data (Experian, 2016).

According to this research, the level of data management has improved in the last few years. Organizations across the globe are aware of the importance of quality data and the necessity to implement a sophisticated approach to managing data. To ensure successful implementation of data management, organizations should smoothly transfer the ownership of data quality and data

Figure 7. Managing data quality
Experian, 2016.

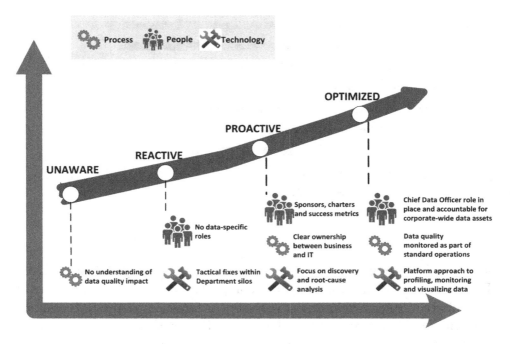

management from the IT portion of their business to business users. Business users are able to quantify the need for accurate data and leverage data in daily operations (Experian, 2016). This shift should empower organizations with high-quality data that can use in the process of decision making, especially when critical business decisions are in question.

Data Security

With more than 90% of data digitally stored (with the Internet and social media enabling easy and world-wide data sharing), data security is becoming increasingly important. Data security is inseparable from privacy, intellectual property, and liability. From a user perspective, data privacy is a top priority, especially in regards to personal data (i.e., health and financial records). The main concern is how to protect competitively sensitive data or other data that should be kept private while simultaneously ensuring the use of scientific and marketing research. For example, personal health records are valuable to medical research. It is necessary to identify trade-offs between privacy and utility.

Data breaches expose both personal consumer information and confidential corporate information. In some instances, national security secrets may be exposed. Figure 8 shows that more than 50% of digital data needing protection is still not protected. With an increase in serious breaches, it will be essential to address data security through technological and policy tools.

Legal Issues

The development and implementation of Big Data raise a number of legal issues, especially because data is fundamentally different from other assets. Data can be easily and perfectly copied, combined with other data, and shared through various communication channels and media outlets. Questions related to intellectual property rights and liability are also attached to data. Who "owns" a piece of data? What rights come attached with a dataset? Who is responsible when an inaccurate piece of data leads to negative consequences?

For organizations and individuals to capture the full potential of Big Data, legal issues must be clarified and resolved. Unfortunately, data issues related

Figure 8. Data security
IDC, 2014.

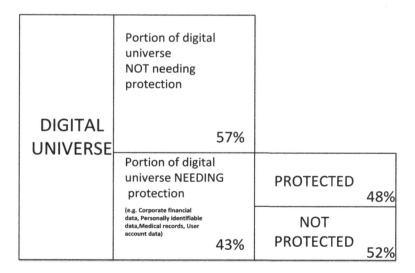

to legal regulation differ between countries (ICLG, 2017). In this chapter, two approaches will be discussed: European Union (EU) and U.S.

In January 2012, the European Commission proposed an overall reform of data protection rules in the EU. On May 4, 2016, the official Regulation and Directive texts were published in all official languages in the EU's Official Journal. While it enters into force on May 24, 2016, it shall apply from May 25, 2018. The Directive enters into force on May 5, 2016. EU member states must transpose it into their national law by May 6, 2018.

The objective of this new set of rules is to give citizens control over their personal data, while simplifying the regulatory environment for business. The data protection reform is a key enabler of the single digital market prioritized by the European Commission.

Under EU law, personal data can only be legally gathered under strict conditions and with a legitimate purpose. Furthermore, persons or organizations collecting and managing personal information must protect it from misuse. Additionally, they must respect certain rights of the data owners as guaranteed by EU law. Common EU rules have been established to ensure that personal data meets a high standard of protection throughout the EU. Data owners have the right to complain and obtain redress if their data is misused within the EU. The EU's Data Protection Directive also foresees specific rules for the transfer of personal data outside the EU to ensure high-quality protection when data is exported.

Under EU General Data Protection Regulation (GDPR), the definition of personal data is expanded to include online identifiers, as well as biometric and genetic information. The aim of the EU GDPR is to harmonize businesses that trade inside and outside of Europe It required those organizations to ensure an adequate level of protection for the rights and freedoms of individuals in relation to the processing of personal data as specified by the regulation. Any organization holding EU citizen data is bound by the regulation. Organizations must ensure that changes in regulation can be recognized and comprised by their data policies. They should remain dynamic and responsive, as well as adaptable to evolving business and regulatory landscapes (Love, 2016).

The U.S. does not have a comprehensive, consolidated data protection law. Data protection in the U.S. is primarily regulated through a number of sectors, specifically federal and state laws. For example, section 5 of the Federal Trade Commission (FTC) Act prohibits "unfair or deceptive acts or practices in or affecting commerce" (FTCA, 2016, p.1). The FTC has brought forth several enforcement actions under section 5 of the FTC Act related to data processing practices considered unfair or deceptive (Simpson & Rode, 2017):

- **The Health Insurance Portability and Accountability Act (HIPAA) of 1996:** This applies to protected health information.
- **The Gramm-Leach-Bliley Act (GLBA):** This applies to financial institutions and "nonpublic personal information."
- **The Children's Online Privacy Protection Act (COPPA):** This regulates the online collection and processing of personal data of children under the age of 13.
- **The Telecommunications Act:** This regulates telecommunications carriers' use of customer information.
- **The Fair Credit Reporting Act (FCRA) and Fair and Accurate Credit Transactions Act:** These govern data protection in the consumer reporting industry.
- **The Video Privacy Protection Act:** This restricts certain entities from processing personal data identifying a consumer as having requested or obtained specific video materials or services.

Some U.S. states have laws defining minimum information security requirements on entities that process information about a resident of those states. The most stringent of these state laws is in Massachusetts, which requires applicable organizations to develop, implement, and maintain a comprehensive and written information security program. The Massachusetts law requires encryption of files that contain personal data and are transmitted across public networks or wirelessly.

The EU and U.S. examples confirm the importance of data protection, as well as the need for adequate legal regulations. The main concern is the differing approaches to data protection across countries. Data can be easily transferred and copied throughout the globe. Therefore, stronger international cooperation related to data protection should be ensured.

Readiness to Change

The variety of Big Data definitions stresses the phenomenon's complexity and analytic needs from different perspectives (i.e., domains). Definitions also show the potential of Big Data, such as its effective use and supportive technologies in transforming organizations and economies through productivity. The utilization of Big Data potential rests with organizational leadership. Leaders must be aware of the potential that Big Data brings to their companies. They must show readiness to change, both within themselves and their organizations.

Data quality is in detail presented the Experian Data Quality research, which shows that managers are conscious of internal challenges related to data quality and human factors (i.e., lack of knowledge/skills, lack of human resources/employees, and time-to-value expectations). Organizational leaders are responsible for finding adequate answers to strategic threats presented by Big Data. They must close the eventual gap that exists between their IT capabilities and data strategy.

They have to prepare organizations to be creative and proactive related to the Big Data implementation and usage in order to use the Big Data in creating added value for organizations. Privacy and security is an important issue influencing the full utilization of Big Data (see "Data Security"). Organizations should help their consumers better understand the benefits and risks of Big Data. To achieve success, managers must find and employ Big Data analytical talents and establish an organizational culture that values and encourages Big Data in the decision-making process. They have to set up the institutional framework to enable organizations to create value from Big Data easily. It will also protect the privacy of their consumers and ensure data security.

Readiness to change in fully leverage of the Big Data benefits implies that organizations should support research in areas connected with Big Data. These include: advanced analytics; education of data scientists; innovation; and shared experiences.

The Big Data data challenges described in this chapter illustrate that there is a long way ahead before organizations to reach their full potential related to Big Data. But, an era of Big Data has already started and solving Big Data challenges will require innovative and transformative solutions.

The Google example has shown that one way of resolving Big Data issue lies in developing of an alternative database technology. The examples of other companies faced with Big Data problem, like Yahoo, Amazon, Twitter, additionally confirms that. In the next chapter, the main characteristics of both, Google solution and solutions based on Google innovations are explained.

EMERGE OF HADOOP DISTRIBUTED FILE SYSTEM

The first companies to face Big Data challenges were Google, Yahoo, and Amazon. However, Google's innovative approach to the development of data architecture, along with its willingness to share solutions, were key to the development of other innovative solutions. This eventually led to the emergence of the NoSQL database.

Google Architecture and MapReduce

When Google was beginning its business, its hardware platform consisted of standard servers, not a bit different from servers in other companies. A few years later, Google was faced with an enormous growth of data and forced to change its hardware architecture. It shifted to masses of rack-mounted servers in commercial-grade data centers. As data rapidly increased, this architecture became a bottleneck of growth and development. Google had to find solutions for both hardware and software architectures. The basic requirement was that the new architecture needed to support a steady growth of data operated by Google. In inventing and developing the new architecture, Google relied solely on its own resources. It utilized the knowledge and innovation of its engineers who, when confronted with Big Data challenges, gained practical experience and offered a new data architecture adapted to the company's needs.

By 2005, Google abandoned the concept of individual servers as basic data processing units. Instead, Google designed the Google Modular Data Center, which consisted of shipping containers housing approximately 1,000 custom-designed Intel servers running Linux. Each module included an independent power supply and air conditioning. Data center capacity did not increase by adding new servers. It added new 1,000-server modules, with storage directly attached to disks within the same servers as would be providing computing power (Harrison, 2015). This unique architecture needed an appropriate software support. At that time, the available operating systems and databases were unable to operate their large number of servers. To enable operation of the described hardware architecture, Google developed three major software layers (Harrison, 2015):

- ***Google File System (GFS):*** *A distributed cluster file system allowing all disks within the Google data center to be accessed as one massive, distributed, redundant file system*
- ***MapReduce:*** *A distributed processing framework for parallelizing algorithms across large numbers of potentially unreliable servers and capable of dealing with massive datasets*
- ***Big Table:*** *A nonrelational database system using the GFS for storage. (p. 25)*

Google shared its solutions and described the basic design of these software layers in papers published from 2003 to 2006. All three technologies were used as the foundation for the development of new solutions, both within Google and other companies. MapReduce attracted the most attention. It served as the foundation for the development of the HDFS.

MapReduce is a programming module based on the concept of parallel programming. It is intended for processing exceptionally large amounts of data. In the MapReduce approach, data processing is divided into a mapping phase, and a reduce phase.

In a mapping phase, data is divided into chunks that can be processed by separate threads whose execution can be on separate computers. A reduce phase combines the output from the mappers into a result. Programmers specify a map function that processes pairs of key/value type to generate a set of intermediate key/value pairs (see Figure 9). The MapReduce library groups intermediate values associated with the same intermediate key. It then passes them to the Reduce function. The Reduce function, which is also written by programmers, allows retrieval of an intermediate key with an appropriate set of values for that key. It also merged these values to form a possibly smaller set of values (Dean & Ghemawat, 2004). Figure 10 illustrates the application of MapReduce with a simple example of calculating the number of occurrences of a particular word within a document.

Figure 9. MapReduce process

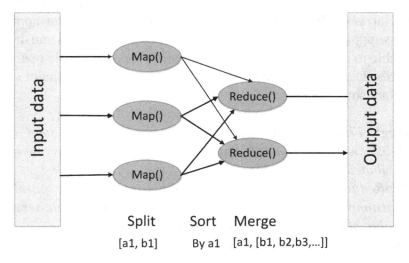

Figure 10. MapReduce simple example

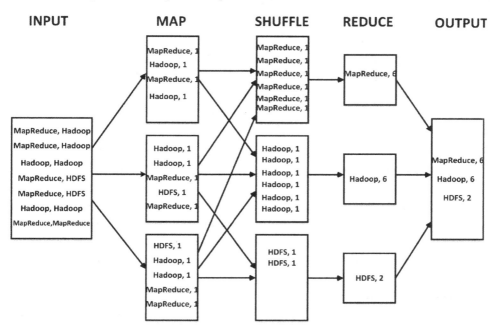

MapReduce processes consist of an arbitrary number of complex pipelines capable of solving many problems in processing large amounts of data. MapReduce can be implemented in different ways. It primarily depends on the environment in which it is implemented. However, the fundamental property of MapReduce is that it uses the "brute force" approach in data processing. This is not necessarily the most efficient or smartest solution. That is why Google, along with and other companies, has been working on more sophisticated and specialized algorithm extensions to MapReduce.

Doug Cutting and Mike Cafarella were working on an open-source project to build a web search engine called Nutch (Harrison, 2015). When Google published its first papers on GFS and MapReduce, they recognized that MapReduce offered a proven architectural foundation for solving Nutch's scalability challenges. After implementing their equivalents for GFS and MapReduce, they realized that the solutions could be applied to various problems in processing large amounts of data. It was concluded that attention should be devoted to additional research and development of this technology. In turn, Hadoop emerged.

HADOOP and HDFS Architecture

In 2006, Yahoo! employed Doug Cutting to develop Hadoop to solve challenges that the Yahoo! platform was already facing. The results were evident already in early 2008 when Yahoo! published results showing that the Hadoop cluster, with more than 5 petabytes of storage and more than 10,000 cores, generated the index that resolved Yahoo!'s web searches. It proved itself on a massive scale (Harrison, 2015).

Facebook was the second large company to adopt Hadoop very early. Facebook tested Hadoop in 2007; by 2008 it had a cluster utilizing 2,500 CPU cores in production. By 2012, Facebook's Hadoop cluster had exceeded 100 petabytes of disk. It overtook Oracle as a data warehousing solution, as well as powered many core Facebook products. The extent to which Hadoop has become the de facto standard solution for storage and processing huge amounts of unstructured data is best demonstrated by the fact that all three top databases vendors—Microsoft, Oracle, and IBM—offered Hadoop in their product portfolio (Harrison, 2015).

Hadoop's first version was developed as an open-source implementation of Google's MapReduce and GFS. Hadoop's architecture is similar to Google's architecture. The possibilities offered by Google through GFS are provided by Hadoop through the Hadoop Distributed File System (HDFS). GFS consists of a single master and multiple chunk servers. Files are split into chunks of fixed length (64 bit). The master is responsible for maintaining all file system metadata, such as the namespace, access control information, mapping from files to chunks, and current locations of chunks. GFS client code linked into each application implements the file system API and communicates with the master and chunk servers to read or write data on behalf of the application (Ghemawat, Gobioff, & Leung, 2003).

HDFS follows the master-slave architecture (see Figure 11). In the case of HDFS, it has the following basic elements (HADOOP, 2016):

- Namenode
- Datanode
- Block

Namenode acts as a master server and is related to commodity hardware with an operating system (GNU/Linux) and namenode software (i.e., software that can be run on commodity hardware). Its main tasks are: managing the

Figure 11. HDFS architecture
Borthakur, 2009.

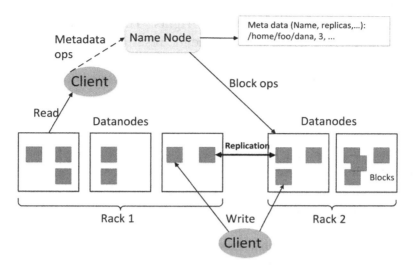

file system namespace; regulating access to client files; and performing file system operations (opening, closing, and renaming files and directories).

A datanode exists for every node of commodity hardware/system in a cluster. This applies to commodity hardware with an operating system (GNU/Linux) and datanode software. Datanodes execute read-write operations on file systems as requested by clients. In addition, datanodes perform operations like creating, deleting, and replicating blocks per instructions received from the namenode.

The file in a HDFS is divided into one or more segments and/or stored in individual data nodes. These file segments are called blocks. A block is the minimum amount of data that HDFS can read or write. Although the initial size of blocks is set to 64 MB, it can be increased as needed.

The Hadoop 1.0 architecture was inspired by the Google architecture and based on MapReduce. Most servers in a Hadoop cluster functioned as data nodes and task trackers (every server provided data storage, CPU, and memory). The job tracker node coordinated distribution of jobs running on the Hadoop cluster. Name node, a type of directory, allowed mapping of data blocks from data nodes to files on HFDS. Although Hadoop 1.0 proved powerful in data processing, its reliance on MapReduce became a constraint in relation to scheduling and resource allocation flexibility.

In 2010, Google granted an Apache license to incorporate the MapReduce model into the Hadoop system. It also allowed for free use and distribution without limitations in terms of patent rights. That provided an impetus for further work on Hadoop improvements, resulting in Hadoop 2.0. This version used yet another resource negotiator (YARN) to improve scalability and flexibility. YARN split the roles of the Task Tracker into two processes (Harrison, 2015):

- **Resource Manager:** Controls access to the cluster's resources (memory, CPU, etc.)
- **Application Manager:** Controls execution of tasks (one per job)

An innovation brought forth by YARN is the assumption that MapReduce is only one possible framework that can run on a cluster. It allows Hadoop to use other approaches or run tasks based on more complex processing models.

The foundation of Hadoop 2.0 architecture (see Figure 12) consists of the following elements (HADOOP1, 2016):

- **Hadoop Common:** Common utilities supporting other Hadoop modules
- **HDFS:** A distributed file system providing high-throughput access to application data
- **Hadoop YARN:** Framework for job scheduling and cluster resource management
- **Hadoop MapReduce:** YARN-based system for parallel processing of large data sets

Today, the Hadoop ecosystem comprises a range of utilities and applications representing an upgrade of the basic Hadoop architecture. Their number constantly increases, as shown in Figure 13. They include (HADOOP1, 2016):

- **Ambari:** This web-based tool is for provisioning, managing, and monitoring Apache Hadoop clusters, including support for: Hadoop HDFS, Hadoop MapReduce, Hive, HCatalog, HBase, ZooKeeper, Oozie, Pig, and Sqoop. Ambari provides a dashboard for viewing cluster health, such as heatmaps and ability to view MapReduce, Pig and Hive applications visually along with features to diagnose their performance in a user-friendly manner.

Figure 12. Hadoop 2.0 architecture
TutorialsPoint, 2014.

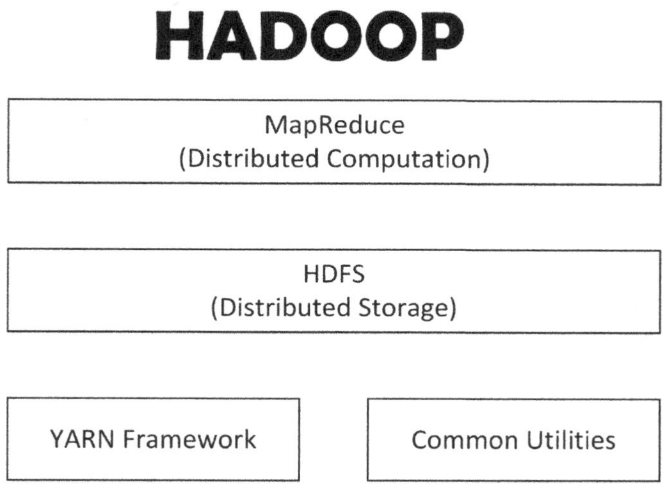

HADOOP

| MapReduce
(Distributed Computation) |

| HDFS
(Distributed Storage) |

| YARN Framework | | Common Utilities |

- **Avro:** This is a data serialization system providing: operation with rich data structures; a compact, fast, binary data format; a container file to store persistent data; remote procedure call (RPC); and simple integration with dynamic languages. Code generation is neither required to read or write data files nor implement RPC protocols. Code generation, as an optional optimization, is only worth implementing for statically typed languages. Avro schemas are defined with JSON to facilitate implementation in languages that already have JSON libraries (Avro, 2012).
- **Cassandra:** Cassandra is a scalable multi-master database without specialized master nodes. For Cassandra, each node is equal and capable of performing any action necessary for cluster operation. Cassandra requires all up-to-date cluster members regarding the current state of cluster configuration and status. This is achieved by using gossip protocols. Every second, members of a cluster transmit information on its state and the state of other nodes it follows (up to three nodes in a cluster). This provides constant cluster status updates across all members of the cluster. It eliminates a single point of failure within a cluster.

- **Chukwa:** This is a data collection system for managing large distributed systems. Chukwa is built on top of the HDFS and MapReduce framework. It inherits Hadoop's scalability and robustness. To make the best use of collected data, Chukwa includes a flexible and powerful toolkit for displaying, monitoring, and analyzing results (Chukwa, 2016).

- **HBase:** HBase uses Hadoop HDFS as a file system in the same way as most relational databases use a file system of an operating system. It is a scalable, distributed database that supports structured data storage for large tables. Thanks to HDFS, HBase can create tables of enormous size.

- **Hive:** Hive is an open-source Hadoop language developed by Facebook. Unlike Pig, Hive is closer to SQL. Therefore, it is often called SQL for Hadoop. Hive provides a catalog for the Hadoop system, as well as a SQL processing layer. It is used for data summarization and ad hoc querying. Hive is significant because it brought Hadoop closer to many developers who were familiar with SQL. Thereby, it laid the groundwork for integrating Hadoop into business intelligence tools.

- **Mahout:** This is a scalable machine learning and data mining library. Mahout provides a simple and extensible programming environment and framework for building scalable algorithms. It includes Samsara, a vector math experimentation environment with R-like syntax working at scale.

- **Pig:** Developed by Yahoo, Pig is part of the Hadoop ecosystem. Pig supports the procedural, high-level data flow language Pig Latin. It is a high-level data flow language and execution framework for parallel computation. It is intended for developers who use a workflow or directed graph programming model. It makes it possible for the model to be parallelized. Pig is more a script language than a SQL alternative.

- **Spark:** Spark is an in-memory, distributed, fault-tolerant, fast, and general compute engine for Hadoop data. Spark provides a simple and expressive programming model to support a range of applications. These include: ETL; machine learning; stream processing; and graph computation. Spark provides a higher level of abstraction than MapReduce. Thus, it increases developer productivity. As an in-memory solution, Spark is valuable in tasks that cause congestion on disk IO in MapReduce. It is also useful in tasks that are iterative on the dataset, which is the case with most machine-learning workloads.

Figure 13. Hadoop ecosystem
BigData, 2016.

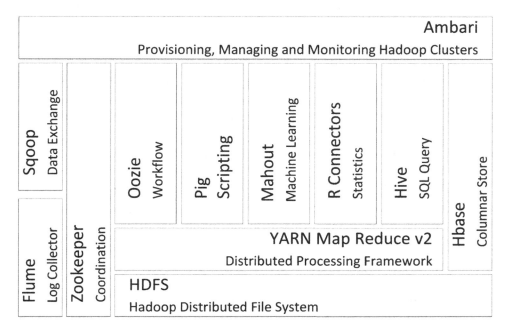

- **Tez:** Tez is based on the flexible processing paradigm known as directed acyclic graph (DAG). It is a generalized data flow programming framework, built on Hadoop YARN, which provides a powerful and flexible engine to execute an arbitrary DAG of tasks to process data for both batch and interactive use-cases. Tez is being adopted by Hive, Pig, and other frameworks in the Hadoop ecosystem. It is also being adopted by other commercial software (e.g., ETL tools) to replace Hadoop MapReduce as the underlying execution engine.
- **ZooKeeper:** This is a high-performance coordination service for distributed applications. ZooKeeper provides coordination and synchronization of services within a cluster.

Although other systems are also available (e.g., Kafka, Mesos, Docker, Databricks, etc.), it is mainly Hadoop that is viewed as the first solution to implementing Big Data storage and processing solutions. Some key reasons include (Wu, Buyya, & Ramamohanarao, 2016):

- Hadoop is an open-source platform without licensing costs.
- Programmed in the Java programming language, it is generally adopted the standard in the developer community.
- It is a fault-tolerant system.
- The Hadoop platform provides storage and processing of huge amounts of data, with tens of terabytes being the basic measurement unit.
- It leverages a commodity type of hardware.
- It is based on the "schema-on-read" concept (i.e., it supports data agility).
- It is suited to work with different data sources.

When comparing Hadoop with conventional or relational databases, is should be considered that Hadoop is not a database. Instead, it is a distributed storage and computational framework. As explained, it is an open-source ecosystem with the following characteristics (Wu, Buyya & Ramamohanarao, 2016):

1. **Scale-Out With Distributed Computing:** With increasing amounts of data, costs of online storage increase too. Since Hadoop is operated on commodity hardware utilizing commodity disks, it follows that the price per terabyte is lower than with other technologies. Due to the application of many commodity devices, the overall IO and network capacity is higher. The addition of new servers to Hadoop simultaneously adds storage, IO, CPU, and network capacity.
2. **Expect Failures With Redundancies:** Hadoop ensures reliability by storing data redundantly on multiple servers. In this case, failure of a server does not result in data loss. Hadoop will continue running the job as processing is only switched to another server.
3. **Share-Nothing Architecture:** This is a scalable processing model. Although MapReduce may not be the most efficient way to implement algorithms, it is capable of brute-forcing acceptable performance.
4. **Schema on Read:** Hadoop allows data loading without converting data into a structured format. This feature allows retrieval and processing of data in different formats. The enforcement of structure can be postponed until access to data is requested. Schema on read distinguishes from the schema on write mode, which is used in relational databases.
5. **Development of Applications:** Hadoop framework is focused on the development of applications rather than infrastructure.

The most valuable Hadoop feature is its support for a large number of auxiliary tools. These are primarily administrative tools allowing easier monitoring, management, and maintenance of Hadoop systems. Hadoop has many APIs to connect with other Big Data applications.

The main advantages of Hadoop are (TutorialsPoint, 2014):

- The Hadoop framework allows users to write and test distributed systems quickly. It is efficient and automatically distributes data and jobs across machines. In turn, it utilizes the underlying parallelism of the CPU cores.
- Hadoop does not rely on hardware to provide fault-tolerance and high availability (FTHA). The Hadoop library is designed to detect and handle failures at the application layer.
- Servers can be dynamically added to or removed from a cluster. Hadoop continues its operation without interruption.
- In addition to being open-source, Hadoop is Java-based. Therefore, it is compatible with all platforms.

Like other technologies, Hadoop has weaknesses or limitations:

- **Security:** Hadoop security model is initially disabled due to the exceptional complexity of the Hadoop system. The person responsible for administering Hadoop should have the knowledge to establish the security model. Otherwise, all data stored in Hadoop run a high security risk. Moreover, Hadoop does not support data encryption at the storage or network level. This can be a key limitation for its implementation in the government sector or in any organization desiring to protect its data.
- **Vulnerability:** Hadoop is an open-source platform written in the Java programming language. This can be an advantage because the Java programming language is generally accepted by the developer community. Open source allows for development and improvement by many developers. On the other hand, this can be a weakness because Java is exploited by cybercriminals. Open-source allows cybercriminals to locate details on the internal structure of the Hadoop system. This makes it vulnerable to security breaches.
- **Stability:** Hadoop is an open-source platform resulting from the work of many developers. Like other open-source platforms, the involvement of many developers means constant changes to improvement and expand

functionalities. This may compromise the stability of the system. To avoid stability issues, organizations are advised to use the last stable and not the latest version. Another suggestion is to use Hadoop under a third-party vendor equipped to handle such problems.

- **Complexity:** Hadoop is a powerful framework for many distributed problems. It requires developers with high levels of specific knowledge and expertise. These developers can be hard to locate. MapReduce is especially difficult to leverage for more than simple transformational logic.

Initially, Hadoop was simple and based exclusively on HDFS and MapReduce. However, as Hadoop implementation increased, it became clear that it could not meet user expectations. Thus, the Hadoop developer community worked on the development of new tools to make the Hadoop ecosystem. It inevitably reached the status of overshooting and significantly increased Hadoop's complexity. Experience shows that most users do not need all the tools.

- **Cloud:** When the development of Hadoop started 10 years ago, cloud solutions were not widely used. Hadoop was essentially designed to run on premises in data centers. Its development was based on Google GFS and MapReduce. However, 10 years is a long period of time, especially when it comes to development and application of information technology. Today cloud solutions are generally adopted, and many companies are moving to cloud While Hadoop can formally work on the cloud, HDFS proved not to be cost-effective (Li, 2016).

It can be expected that Hadoop developers will work to solve limitations and weaknesses of this framework in the coming years. Research results presented in a 2015 Gartner report that 54% of surveyed organizations have no plans to use Hadoop in the near future. The lack of interest surrounding Hadoop is the first signal of upcoming technologies. These new technologies include: Spark; Kafka; Messos; and Docker. They prove to be better than their counterparts or fill in blank space. Realizing the challenges, Hadoop vendors have tried to integrate new sophisticated, state-of-the-art details in their products (Li, 2016). For a user, the final result is a Hadoop ecosystem that is too complex, difficult to understand, and confusing to implement and use.

This may be one reason why Arun Murthy, presently an architect at Hortonworks (the Hadoop company he has founded after working on Hadoop within Yahoo! more than 10 years ago), thinks that the Hadoop community needs to refocus on new innovations in HBase, Spark, or Flink. In doing so, needs to start thinking how to make it easier for users to develop new applications that would help them make use of all the advantages of data on the Hadoop platform. He believes that the focus should be on business customers, and on how to make Hadoop more user-friendly by developing products and solutions available out of the box, so the users do not have to understand Hadoop at all. According to Murthy, users should be able to download an app on Windows or Mac and do not care much about the underlying OS, i.e. Hadoop. Hadoop should be less about technology, and more about applications of the technology. Namely, the Hadoop developers need to make getting the value of data a trivial task for the end user (Handy, 2015).

Doug Cutting, the creator of Hadoop, believes that cloud computing and IoT will be the basis for the next stage in the growth and development of the Hadoop framework. He noted recent developments of tools to facilitate the faster exchange of information (such as Flume, Kafka, and Apache Kudu). Kudu provides real-time updating. While HDFS also provides updates, Kudu proved more convenient. With the fast development of cloud solutions, cutting pointed out developers must embrace this technology in their offerings (Kognitio, 2016).

NoSQL GENESIS

Over the last 10 years, the Big Data phenomenon and its challenges have been the main driver behind NoSQL database movement. The first NoSQL databases were developed within major companies, including Google (Google Big Table), Amazon (Dynamo), Facebook (Cassandra), and Yahoo! (PNUTS). Those internal solutions were created out of necessity rather than an intention to abandon relational databases. These companies initially used relational databases. However, because of the rapid growth of data they operate with, they very soon faced Big Data challenges. These included: unprecedented transaction volumes; expectations of low-latency access to massive datasets; and nearly perfect service availability while operating in an unreliable environment.

Attempts to find a solution to these challenges in the context of the relational world did not give satisfactory results. An attempt was made to find a solution by adding newer, faster hardware resources. Next, when that was not enough anymore, they looked for solutions by simplifying database schema; by relaxing referential integrity; and by using data partitioning. Although these techniques expanded some functionalities of relational databases, they were unsuccessful in solving existing problems. In fact, it made the application of relational technology more complicated and costly.

This was caused by dramatic changes in IT operations (the hardware model). Relational databases emerged when the dominant hardware model was based on large servers attached to dedicated storage area networks (SANs). Hardware relational databases were based on was a single server that was responsible for managing consistency of the stored database. At that time, the need to replicate data to a larger number of servers for scalability and concurrent access was not dominant. The hardware model with a single server with a hot stand-by ready to take over query processing in the event of master failure was enough to meet most application demands. However, the explosive growth of the Internet and Web brought new challenges, new hardware models, and Web servers in which a nearly linear increase in speed was achieved by the simple addition of commodity hardware. Databases were expected to scale like Web servers. Relational databases could not meet these expectations and companies were forced to seek new solutions.

In 1998, Carlo Strozzi was the first to use the term *NoSQL*. Strozzi used it to describe a simple, open-source relational database that did not use a standard SQL interface. The database stored tables as ASCII files, with each tuple represented by a line with fields separated by tabs. The name NoSQL resulted from the fact that the database, instead of SQL, used shell scripts that could be further combined into usual UNIX pipelines (Sadalage & Fowler, 2013). However, except the terminological coincidence, Strozzi's database, however, did not have any impact on the development of the NoSQL database discussed in this book.

The first use of the term NoSQL in the present sense of the word was registered in 2009 as the name of a meetup organized by Johan Oskarsson. Oskarsson was inspired by the Hadoop Summit in San Francisco. He decided to organize a meetup where open-source distributed databases, like Big Table and Dynamo, could be discussed. Looking for a convenient name for his meetup, which would be appropriate for the Twitter hashtag (i.e., short, memorizable, and without too many Google hits so that it could be easily found), he asked for suggestions on the #cassandra IRC channel. Out of those received, he selected Eric Evans' proposal, NoSQL, from Rackspace. NoSQL Meetup was about open-source, distributed, nonrelational databases. The meetup discussed databases, such as Voldemort, Cassandra, Dynomite, HBase,

CouchDB, Hypertable, and MongoDB (Saldage & Fowler, 2013). NoSQL was not used in terms of terminological integration of these databases. The original idea was only to name the meetup. The term NoSQL unexpectedly spread and was adopted by the IT community to designate the new trend in the development of databases.

Although NoSQL has become generally accepted, there is no universally adopted definition for the term. Some IT experts believe that the term is misleading because it suggests that NoSQL databases do not use SQL at all, which in the case of some NoSQL databases do not correspond to facts (Cassandra's CQL). Most agree that "no" stands for "not only." They believe that it emphasizes that NoSQL databases aim to overcome technical limitations of the relational databases rather than abandon SQL.

Essentially, NoSQL is not about abandoning some software and hardware database architectures, but it is about a specific technology. As noted in this chapter, NoSQL solutions are based on a different set of objectives and hardware models than was the case with relational databases.

There are many approaches to defining the term NoSQL database. The NoSQL archive defines NoSQL databases as "nonrelational, distributed, open-source, and horizontal scalable" (NoSQL, 2017, p.1), Nonrelational means that databases are not based on the relational data model or relations/tables. Distributed means that data is stored and managed on different hardware machines. Open-source means that everybody can use their source code and change it free of charge. Horizontally scalable means that as more database servers are added, the performance increases almost linearly.

McCreary and Kelly (2014) define NoSQL as "a set of concepts that allows the rapid and efficient processing of data sets with a focus on performance, reliability, and agility" (p. 4). Their definition does not exclude SQL or relational databases. They have identified the core issue behind NoSQL within their definition (McCreary & Kelly, 2014):

- **Tables Are Not Basic Structures:** NoSQL databases store and work with data in different formats (key-values, graphs, column-family [Bigtable], documents, and tables).
- **There Are No Joins:** NoSQL databases allow data processing through simple interfaces, without the need for joins.
- **They Are Schema-Free:** NoSQL databases allow data manipulation without the need for their previous modeling (e.g., entity-relational model).

- **There Are Many Processors:** NoSQL databases allow storage on multiple processors while keeping high levels of performance.
- **They Use Shared-Nothing Commodity Computers:** Most NoSQL databases are based on hardware architecture consisting of low-cost commodity processors that have separate random access memory (RAM) and disk.
- **They Support Linear Scalability:** The addition of a larger number of processors is manifested in a consistent increase in performance.
- **Innovation:** NoSQL databases offer several options to store and process data, including SQL. NoSQL supporters advocate an inclusive approach, aware that there is not only one solution to any problem. For them, NoSQL means "not only SQL."

Since NoSQL databases are not strictly defined, one way to explain them is to specify what NoSQL databases are not or should not be (McCreary & Kelly, 2014):

- **It Is Not About SQL:** The definition of NoSQL databases does not mean that they exclusively use other languages rather than SQL. SQL, as well as other query languages, are used in NoSQL databases.
- **They Are Not Only Open-Source:** While many NoSQL databases are developed as open-source, there is an increasing number of commercial databases that use the NoSQL concept.
- **It Is Not Only About Big Data**: While Big Data is the driving force behind the creation and application of NoSQL databases (as well as volume and velocity), NoSQL focuses on variability and agility.
- **It Is Not Only Cloud Computing:** Many NoSQL databases are stored in the cloud to make use of its ability to rapidly scale when the situation dictates. However, that does not mean that they cannot efficiently work with a corporate data center.
- **It Is Not Only About the Smart Use of RAM and Solid State Disks (SSDs):** Efficient use of RAM or SSDs is important to boost performance. However, NoSQL databases can also be used on standard hardware.

To understand NoSQL databases, this chapter will analyze their basic features.

THE FEATURES OF NoSQL DATABASES

This chapter will describe common features for most NoSQL databases. It was discussed that NoSQL is an umbrella term related to numerous databases. Each NoSQL database has different architecture and purpose. NoSQL supporters believe that a universal solution which could be applicable to all data types, volumes, and objectives does not exist. The definition of NoSQL databases comprises main features of those databases: nonrelational; distributed; open-source; and horizontally scalable (NoSQL, 2017).

NoSQL archive as additional features common for most NoSQL databases lists the following (NoSQL, 2017): schema-free; easy replication support; simple API; eventually consistent/BASE (not ACID); a huge amount of data, etc. Authors propose diverse features common to NoSQL databases. This chapter will incorporate those approaches to discuss the following main features of NoSQL databases:

- Based on nonrelational model
- Distributed and cluster oriented
- Schema-free/Schemaless
- Use CAP and BASE approach
- Support Big Data
- Open-source
- Horizontally scalable
- Right data model for the right problem

Based on Non-Relational Model

As opposed to relational databases, which are based on relational model (i.e., whose structure is composed of relations [tables] and highly normalized, while the structure of NoSQL databases is denormalized (redundant) and very flexible, meaning that data is stored together depending on their usage, and different structure like JSON, XML, etc. can be used. NoSQL databases avoid join operations due to complexity. This is true, especially when data is stored in many different tables, which is often the case in relational databases. In relational databases, tables consist of rows (tuples) and columns (attributes). A relation (table) is a restrictive data structure because columns (attributes) can have only a single value. This means that complex structures, like nesting one tuple within another, are not allowed. If data stored in different tables (relations) need to be analyzed or presented together, relational databases have to use joins to link tables. In the case of many tables, this can be a complex operation.

NoSQL databases have a different approach since they recognize the necessity to operate on data that have a more complex structure than tables (relations) (for example, lists and other record structures to be nested inside it). Term aggregate (which comes from domain-driven design) can comprise a collection of relates objects that must be treated as a unit. Using aggregates makes it easier for NoSQL databases to handle operating on a cluster. The aggregate makes a natural unit for replication and sharding. Aggregates are often easier for application programmers to work with since they manipulate data through aggregate structures (Sadalage & Fowler, 2013).

Consequently, NoSQL databases do not store information on how data relate to each other (i.e., the same data can be stored multiple times). Although multiple storages of the same data requires extra storage space and additional application software efforts, there are two benefits of the approach (Flower, 2015):

- **Easy Storage and Retrieval:** Data is stored and retrieved as a single record.
- **Query Speed:** Data required by a query is stored as a single record. In the relational model, data is stored in different tables, and queries use joins to integrate necessary data. This reduces query speed.

These benefits should not be the main driver for the use of NoSQL databases. Relational (normalized) and NoSQL (denormalized) approaches are different solutions related to data spread across records. Both approaches have advantages and disadvantages. The main disadvantages of nonrelational models are that software must take into account managing of multiple storages of the same data. This increases the cost of data storage.

Distributed and Cluster Oriented

The first NoSQL databases arose as an answer to requirements for storing enormous data quantities by using huge numbers of commercial hardware (see Google example in "Google Architecture and MapReduce"). The distributed approach is crucial in efficient Big Data storage and management. Even the largest available single server is not sufficient for storing and managing necessary data. The key advantage of distributing database is cheaper servers (i.e., commodity hardware can replace expensive servers). Performance improvement can be achieved by adding new machines to the cluster. In the case of individual machine failures, clusters are more resilient. The overall cluster provides high reliability because it keeps going despite failure.

However, relational databases are not designed to run on clusters. Some relational database vendors try to find solutions (for example, Oracle with Oracle RAC or Microsoft with Microsoft SQL Server). The solution is based on the concept of a shared disk subsystem and uses a cluster-aware file system to write to a highly-available disk subsystem. This means that the cluster still has the disk subsystem as a single point of failure. Relational databases could also run as separate servers for different sets of data. This effectively sharding the database. Although this separates the data load, sharding must be controlled by the application. The application must keep track which database server to talk to for each bit of data. It is necessary to lose querying, referential integrity, transactions, or consistency controls that cross shards. In that situation, relational databases are acting unnatural (Sadalage & Fowler, 2013).

Licensing costs are another issue. The mismatch between relational databases and clusters forced organizations with Big Data issues to consider alternative solutions to data storage (Google, Amazon, etc.). As explained, this was the beginning of NoSQL database development. For NoSQL databases, data distribution and clusters are natural situations.

SCHEMA-FREE/SCHEMALESS

Relational databases expect the existence of a schema to enable data storing. The schema defines database structure and the relations between them (i.e., tables, columns [fields]). NoSQL databases have a more liberal approach to data storing. They operate without a schema; they do not need to define database structure to store and manage data. This schema-free or schemaless approach can be efficient in working with nonuniform data (i.e., data where each record has a different set of fields). As will be explained in the next chapter, a key-value store allows storing of any data under a key. A document database is similar, making no restrictions on the structure of the stored document. A column-family database allows storing any data under any column, while graph databases allow free adding of new edges and properties to nodes and edges (Sadalage & Fowler, 2013).

Without a schema, it is not necessary to define the data structure in advance (i.e., without a schema binding it is easier to store whatever is needed). This enables an easy change of data and addition of new data as they appear. If some data is no longer needed, their storage can be stopped without concern for losing old data. It is opposite to deleting columns in a relational schema.

Although a schema-free approach avoids problems related to fixed-schema databases, it has problems of its own. Schema-free databases shift the schema into the application code that accesses it because each program with access to data almost always relies on some form of implicit schema. The implicit schema is a set of assumptions about the data's structure in the code that manipulates the data. The database cannot use the schema to decide how to store and retrieve data efficiently or to apply its own validations upon that data to ensure that different applications do not manipulate data in an inconsistent way (Sadalage & Fowler, 2013).

One way to reduce these problems is to encapsulate all database interaction within a single application and integrate it with other applications using web services. This works well in situations where web services are used for integration. Another approach is to clearly identify areas of an aggregate for access by different applications (i.e., creating different sections in a document database or different column families in a column-family database (Sadalage & Fowler, 2013).

NoSQL advocates are critical toward relational schemas because they must be defined in advance and reduce flexibility. However, this is not completely true. Relational schemas can be changed whenever it is necessary by using regular SQL commands. This can be done in a controlled way. Changing the way data is stored in a schema-free database requires additional control to ensure access to both old and new data. Flexibility, as the most cited advantage of schema-free databases, applies only within an aggregate. Changing aggregate boundaries can be as complex as in the relational schema.

Use CAP and BASE Approach

NoSQL databases are distributed and cluster oriented. Data consistency and availability should be resolved differently than when a central data server is in question. The CAP theorem stresses that distributed databases can have no more than two of three desirable properties: consistency; high availability; and partition tolerance. According to the CAP theorem, in a situation when data is partitioned and distributed, it is necessary to have a different approach related to availability and consistency. This is especially true in the case of network failures. This theorem allows organizations to find a response (sacrificing tolerance, sacrificing consistency, or sacrificing availability) to best match their business requirements. For example, CAP theorem forces organizations to determine if they are prepared to accept a write operation if the network communication fails between the nodes. If an organization decides to accept this write, it must take responsibility to ensure a later update for the remote node and accept the risk that a client is reading inconsistent data until communication is restored. On the other hand, if an organization chooses to refuse the write, it sacrifices availability and forces the client to retry accessing data later. The CAP theorem is an effective tool in guiding database selection discussions within organizations, as well as prioritizing properties (consistency, availability, and scalability). If an organization concludes that high consistency and update availabilities are simultaneously required, then a faster single processor would be the best choice. On the contrary, if an organization needs the scale-out benefits offered by distributed systems, then it can make decisions about its need for update availability vs. read consistency for each transaction type. The CAP theorem offers a formal process to weigh the pros and cons of SQL or NoSQL databases (McCreary & Kelly, 2014).

Transaction control is an important aspect in distributed environments which focuses on performance and consistency. One of two types of transaction control models are used: ACID (in RDBMS) and BASE (found in many NoSQL databases). BASE originated as an alternative for ACID transaction properties. Its main purpose was to provide additional options to expanding distributed systems, as well as the simple integration of more hardware to expand data operations. The main difference between these models is the effort required by application developers and the location (tier) of the transactional controls. In relational databases, the transaction management is fully under control of the database system.

Software developers must deal with transaction failures to find a way to notify a user or to retry until the transaction is complete. Software developers do not need to worry or know how to undo parts of a transaction because transaction management is built into the database. Unlike RDBMSs that focus on consistency, BASE systems focus on availability. BASE systems store new data, even at the risk of being out of sync for a short period of time. They relax the rules and allow reports to run even if not all portions of the database are synchronized (McCreary & Kelly, 2014).

BASE systems are optimistic because they assume that eventually all systems will catch up and become consistent. BASE systems tend to be simpler and faster because they do not deal with data locking and unlocking. Their main goals are to enable that the process is moving and to deal with failures later. This makes them ideal for web stores, where filling a shopping cart and placing an order is the high priority.

Support Big Data

The origin of NoSQL databases is a consequence of Big Data challenges unresolved with the relational database technology of that time. Big Data has requests for storing and management of an enormous quantity of complex, dynamic, evolving, distributed, and heterogeneous data from different sources and platforms.

NoSQL databases emerged as an answer to those challenges. Today, NoSQL databases are a possible solution when different kinds of big are in question. For example, Big Data, a big number of users, big number of computers, big supply chains, big science, etc. This will be discussed in Chapter 4.

Open-Source

Open-source systems are one of the first associations to NoSQL databases. However, not all NoSQL databases are open-source systems. Most of the today's commercial database vendors (Oracle, Microsoft) have developed commercial NoSQL databases. Many NoSQL databases are open-source, meaning that they are the work of many developers. A NoSQL open-source community is very strong. As in other open-source platforms, the involvement of many developers usually means constant changes aimed at improvements and functionality expansion. This may compromise the stability of the system. To avoid stability issues, organizations are advised to use the last stable and not the latest version of NoSQL databases.

Horizontally Scalable

Horizontally scalable refers to a situation where database servers are added to improve performance in a nearly linear way. This is often called scale-out. When data is distributed over many servers, it enables scaling of data set and distribution of the processing load. A characteristic of the most NoSQL databases is the automatic distribution of data to new servers added to the cluster, and the performance improvement as a final result.

Right Data Model for the Right Problem

The appearance and development of NoSQL databases confirm that there is no single solution for different data problems. There have been many attempts to use the relational database for solving problems that are contrary to the real nature of these databases. NoSQL databases focus on the fact that different data models have to be used in solving different problems. For this reason, many different (by structure and purpose) databases have been developed under the umbrella of NoSQL databases.

NoSQL DATABASES CLASSIFICATION

Today, different types of Big Data problems are, with more or less success, resolved with different NoSQL database architectures. According to that, NoSQL database can be classified in four basic categories, each resolving the different type of Big Data problems:

- Key-Value
- Column-Family (Bigtable)
- Document
- Graph

Key-Value Stores

The key-value type of NoSQL databases uses a key to locate a value (traditional data, BLOBs – Binary Large OBjects, files, etc.) in simple, standalone tables, known as hash tables. In that case, searches are performing against keys, not values, and they are restricted to exact matches. The key can be accessed by hashing, indexing, brute-force scans, or any other appropriate method. This is the most primitive model for data retrieval.

The term *data store* is often used instead of the term *database* when referring to NoSQL databases to emphasize that these databases do not have all the properties and possibilities of relational databases. Key-value stores are also different from relational databases terminologically (Table 2).

McCreary and Kelly (2014) compare a key-value store with a dictionary where each word has at least one definition. Using key-value store terminology, the dictionary is organized so that each word can be said to represent a key and definition represents a value.

From the perspective of the programming interface, key-value stores are the simplest form of NoSQL databases because the client can only either get the value for a particular key, put a value to a key or delete a key from the database. The value is only a BLOB that is stored in the database without a need to know what is inside the BLOB. It is the applications that should know what is stored (string, XML file, binary image, PDF document, web page, etc.). Also, keys in a key-value store may have different formats: file path name, web page URL, REST web service call, image name, SQL query, etc.

It is easiest to describe a key-value store as a table with two columns where the first column is called the key and the second is called the value. Three operations are performed on a key-value store: put, get and delete, and they are the basis of the program interface (API - Application Program Interface) for work with a key-value store (see Figure 14).

So, instead of SQL or some other query language, it is the functions put, get and delete that are used to work with key-value stores. The put function adds a new key-value pair and updates a value if the key already exists. The get function returns the value for a particular key or returns an error message if such key does not exist, while the delete function removes a key and its value, or returns an error message if the key does not exist. In addition to these functions, two rules are the basis of a key-value store (McCreary & Kelly, 2014):

Table 2. Terminological comparison of relational and key-value stores

RDBMS	Key-Value Store
Database instance	Cluster
Table	Bucket
Row	Key-value
Rowid	Key

Sadalage & Fowler, 2013.

Figure 14. Key-value store API
McCreary & Kelly, 2014.

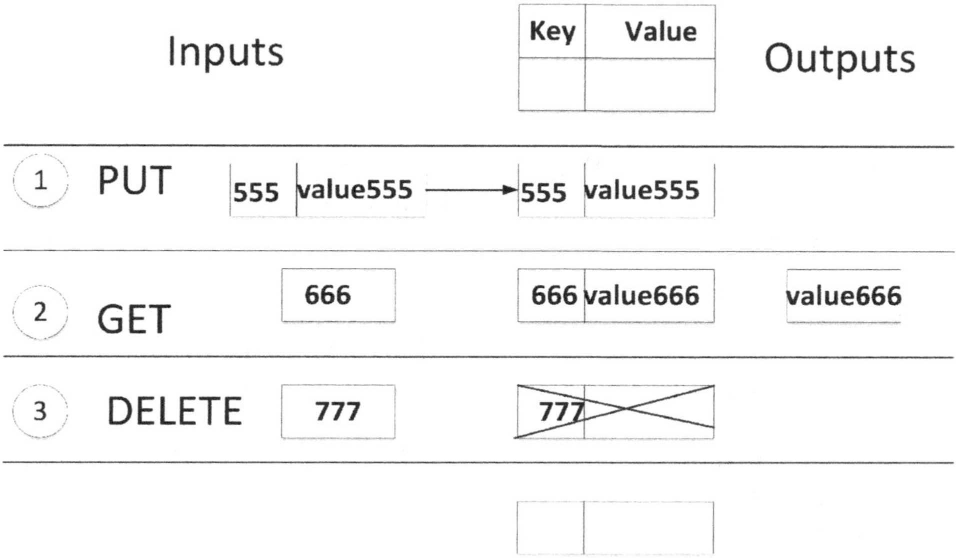

1. **Distinct Keys:** Speaking in terms of relational databases, unique keys, which means that there can never be two rows with the same value for a key.
2. **No Queries on Values:** To perform a query, it has to based exclusively on a key, in other words, it is not possible to perform a query based on value.

The main advantages of key-value stores are:

- **Scalability:** Most key-value stores use sharding to provide scalability. Sharding uses the value of a key to determine in which node the key will be stored. This way of sharding can result in increased performance, especially when a large number of nodes is added to a cluster (Sadalage & Fowler, 2013).
- **In-Memory Caches:** Serve great in-memory caches because they are optimized for queries based on keys.
- **Precision Service Levels:** Simple interface allows setting and allocating resources to new data services and their quick reconfiguring.

Since service levels can be adapted to application needs, that in turn has a positive effect on system reliability and performance.

Advantages of key-value stores come into play when dealing with business issues such as:

- **Storing Data on Web Pages:** Every web page is defined by a unique uniform resource locator (URL), which essentially represents the key of the web page, and the value is the web page or resources located on this URL. This allows storing of all static components of the web page (images, static HTML pages, CSS, JavaScript) in a key-value store, which is the option used by many websites. Only the dynamic part of a website, which is generated by script languages, is not stored in key-value stores (McCreary & Kelly, 2014).
- **Storing Customer Profiles and Preferences, as Well as Product Profiles:** Both customers and products usually have their unique identification number (ID), which is an ideal candidate for the key in a key-value store.
- **Storing Shopping Cart Data:** Online shopping websites have to link shopping carts with customers, or their unique keys (IDs) to ensure the availability of information on the purchase of a particular user at all times.

Some of the best-known key-value stores are Amazon DynamoDB, Berkeley DB, HamsterDB, Memcached DB, Redis, and Riak.

Key-value stores have certain limitations and are not the best solution in the following cases (Sadalage & Fowler, 2013):

- **Relationships Among Data:** If it is necessary to establish relationships between different sets of data, key-value stores are not the best solution.
- **Multioperation Transactions:** If multiple keys are stored, and there is an error when storing any of them, and it is necessary to perform rollback operations, key-value stores are not a good solution.
- **Query by Value:** As a rule, key-value stores do not provide queries based on values, although there are exceptions like Riak Search.
- **Operations by Sets:** Since operations are limited to one key at a time, there is no way to work with multiple keys at the same time.

Column-Family (Bigtable) Stores

Column-family (Bigtable) or column-oriented NoSQL databases were named for their design with data stored in columns. In contrast, a row-oriented database (like RDBMS) keeps information about a row together (see Figure 15). In column-family stores, adding columns is inexpensive; it is applied on a row-by-row basis. With respect to structure, columns are midway between relational and key-value (Redmond & Wilson, 2012). Column-family stores are useful in situations where data exist whose columns can change and need to be retrieved as a group or aggregate (Fowler, 2016).

Table 3 shows terminological differences between relational and column-family databases.

Figure 15. Column vs. row data storage

ID	Product description	Price	Quantity
10	Milk	1.20	5.00
22	Chocolate	2.10	10.00
23	Bread	1.00	22.00
54	Juice	1.56	11.00

Storing data in relational database
10, Milk, 1.20, 5.00
22, Chocolate, 2.10, 10.00
23, Bread, 1.00, 22.00
54, Juice, 1.56, 11.00

Storing data in column-family store
10, 22, 23, 54
Milk, Chocolate, Bread, Juice
1.20, 2.10, 1.00, 2.56
5.00, 10.00, 22.00, 11.00

Table 3. Terminological comparison of relational and column-family stores

RDBMS	Column-Family Store
Database instance	Cluster
Database	Keyspace
Table	Column family
Row	Row
Column (same for all rows)	Column (can be different per row)

Sadalage & Fowler, 2013.

Figure 16. Key structure in column-family store
McCreary & Kelly, 2014.

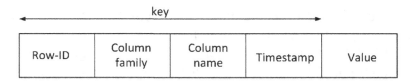

McCreary and Kelly (2014) compare the basic logic of column-family stores with the logic of spreadsheets. Unlike key-value stores, spreadsheets use two keys instead of one to access a value (data): the row number and the letter mark of the column number. For example, C8 designates the value stored in the cell located at the intersection of column C and row 8. Column-family stores use a similar concept. Finding a piece of data requires information on the row and the column. However, in addition to row and column, the key in a column-family store has two additional attributes in its structure: column family and timestamp (see Figure 16). A column family groups similar column names; a timestamp allows storage of multiple versions of each value over time.

Not all column-family stores use the column family attribute as part of the key. When used, it is necessary to take that into consideration when storing data, because since column family is an integral part of the key, it is impossible to access data without it.

Column-family stores have several advantages.

- They are fully adapted to distributed file systems (Hadoop) and MapReduce.
- Higher scalability results from the simplicity of the concept in which data is identified by keys containing row and column numbers. This simple interface allows queries to be distributed to many processing nodes without the use of join operations.
- Higher availability is the result of high scalability levels that allow data to be replicated on multiple nodes in a network. Nonuse of join operations allows storage of any part of a column family matrix on remote computers. In the case of failure of the server storing that column family the matrix, other computers can access the data on remote computers (McCreary & Kelly, 2014).

- It is simple to add new data. It is not necessary to define the entire data model before starting to work with these types of databases. If a column family is used as part of the key, it is necessary to define grouping or what belongs to a column family prior to beginning the work. New columns can be added over time without having to worry about filling in default values for the existing rows for the new columns.
- It performs better work with a subset of the available columns, especially when calculating maximums, minimums, sums, or averages on huge datasets.

The above advantages of column-family stores are manifested in solving business problems:

- **Storing Analytical Information:** A typical example is the Google Analytics service, which uses Google Bigtable to store information on website use. Every time a user clicks on a web page that is stored in a single row-column entry that as the URL and the timestamp has the row ID. The row IDs are organized in such a way that all page hits for a specific user session are together (McCreary & Kelly, 2014). Google Analytics is an example of a huge database that scales in almost linear fashion as the number of users increases. As new transactions appear, new hits are immediately added to the table.
- **Storing Geographic Information:** Geographic information systems (GIS), like Google Maps, store geographic points on the Earth, moon, or other planets. It identifies locations using longitude and latitude coordinates. GIS is organized by clustering similar row IDs, which results in an extremely fast finding of all images/points that are close to each other on the map (McCreary & Kelly, 2014).
- **Event Logging:** The ability to store any data structures allows column-family stores to store event information (application status or errors) with their own columns and the rows (Sadalage & Fowler, 2013).
- **Content Management Systems and Blogging Platforms:** Column-family stores allow efficient storage of blog entries with tags, categories, links, and trackbacks in different columns. Comments can also be stored in the same row or moved to another keyspace. Column families can be used to organize blog users and actual blogs in different column families (Sadalage & Fowler, 2013).

Publication of the Google paper on Google Bigtable (Ghemawat, Gobioff, & Leung, 2003; Dean & Ghemawat, 2004) had a decisive effect on the development of the Google Datastore, as well as other column-family stores, including Apache Cassandra, HBase, Hypertable and Amazon SimpleDB.

Column-family stores also have limitations.

- They do not support SQL queries in real time.
- Although they may have higher-level query languages, they usually generate batch MapReduce jobs.
- For faster access to data, it is necessary to use a custom API written in programming languages such as Java or Python.
- They are not recommended for systems that require ACID transactions for writes or reads.
- If it is necessary to aggregate data using queries (e.g., SUM or AVG), this must be done on the client side using data retrieved by the client from all rows (Sadalage & Fowler, 2013).

Document Stores

Document-oriented NoSQL stores were designed to store and manage documents. The documents are encoded in standard data exchange formats (XML, JSON [JavaScript Object Notation], BSON [Binary JSON]). The document is similar to a hash, with a unique ID field and values that may be any of a variety of types, including more hashes. Documents can contain nested structures; they exhibit a high degree of flexibility, which allows for variable domains.

A document store can be represented in the form of a tree structure (see Figure 17). Document trees generally have a single root element, although they may have multiple root elements. Under the root element are several branches, sub-branches, and values. Each branch has a related path expression (document path) showing how to navigate through the tree (McCreary & Kelly, 2014).

Table 4 shows terminological differences between relational and document stores.

A primary feature of a document store is that everything inside a document is automatically indexed when a new document is added. Although indexes are large, it is possible to search everything stored within the database. If any property of a document is known, it is possible to quickly find all documents

Figure 17. Tree structure of the document store
McCreary & Kelly, 2014.

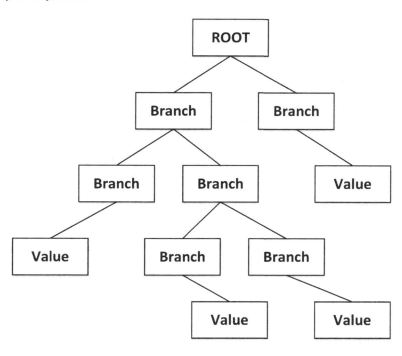

Table 4. Terminological comparison of relational and document stores

RDBMS	Document Store
Database instance	Document store instance
Schema	Database
Table	Collection
Row	Document
Rowid	Id

Sadalage & Fowler, 2013.

with the same property. In addition, it is possible to exact locations using the document path, which is a type of key for accessing the leaf values of a tree.

Most document stores group documents into collections that are like the structure of directories of operational systems (for example, Windows or UNIX). Collections allow for the organization of document stores by grouping similar documents, storing business rules, and navigating through document hierarchies. Collections can be further grouped like trees or may contain other collections. Document collections can also be used as application collections or as containers for data, scripts, views, and transforms of the software application (McCreary & Kelly, 2014).

It is typical for document stores to have an API or a query language that specifies the path or path expression for any node or group of nodes. Nodes do not need different names because position numbers determine nodes in the tree.

Different document stores offer different query options. For example, CouchD allows queries over views that can be materialized or dynamic. Further, CouchDB allows aggregation and calculation of averages by adding views implemented via MapReduce to return a count or average.

MongoDB uses a query language expressed via JSON. $query is an expression for the where clause. $orderby is an expression for data sorting. $explain is an expression to display the query execution plan (Sadalage & Fowler, 2013). These and other similar expressions can be combined when creating queries in MongoDB.

Several advantages exist for document stores.

- In a situation with multiple requests, it is not necessary to calculate the count or average for each request. Instead, it is possible to add a materialized view that precomputes the values and stores the results in the database (Vaish, 2013).
- Document stores allow queries on data within a document without having to retrieve the entire document by its key. A search within the document is then possible.
- The content in document stores is schemaless or very loosely defined. This proves useful in web-oriented applications that ensure storage of different contents that change over time.
- For document stores based on XML, BSON, JSON, and YAML, it is possible to partially retrieve or update a record (Vaish, 2013).
- Document stores allow for the creation of indexes.
- Document stores based on JSON allow for the creation of so-called projections (Vaish, 2013). Top-level key for a JSON object can be the entity's projection across other parts of the system. This allows the schema to evolve over time, providing the backward compatibility.

Advantages of document stores come into play when solving different types of business problems:

- **Content Management and Blogging Platforms:** As noted, document stores do not require predefined schemas because most of them work with JSON documents, store Web content, and photographs. They can use geolocation indexes to find data, which makes them convenient databases for content management systems, user comment management, user registration, Web site applications, etc.
- **Real Time and Web Analytics:** Since document stores allow updating to only a part of documents, they are convenient for the storage of page views. Since there is no schema, adding a new metric does not require a change of schema. They are used for real-time sentiment analysis, social media monitoring, etc.
- **E-Commerce:** Data stores allow storage and queries for very complex and changeable data on products.

Some of the best-known document stores are MongoDB, CouchDB, Terrastore, OrientDB, and RavenDB.

Document stores also have limitations (Sadalage & Fowler, 2013):

- **Complex Transactions Spanning Different Operations:** Document stores are not appropriate to perform atomic cross-document operations.
- **Queries Against Varying Aggregate Structure:** Since document stores are based on the flexible schema, data is stored in the form of application entities or aggregates. This means that if the design of the aggregate keeps changes, it is necessary to store aggregates at the lowest level of granularity. Another option is to normalize data, which is contrary to the basic idea of document stores.

Graph Stores

Graph NoSQL databases excel at dealing with highly interconnected data. They focus on relationships rather than data. A graph store consists of nodes and relationships between nodes. Both nodes and relationships have properties (or key-value pairs) to store data (see Figure 18). The real strength of graph databases is traversing through the nodes by following relationships (Redmond & Wilson, 2012).

A graph store consists of three data fields: (1) nodes; (2) relationships; and (3) properties (see Figure 19). Node-relationship-node structures are also called triple stores (McCreary & Kelly, 2014).

Figure 18. Graph presentation
Vaish, 2013.

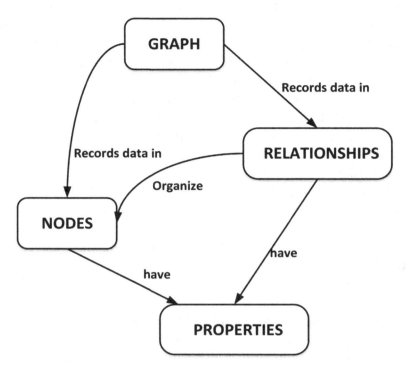

Figure 19. Structure of the graph store
McCreary & Kelly, 2014.

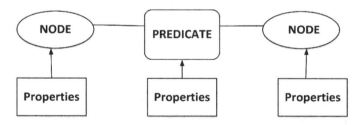

Graph stores link nodes know that two nodes with the same identifier are the same node. Graph stores assign internal identifiers to nodes and use these identifiers to connect networks. However, graph store joins are by their nature small and, unlike RDBMS joins, computationally lightweight and fast because they can be kept in RAM. Retrieving data does not require disk input and output operations (McCreary & Kelly, 2014).

When loading nodes into RAM, most graph stores assign an internal ID to each node. The World Wide Web Consortium (W3C) is an international community where member organizations, a full-time staff, and the public work together to develop Web standards. They have established identifiers similar to URL identifiers, which are called uniform resource identifiers (URIs). These create explicit identifiers for each node. This standard is called W3C resource description format (RDF) and is designed to allow joining external datasets created by different organizations. Thanks to this standard, it is possible to load two external datasets into one graph store and execute graph queries on such joined data. This is because RDF uses direct graphs, where the relationship directly points from the source node to the destination node (McCreary & Kelly, 2014). The terms *subject*, *predicate*, and *object* are often used to describe this situation (see Figure 20).

These terms are taken from the formal system logic and language. The RDF standard calls each node-arc-node relationship a triple. The fact that two nodes in different groups reference the same physical object generates the ability to traverse a graph. Through the RDF standard, the W3C is trying to maintain consistency of all its standards. However, unlike a URL, a URI does not need to point at any actual website or web page. It must be globally consistent throughout the Web, as well as fully matching when comparing two nodes.

Pure triple stores are rarely found in practice because they relate additional information (e.g., date of creation or last update, group to which the graph belongs, etc.). These additional attributes are called link metadata because they give context to the link while facilitating data management and auditing.

Graph stores use query languages. For instance, Gremlin is a domain-specific language for traversing graphs or graph stores that implement the Blueprints property graph. The Neo4J graph store uses the Cypher query language for querying graphs.

Graph stores have several advantages:

Figure 20. RDF specific names
McCreary & Kelly, 2014.

- In a situation with many complexly interrelated items, they are ideal. When their relationships have properties, they allow simple queries to show the closest neighboring node. They also produce queries to search deeper and more quickly for patterns in networks.
- Graph stores find paths between two nodes. This establishes whether there are multiple paths. They are able to locate the shortest path.
- Graph stores allow indexing properties of a node, as well as indexing properties of relationships or edges. It is possible to find a node or edge by the value. Indexes should be queried to find the starting node to begin a traversal (Sadalage & Fowler, 2013).
- Interaction with graph stores is similar to that with relational databases (load, query, update, and delete data). However, there is a difference in query types. A graph query returns a set of nodes that are used to create a graph image on display to show relationships between data (see Figure 21).

The graph store advantages are manifested when solving business problems such as:

- **Social Networks:** They are a natural environment for graph stores, although every field rich in relationships is convenient for graph stores (spatial, telephone, or e-mail records). Graph stores bring an additional value, especially in a situation when relationships between entities from different domains are in the same database (social, spatial, commerce data). They allow traversing across domains.

Figure 21. Example of a graph

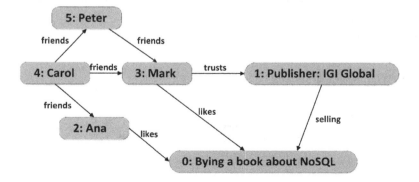

- **Location-Based Services:** Delivery locations or addresses are convenient for graph stores because a delivery is treated as a node. Nodes, where the delivery should be made, can be modeled as a graph of nodes. Relationships between nodes can have distance as property, which can calculate the quickest delivery path or recommend a restaurant or shop closest to the user's location.
- **Recommendations:** Nodes and relationships between nodes in graph stores create recommendations like "users who bought this book, also bought the following books... ." Recommendations can be created to endorse places to visit in a city. This is based on information from others who have already visited the city. As the number of data grows, so do the number of nodes and relationships that can be used to create recommendations. Data from graph stores can be used as a basis for data mining analyses (e.g., which products are purchased together [analysis of shopping cart]) or to find patterns in relationships to locate fraudulent transactions.
- **Rules and Inference:** These perform queries on complex structures, including class libraries, taxonomies, or rule-based systems.
- **Integrating Linked Data:** This is used when it is necessary for a large amount of open linked data to provide real-time integration and build mashups without storing the data.

Some of the better-known graph stores are Neo4J, Infinite Graph, OrientDB, and FlockDB. FlockDB is a special case because it only supports single-depth relationships or adjacency lists; it cannot traverse more than one level deep for relationships (Sadalage & Fowler, 2013).

In addition to the said advantages, graph stores also have limitations:

- Unlike other types of NoSQL databases, graph stores have problems with scaling on a large number of servers because of the relatedness of nodes in a graph.
- Although the triple structure of graph stores seems simple, each database has complex and inconsistent jargon, which complicates implementation.

It is important to stress that the four main categories of NoSQL databases are described globally to present the basic characteristics, advantages, and disadvantages that apply to most of these database types. This does not mean that some do not have different possibilities and implementations. Possibilities

Figure 22. NoSQL databases and Big Data problems
Gašpar & Mabić, 2016.

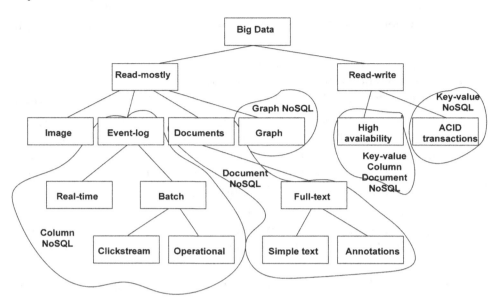

for application or business problems that each of these databases effectively solves are specified.

Figure 22 shows how these categories of NoSQL databases respond to Big Data problems presented in Figure 2. When high availability is in question, most NoSQL databases resolve that problem. When ACID transactions are in question, only key-value databases, which are the closest to relational databases, can compete. Wide column databases are more suitable for event-log problems, while document databases are best in document management. Graph databases are best in graph management.

REFERENCES

Avro. (2012). *Welcome to Avro!*. Retrieved December 12, 2016 from https://avro.apache.org/docs/1.2.0/

BigData. (2016). *Hadoop ecosystem overview*. Retrieved October 17, 2016 from http://thebigdatablog.weebly.com/blog/the-hadoop-ecosystem-overview

Borthakur, D. (2009). *Hadoop architecture and its usage at Facebook.* Retrieved February 7, 2017 from http://borthakur.com/ftp/hadoopmicrosoft.pdf

Chukwa. (2016). *Welcome to Apache Chukwa.* Retrieved, January 23, 2017 from https://chukwa.apache.org/

CrowdFlower. (2016). *Data science report.* Retrieved July 23, 2017 from http://visit.crowdflower.com/rs/416-ZBE-142/images/CrowdFlower_DataScienceReport_2016.pdf

CSC. (2012). *Taking on the explosion with radical new databases.* Retrieved July 23, 2017 from http://assets1.dxc.technology/insights/downloads/CSC_Infographic_Big_Data.pdf

DAMA. (2013). *The six primary dimensions for data quality assessment - Defining data quality dimensions.* DAMA UK and the Data Quality Dimensions Working Group. Retrieved July 11, 2017 from https://www.dqglobal.com/wp-content/uploads/2013/11/DAMA-UK-DQ-Dimensions-White-Paper-R37.pdf

Dean, J., & Ghemawat, S. (2004). *MapReduce: Simplified data processing on large clusters.* Retrieved November 20, 2016 from https://static.googleusercontent.com/media/research.google.com/hr// archive/mapreduce-osdi04.pdf

Elliott, T. (2013). *7 definitions of big data you should know about.* Retrieved July 24, 2017 from http://timoelliott.com/blog/2013/07/7-definitions-of-big-data-you-should-know-about.html

Experian. (2016). *The 2016 global data management benchmark report.* Experian Data Quality.

Fowler, A. (2015). *NoSQL for dummies.* John Wiley & Sons, Inc.

FTCA. (2016). *Federal Trade Commission Act section 5: Unfair or deceptive acts or practices.* Retrieved July 24, 2017 from https://www.federalreserve.gov/boarddocs/supmanual/cch/ftca.pdf

Gašpar, D., & Mabić, M. (2016). NoSQL Databases for Big Data Management. *Proceedings of 27th Central European Conference on Information and Intelligent System*, 3-10.

Ghemawat, S., Gobioff, H., & Leung, S.-T. (2003). *The Google file system.* Retrieved August 2, 2016 from http://static.googleusercontent.com/media/research.google.com/hr//archive/gfs-sosp2003.pdf

HADOOP1. (2016). *What is Apache Hadoop?.* Retrieved October 29, 2016 from http://hadoop.apache.org/

HADOOP. (2016). *Hadoop – HDFS overview.* Retrieved October 29, 2016 from http://www.tutorialspoint.com/hadoop_hdfs_overview.htm

Handy, A. (2015). *Arun Murthy discusses the future of Hadoop.* Retrieved October 29, 2016 from http://sdtimes.com/arun-murthy-discusses-the-future-of-hadoop/#sthash.VSQfj4YQ.dpuf

Hilbert, M., Lopez, P. (2011). The world's technological capacity to store, communicate, and compute information. *International Journal of Communication, 6*(2012), 956–979.

ICLG. (2017). *Data protection 2017.* Retrieved July 11, 2017 from https://iclg.com/practice-areas/data-protection/data-protection-2017#general-chapters

IDC. (2014). *The digital universe of opportunities: Rich data and the increasing value of the internet of things.* Retrieved November 6, 2016 from http://www.emc.com/leadership/digital-universe/2014iview/executive-summary.htm

Internetlivestats. (2017). *Internet live stats.* Retrieved July 25, 2017 from http://www.internetlivestats.com/

Kognitio. (2016). *IOT and cloud "the future of Hadoop".* Retrieved November 6, 2016 from http://kognitio.com/iot-and-cloud-the-future-of-hadoop/

KPMG. (2016). *Now or never CEOs mobilize for the fourth industrial revolution - U.S. CEO outlook 2016.* Retrieved November 6, 2016 from https://assets.kpmg.com/content/dam/kpmg/pdf/2016 /07/2016-ceo-survey.pdf

Li, H. (2016). *The future of Hadoop is misty.* Retrieved November 11, 2016 from https://haifengl.wordpress.com/2016/03/03/the-future-of-hadoop-is-misty/

Liu, J., Li, J., Li, W., & Wu, J. (2015). Rethinking big data: A review on the data quality and usage issues. *ISPRS Journal of Photogrammetry and Remote Sensing.*

Loshin, D. (2015). *Addressing five emerging challenges of big data*. Progress White Paper.

Love, S. (2016, Sept.). Change is coming. *Information Age*. Retrieved November 8, 2016 from www.information-age.com

McCreary, D., & Kelly, A. (2014). *Making sense of NoSQL: A guide for managers and the rest of us*. Manning Publications Co.

NoSQL. (2017). Retrieved June 27, 2017 from http://nosql-database.org/

Pierce, E., Yonke, C.L., & Youn, M. (2016). *The state of information quality and data governance*. 2016 Industry Survey & Report.

Price, D. (2015). *Surprising facts and stats about the big data industry*. Retrieved November 1, 2016 from http://cloudtweaks.com/2015/03/surprising-facts-and-stats-about-the-big-data-industry/

Redmond, E., & Wilson, J. (2012). *Seven databases in seven weeks: A guide to modern databases and the NoSQL movement*. Pragmatic Bookshelf. Kindle Edition.

Sadalage, P. J., & Fowler, M. (2013). *NoSQL distilled - A brief guide to the emerging world of polyglot persistence*. Pearson Education, Inc.

Simpson, A. P., & Rode, J. (2017). *USA data protection*. Retrieved July 11, 2017 from https://iclg.com/practice-areas/data-protection/data-protection-2017/usa

SINTEF. (2013, May 22). Big Data, for better or worse: 90% of world's data generated over last two years. *ScienceDaily*. Retrieved November 1, 2016 from www.sciencedaily.com/releases/2013/05/130522085217.htm

TutorialsPoint. (2014). *Hadoop big data analysis framework*. Retrieved November 12, 2016 from https://www.tutorialspoint.com/hadoop/hadoop_tutorial.pdf

Vaish, G. (2013). *Getting started with NoSQL*. Packt Publishing Ltd.

Wu, C., Buyya, R., & Ramamohanarao, K. (2016). BDA = ML + CC. In Big data principles and paradigms. Elsevier Inc.

Chapter 3
NoSQL Data Modeling

ABSTRACT

The chapter discusses the necessity for data modeling in NoSQL world. The NoSQL data modeling is a huge challenge because one of the main features of NoSQL databases is that they are schema-free, that is they allow data manipulation without the need for the previous modeling or developing an entity-relationship (ER) or similar model. Although the absence of a schema can be an advantage in some situations, with the increase in the number of NoSQL database implementations, it appears that the absence of a conceptual model can be a source of substantial problems. In order to better understand the need for data modeling in NoSQL databases, first the basic structure of an ER model and an analysis of its limitations are summarized, especially regarding an application in NoSQL databases. The concept and Object modeling notation is presented as one of the possible solutions for data modeling in NoSQL databases.

INTRODUCTION

One of the more complex aspects of database design is the fact that designers, developers, and users typically see and use data in different ways. Unfortunately, if there is no common understanding of how the organization operates and what data is needed, the database design will not fully meet

DOI: 10.4018/978-1-5225-3385-6.ch003

the user's requirements. In order to have an accurate understanding of the nature of data and its use in the organization, it is important to develop a model for communication that, by its nature, would be nontechnical and free of ambiguity or vagueness. In this sense, a model is an abstraction that is focused on the essential, typical aspects of the organization and ignores its accidental characteristics. It needs to provide the basic concepts and notations that would allow database designers and users to communicate with each other unambiguously and accurately and to understand organizational data.

In the terminology of relational databases, the term logical model is used to mean a data model. A logical model represents a global view of the whole database, or as seen from the level of the entire organization. It is the basis for the identification and high-level description of the main data objects while avoiding any specifics of individual database models (Coronel, Morris & Rob, 2011). The logical level provides a view of data independent of the physical implementation. Namely, a logical model is independent of both software and hardware. Software independence means the model is independent of the database management software that is used for its implementation, whereas hardware independence means the model is independent of the hardware that is used for its implementation.

Relational databases are generally based on the Entity-Relationship (ER) logical model. However, as explained in Chapter 2, one of the main features of most NoSQL databases is that they are schema free, or they allow data manipulation without the need for the previous modeling or developing an ER or similar model. Although the absence of a schema can be an advantage in some situations (Chapter 2), with the increase in the number of NoSQL database implementations, it appears that the absence of a conceptual model can be a source of certain problems. That is why this chapter emphasizes the need for data modeling with NoSQL databases as well. In order to better understand the need for data modeling in NoSQL databases, first the basic structure of an ER model and an analysis its limitations are summarized, especially in terms of application in NoSQL databases. Hill's COMN (Concept and Object Modeling Notation) model is then presented. COMN is designed to make it possible to present the real world, or its objects and concepts—data about the real world—but also objects in a computer's memory, or to present everything from the naming of requirements to a functional database running by either a NoSQL or a SQL database management system.

DATA MODELING IN RELATIONAL DATABASES

The purpose of this chapter is to explain the main concepts of ER modeling so that readers (especially those without prior knowledge of ER modeling) can more easily understand the need for modeling in NoSQL databases and a COMN model ("The Concept and Object Modeling Notation").

The ER model is the primary model used in modeling relational databases. ER modeling involves a top-down approach to database design that starts by identifying important data that comprises *entities* and *relationships* between the data represented by the model. Then details are added, such as the information needed on the entities and relationships, called *attributes*, as well as constraints on the entities, relationships, and attributes.

An ER model is a detailed, logical presentation of data of an organization or a business field. It is expressed in terms of entities in the business environment, relationships (associations) between these entities, and attributes (properties) of both the entities and the relationships. An entity-relationship diagram represents an ER model, also called an ER diagram or ERD (Hoffer, Ramesh & Topi, 2011).

The ER model quickly became popular because of its complementarity with the relational data model concepts, and after decades of use, the ER model remains the leading approach in conceptual data modeling. Its popularity results from factors such as relative ease of use, support by CASE (computer-aided software engineering) tools, and the widespread belief that entities and relationships are natural modeling concepts in the real world.

Many different notations are used for graphical representation of ER model elements and concepts. One of them is the graphical notation in *Unified Modeling Language* (UML). This notation is extensively used in object-oriented programming, and although it was not initially intended for data modeling, it is increasingly being used for this purpose because it is widespread and accepted in the developers' world. The UML notation is also used in this chapter to represent the ER model.

The basic structure of an ER model consists of the following elements:

- Entity
- Attribute
- Relationship
- Domain

The term *entity* can be defined in different ways. Some of the typical definitions include the following:

- An entity is a thing or object of importance, whether realistic or imaginary, for which it is necessary to know and store some information (Connolly & Begg, 2005).
- An entity is a person, a place, an object, an event, or a concept in the user environment about which the organization wishes to maintain data (Hoffer, Ramesh & Topi, 2011).
- An entity is a collection of information about something that the business deems important and worthy of capture (Hoberman, 2009).

The common thread running through these and other definitions of an entity is the importance of what the organization considers an entity. To call something an entity, it has to be so important to the organization that it wants to collect and maintain data about it. It follows that the same thing, person, object, or the like does not necessarily need to be important for every organization. Although things, persons, objects, etc., are important for many organizations and will be viewed as entities in most of them (e.g., CUSTOMER, EMPLOYEE, BILL, etc.), that still does not necessarily mean that these will be entities in all organizations.

An instance of an entity is an individual entity, and all instances of an entity of the same type have the same attributes, although they differ in the values of attributes of individual instances.

It is essential to distinguish between an entity type and an entity instance or manifestation. An entity type is a collection of entities that have the same properties.

Every entity type in an ER model has a name. Because the name represents a collection or a set of instances, it is always singular. Names of entity types are normally written in capital letters. UML class diagrams are used to represent entity types (Figure 1) graphically.

An instance, or a manifestation of an entity, is an individual occurrence of an entity type. Figure 2 shows the difference between an entity type and its instances. An entity type is described only once in a database, whereas its instances (which are usually numerous) are represented by data stored in the database.

An attribute is any detail that specifies, identifies, classifies, quantifies, or expresses the state of an entity and represents a description of an entity. Each

Figure 1. UML class diagram: representation of an entity

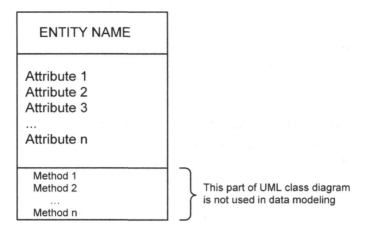

Figure 2. The difference between entity types and entity instances

Entity type						
STUDENT	ID number	Name	Surname	Date of birth	Status	Year of study
ID number	12342/R	Petra	Peric	18.07.1990.	Full time	4
Name	12784/R	Karla	Karlovic	11.11.1991.	Full time	4
Surname	13120/RP	Mario	Gaspar	02.02.1994.	Part time	2
Date of birth	14002/I	Jure	Juric	15.06.1995.	Part time	1
Status	12875/I	Ante	Antic	05.05.1990.	Part time	4
Year of study	13243/R	Marija	Marijanovic	12.10.1993.	Full time	3
	13286/R	Ana	Anicic	19.03.1992.	Full time	3
	13577/RP	Petar	Petrovic	22.06.1994.	Part time	2
	13601/RP	Karlo	Matic	18.08.1994.	Full time	2

entity has attributes associated with it. These are properties or characteristics of the entity that are important for the organization (Hoberman, 2009).

The name of an attribute is a noun. Figure 3 gives a graphical representation of the entity CUSTOMER and its attributes.

Figure 3. Example of an entity and attributes

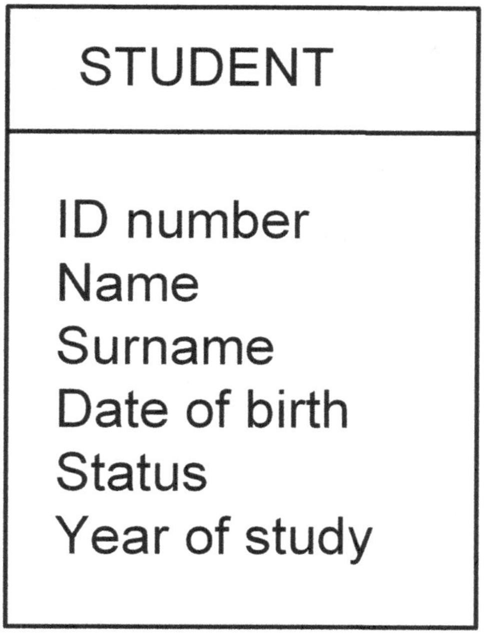

```
┌─────────────────────────┐
│                         │
│      STUDENT            │
│                         │
├─────────────────────────┤
│                         │
│  ID number              │
│  Name                   │
│  Surname                │
│  Date of birth          │
│  Status                 │
│  Year of study          │
│                         │
└─────────────────────────┘
```

Relationships are the "glue" that holds together different entities in an ER model. Namely, a relationship is an association representing an interaction between one or more entities that is of interest for the organization. Through the classification process, instances of an entity are grouped by common attributes into entity types. The real world is thus simplified and "put in order" in order to better understand the basic relationships or data. However, after the real objects are "broken down" into entities for ease of understanding and maintenance, there is a question of their mutual relation. That is, real objects are normally constantly in a mutual interaction, and in the real world they are intertwined, or their mutual relation is defined by certain rules that are usually business rules. These rules may apply to data or actions. Data rules are instructions on how data objects relate to one another, whereas action rules are about what to do or what action to take for certain values of attributes (Hoberman, 2009).

It is clear from what has been said that not all interactions are of interest to the organization, particularly when things are viewed from the aspect of data. However, in order to relate data that is of interest to the organization or to be able to represent real data rules, it is necessary to establish relationships among entities. The abstraction method known as aggregation is used for establishing relationships between entities. These relationships are also abstractions, i.e. the relationship type. A relationship instance, which essentially represents an association of entity instances, is especially emphasized. The illustration in Figure 4 is used to understand the difference between relationship type and relationship instance better.

A relationship type, or a relationship, is an important association between entity types. The term *important association* means that a relationship provides answers to the questions that cannot be answered using entities only. A relationship instance is an association between entity instances, where each relationship instance relates exactly one entity instance from each entity participating in the relationship (Elmasri & Navathe, 1994). Figure 5 illustrates a relationship using UML.

Figure 4. The difference between a relationship type and an instance

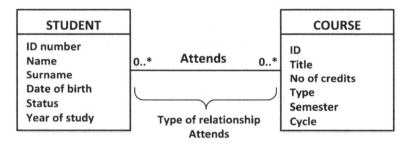

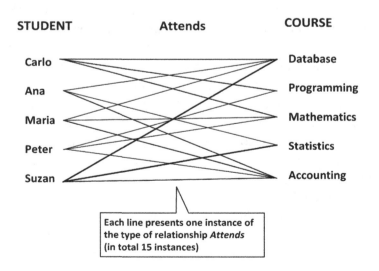

Figure 5. Illustration of a relationship using UML

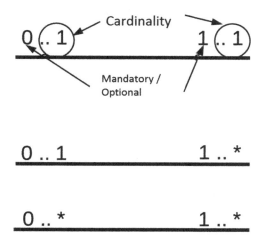

It is evident in Figure 5 that there are two distinct concepts when defining a relationship:

- Cardinality of participation in a relationship
- Mandatory or optional participation in a relationship

Cardinality defines the number of instances of each particular entity participating in a relationship. To represent cardinality, UML uses the following notation (Figure 5):

- 1 – only one entity instance (occurrence) can participate in the relationship.
- * – multiple entity instances (occurrences) can participate in the relationship.

Regarding cardinality, we can distinguish three basic types of relationships:

1. One-to-one (1:1)
2. One-to-many (1:N)
3. Many-to-many

Mandatory or optional participation of an entity instance in a relationship is concerned with whether each occurrence or instance of an entity has to participate in the relationship. To represent mandatory or optional participation in a relationship, UML uses the following notation (Figure 5):

- 0 – optional participation, or not every instance of an entity has to participate in the relationship.
- 1 – mandatory participation, or each instance of an entity must participate in the relationship.

The name of a relationship is indicated by using a verb because the relationship is usually a result of an occurrence in the organization. The verb should be specified in the present tense and descriptive. Certainly, there are different ways to represent relationships. When it comes to naming, some analysts prefer the form with two names for a relationship, one for each direction of the relationship, whereas others use only one verb.

Figure 6 gives an example of an ER model for customer orders. The ER diagram shows that information on the customer and products are contained in the entities CUSTOMER and PRODUCT, whereas the entity ORDER

Figure 6. ER diagram of orders from customers

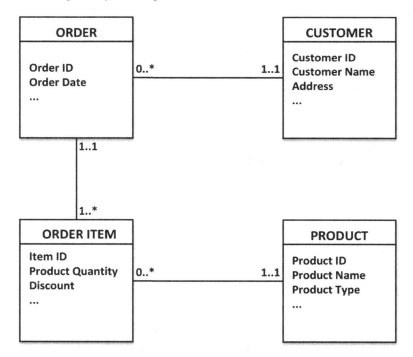

contains only basic data on order, and the entity ORDER ITEM data contains information on each item of the order. In order to know which customer ordered what, ORDER needs to be related to CUSTOMER, and it can be read from this relationship that each ORDER must have information on CUSTOMER, and only one CUSTOMER (each ORDER has one and only one CUSTOMER), whereas on the other hand each CUSTOMER does not need to have an ORDER, but can have many orders as well. The relationship between ORDER ITEM and PRODUCT is interpreted similarly. Each ORDER ITEM must have information on each PRODUCT that is ordered, and there should be only one (on each ORDER ITEM, there is only one PRODUCT), whereas PRODUCT does not need to be on any ORDER ITEM, but can be found on many items as well.

Along with entity, attribute, and relationship, the structure of an ER model includes a domain. That is the full set of all possible values that an attribute can assume. A domain is a set of validation criteria that can be applied to one or more attributes (Hoberman, 2009). An attribute can never have a value that would be outside of the set of values defined by the assigned domain, and domain values are defined by specifying the actual list of values or set of rules. For example, for the attribute Status (Figure 6), the entity ORDER can have the domain *OrderStatus* that defines the status of a particular order (received, approved, delivered, paid), and thereby execution of certain program steps.

The basic ER model has proven suitable for modeling many business problems, which greatly contributed to its widespread use. However, to better handle constant changes, database designers were forced to keep extending the ER model in order to represent as accurately as possible complex relationships from the modern business environment. The term Enhanced Entity Relationship model (EER) is used to denote a model that has resulted from extending the original ER model with new elements or modeling structures. The most important new structure element contained in the EER model is the relationship *supertype/subtype*). This relationship allows modeling a general entity (called a supertype) and then its division into several specialized entities (called subtypes). For example, the entity CAR can be modeled as a supertype, with subtypes SPORTS CAR, SUV (suburban utility vehicle), SEDAN, etc. Each subtype inherits attributes from its supertype and can additionally have specific attributes and be involved in its own relationships. The addition of new notation for modeling supertype/subtype relationships has significantly contributed to the flexibility of the basic ER model.

The ER and particularly EER diagrams can become large and complex, requiring multiple pages (or very small fonts) in order to view. Some commercial databases have hundreds of entities. Most users and managers that define requirements for database development do not need to see all the entities, relationships, and attributes to understand the part of the database in which they are interested the most. Entity clustering is a way of converting a part of ER/EER data into a higher, macro-level view of the same data using a technique of hierarchical decomposition (a nested process of dividing systems into further and further subsystems) that can make an ER/EER diagram readable and facilitate database design. By grouping entities and relationships, a diagram can be represented in such a way that attention is paid to the details that are most important for a given modeling task.

Universal and industry-specific generalized data models that extensively use EER features are becoming very important for modern data modeling. These data model packages and patterns have made data modeling more efficient and better.

The EER supertype/subtype feature is a basis for creating generalized data models, and additional general constructs, such as typified entities and relationships, are used. In modern modeling, it has become very important during the process of modeling to know how to adapt the data model pattern or the data model to big, ready-made software packages like ERP (Enterprise Resource Planning) or CRM (Customer Relationship Management). Thus, data modeling has become the contact point, or the place where business users necessarily meet and communicate with the information system (IS) designers in charge of adapting off-the-shelf software suites and components to needs of the organization.

BEYOND ENTITY-RELATIONSHIP MODELING

Since 1976, when Chen published his paper on ER modeling (Chen, 1976), appropriate use of ER modeling enabled efficient and smooth running of countless database design processes and all related steps, from analysis of requirements to data modeling and design, to database implementation. As explained in the previous chapter, conceptual database modeling has become an essential and inevitable step in database development. Certainly, during the decades of its use, it became clear that the ER model, like other models, is not perfect. Attempts to overcome some limitations of the ER model were made by extending it, which resulted in the EER model. However, the use of the EER model in practice has shown that certain limitations remain, especially when it comes to representing complex phenomena and relationships between them, as well as representing data and the behavior of the system in a consistent and integrated manner. These limitations are the result of the assumption underlying the ER or EER model, which is that data will be stored in tables or implemented in a relational database. However, the possibilities of NoSQL databases to store data in structures other than tables, like arrays and nested data structures (nested documents), have reemphasized the limitations of the ER model in representing such data structures.

From the aspect of NoSQL databases, the main limitations of the ER model are as follows (Hills, 2016):

- It is not possible to represent data structures that are interrelated without using keys. Thus, arrays and nested data structures in an ER model are separated into tables and linked with one another through relationships implemented in a relational database using foreign keys. Unlike relational databases, NoSQL databases support direct aggregation of arrays and nested data structures without using keys. However, because it is not possible for an ER model to represent these structures, this model is usually avoided when developing NoSQL databases.
- It is not possible to represent composite types or types of attributes that have multiple components. Entity attributes in an ER model are a simple type because they do not have components. In an ER model, there is no way to represent composite attribute types because the ER model is implemented in a relational database that does not allow multiple attribute values. However, in reality, there are attributes that are composite attributes, such as a postal address that consists of a street, number, postal code, city, state, etc. When designing relational databases, it is assumed that composite attribute types cause data redundancy, which is essentially true, especially when it comes to simple use. However, in many cases, the use of composite types may lead to simpler and more robust database design. For example, it can be very useful to specify a postal address only once and then to incorporate it in multiple places, possibly also in models for multiple databases. The use of composite types is especially helpful when data needs to be represented as a structural pattern and organization with keys is not of any use.

- It is not possible to represent all the complexity of mapping from logical entities to physical tables. The ER model represents a database as logically unique. However, it does not mean that one logical database cannot be implemented as several physical databases (distributed databases). The consequence of such an implementation is that data belonging to one logical record (entity) may be located in multiple physical records and multiple databases. The ER model supports one-for-one mapping of logical record type to physical table and therefore cannot represent all the complexity of actual mapping in distributed database systems. In an ER model, it is not possible to show that one logical record type has many instances in multiple databases. Also, an ER model cannot show the mapping of two or more logical tables to a single physical one that may result from the data denormalization process at the physical level aimed to ensure faster database operation.
- The ER model provides support for database development without taking into account any needs related to software development. Software developers cannot use the ER notation to represent software design. Nowadays they mostly use object-oriented modeling and UML diagrams to visualize the software development process. However, a consequence of such an approach is the gap, or impedance mismatch, between the modeling notation used by database developers and the modeling notation or programming languages used by software developers.

These limitations of the ER model are probably one of the reasons why the data modeling step is skipped when developing NoSQL databases, proceeding instead with the implementation or data storage. The next section explains the pitfalls of such an approach.

THE IMPORTANCE OF MODELING DATA IN NoSQL DATABASES

NoSQL databases are mostly designed with application performance in mind rather than business models, data integration, and standardization, which leads to the gap between modeling and physical implementation of data in the databases. On the other hand, the development of relational databases is typically based on business models and data models, which ensured automatic implementation of relational databases (automatic model-based database creation in the relational database management system), more straightforward integration, and standardization of data.

Although the creation of a logical (ER) model is one of the key steps when creating relational databases, that does not mean it is absolutely necessary. In other words, relational databases, too, can be developed by skipping the data modeling stage and moving to database creation and data storage right away. However, over 30 years of experience in implementing relational databases has shown that this is not the wisest way, especially when developing a database for complex organizational systems. Data modeling offers the possibility of "playing" with the database on paper or some other model drawing tool and allows easier correction, communication with users, and testing of different versions in order to choose the best one. It is much easier to redraw a part of the model than to re-create the database schema, move large amounts of data, or change the application code to work with the database.

Therefore, it is just astonishing that this experience is "forgotten" in the development of NoSQL databases, and the schema-less property is specified as one of the main features of these databases. The possibility to quickly start working on the project is emphasized as an advantage of schema-less databases because there is no loss of time to define and create a database schema, and it is possible to start storing data right away. However, the time savings at the beginning of the project are usually the cause of many problems later, both in the data storage itself and in the efficiency of their maintenance and query performance. This is usually manifested when handling large amounts of data, which usually requires data reorganization to speed up the access and update times and find the appropriate balance between consistency, availability, and access speed. In addition, patterns often appear in the data structure, so even in situations when the database does not need a particular database schema, most stored data has a common schema. That is why some vendors reorganize data dynamically, which is good in situations when the amount of data is not large. However, if the amount of data is large, the reorganization can be expensive, both in terms of time and the space necessary for temporary storage during the reorganization, all of which can cause reduced availability of data for users. Also, the schema changes do not apply only to the data—they typically also affect the application code because it is necessary to have at least some basic assumptions on the data schema when writing the code.

If the database is implemented without previously creating a model (schema-less), it follows that the only way to understand the data after the implementation is to speak with the developer or to analyze the code. Being dependent on developers to understand the code significantly reduces the possibility of proposing changes and expansions of data by the user and may create additional pressure on developers.

Furthermore, although being schema-less is one of the basic features of NoSQL databases, some of these databases, like document databases, support schemas such as XML, JSON, etc. However, even in a situation when it is not necessary to do so, it is more than desirable to impose an association with a schema for a part or all of the stored data in order to increase the data quality, in the sense that only valid data is stored, which provides certain guarantees to the application code that there is a certain level of data "purity."

With the increasing number of NoSQL database applications, there is a growing awareness of the need for data modeling in these systems too. When developing NoSQL databases, some organizations try to use the ER model by using additional notes and remarks to leave a record that a relationship, as presented in the ER model, actually does not represent a conventional relationship, but an array or nested data structure. Although such models can be useful, they cannot be used for model-driven development of NoSQL databases because it is not possible to read the difference between relationships implemented by foreign keys and array aggregations or nested data structures directly from the model (Hills, 2016). Hence, efforts are made to find a solution that will enable modeling both relational and NoSQL databases.

Wang (2016) proposes the use of Unified Data Modeling techniques that support features like document schema of NoSQL databases, reverse engineering of data from an existing database, and visual refactoring of existing databases. According to Wang (2016), there is a basic concept of mapping among logical, relational, and NoSQL data models (Table 1).

According to the Unified Modeling Procedure, business requirements can and should be described by a logical model that could then be transformed into the appropriate target physical model, whether relational or NoSQL. The transformation process should be based on query patterns and data production patterns described in the logical model. The transformation rule is predefined as a schema transformation strategy. Which strategy will be used depends on the tags that describe query and data production patterns. It is important that users can change and adapt both tags and rules. At the end of the procedure, raw data can be formatted according to the appropriate physical model and migrated to the database using forward engineering (Wang, 2016).

In the Unified Modeling Procedure query patterns are of exceptional importance for NoSQL data modeling because the process of denormalizing

Table 1. Concept mapping among logical, RDBMS, and NoSQL data models

Conceptual/Logical	RDBMS	NoSQL
Entity	Table	Collection/column family
Entity instance	Row	Document/row
Property	Column	Key/column
Property of an entity instance	Cell value	Field value
Domain	Data type	Data type (some NoSQL databases have no data type; all of the values are plain text)
Relationship	Constraint	Reference, embedded, additional table, row across multiple column families
Key	Index	Index, additional table, reference
Unique identification	Primary Key	Row key

Wang, 2016.

logical to physical models directly depends on how data is queried. That is why in this modeling technique, it is essential to describe query patterns in the data model, where all entities are still viewed as one whole. However, as data in NoSQL databases are normally distributed, the data schema needs to be denormalized according to business requirements—that is, entities described in the logical model need to be aggregated in accordance with the NoSQL physical storage. The schema needs to be designed to allow distributed queries, which means that each data set must contain enough information to allow execution of queries separately in different data nodes (Wang, 2016).

The Unified Modeling Procedure also emphasizes the importance of data modeling, not only for a relational database (where this has long been a standard) but also for NoSQL databases. The assumption is that descriptions of business requirements and denormalized schemas for physical data models are key to building NoSQL databases. The model set consists of one logical model and multiple physical models (Wang, 2016).

Also, Hills (2016) proceeds from the idea that a single model can be used for both relational and NoSQL databases at the logical level, whereas on the physical side there can be multiple models. That is why Hill's (2016) Concept and Object Modeling Notation (COMN) was designed to enable data modeling in both relational and NoSQL databases ("The Concept and Object Modeling Notation").

However, it is important to emphasize that both theorists and practitioners are increasingly aware of the need for data modeling in the NoSQL world as well, primarily recognized as schema-less and schema on read (Chapter 2). Schema on read allows data writing "as is" and the implementation of different views of stored data supported by applications. Essentially, the schema is not needed for data storage, but it is needed for data reading and understanding. The schema is hidden in the MapReduce program, and that can be a problem for the developers who do not work with MapReduce and for database administrators because they cannot directly access the schemas and thereby cannot understand them. That is one of the reasons why data modeling is necessary because it leads to better understanding of the data.

THE CONCEPT AND OBJECT MODELING NOTATION

The Concept and Object Modeling Notation (COMN) introduced by Hills (2016) has the goal of consolidating in a single notation the following:

- *The real world, with its objects and concepts*
- *Data about real-world objects and concepts*
- *Objects in a computer's memory whose states represent data about real-world objects and concepts.* (Hills, 2016, p. 23)

The basic idea of COMN notation is to integrate real objects, data, and implementation to allow all things, from user requests to logical models, to functional databases, to be represented in a single model, regardless of whether it is executed in a relational or NoSQL database management system. This would allow for tracking user requests up to their final implementation and ensure that nothing was lost in translation from one model to another. Changes would be tracked in a similar way, which would enable the expression of reverse-engineered data and the development of logical and conceptual models to give it meaning (Hills, 2016).

Analyzing some of the existing notations most frequently used in data modeling, Hills (2016) concluded that none of them could meet the challenges of NoSQL data modeling and therefore proposed a new notation: COMN. Because UML notation was used in "Data Modeling in Relational Databases" to represent the ER model, the limitations of UML are only briefly stated here (Hills, 2016):

- **Lack of Keys:** Because UML is primarily designed to represent and visualize software development processes, associations were conceived as references between objects in a computer's memory, or usually as pointers. Although the first database management systems used pointers to represent relationships among data, they turned out to be difficult to maintain and were replaced by foreign keys, which are used by most relational databases. However, UML does not have a notation for specifying key attributes and therefore cannot represent foreign keys. Consequently, UML cannot fully specify a relational database design.

- **Middling Level of Abstraction:** UML supports the same abstraction level as object-oriented programs. This means that UML and program classes correspond to real-world entity types (concepts and real-world objects) with similar names. It follows that UML can be used to denote real-world classes and real-world objects; therewith it is necessary to make clear notes on a diagram in order to know which classes and objects will be interpreted as existing in the real world and not in a computer's memory. In addition, UML depends on the "slot" notation, which is not defined anywhere, nor does it allow a "slot" to be represented by a graphical symbol. Such an approach makes it difficult to use UML to represent implementation details because it does not guarantee the rigorousness and completeness required for model-driven development.

- **Lack of Concept:** UML does not have the ability to describe entities that do not have their state or behavior (i.e. it cannot describe concepts). In UML, concepts can be represented only implicitly and only in connection with classes, objects, or other things that UML can represent. However, concepts appear often in user requirements, and the inability to use direct modeling means that a model can represent only things that are related to a concept.

- **Type and Implementation Class:** UML describes a type as a stereotype of a class, which means that a class is used in a restrictive way or only for specifying a subset of objects. An implementation class is another class stereotype that essentially restricts the class to correspond to a programming language class.

- **Repurposed Ordinary English Words in Defining the Relationship, Composition, and Aggregation:** The UML defines a relationship as "a reified semantic connection among model elements. Kinds of relationships include association, generalization, meta relationship, flow, and several kinds grouped under dependency" (Rumbaugh, 1999, p. 411). It is obvious that this definition encompasses various types of connections between model elements, which makes it vague and ambiguous. The UML has a concept called "aggregation," but it is explicitly ill defined and called a "modeling placebo" (Rumbaugh, 1999, p. 148), intended to pacify those who claim that it is important. However, in ordinary English, the term aggregate refers to a composite material, such as concrete, where the components of the aggregate retain their integrity, but there is little chance that they can be separated again (the way COMN uses the term). Although the term aggregation is poorly defined in UML, the composition is defined through aggregation as "a form of aggregation association with strong ownership and a coincident lifetime of parts by the whole" (Rumbaugh, 1999, p. 226).

These limitations of UML, but also of other data modeling notations, motivated Hills (2016) to develop the COMN in such a way that it enables the modeling of data, both in relational and NoSQL databases, starting from user requirements and recognition of real-world entities and concepts, to the logical model, up to views of the database physical model.

COMN Fundamentals

The main starting points underlying the development of COMN notation are:

- Data modeling is necessary for the database development process, regardless of whether it is a relational or NoSQL database ("The Importance of Modeling Data in NoSQL Databases").
- Specify the vocabulary that is used in data modeling by reconsidering definitions of the terms that are key to data modeling and software development.
- Understand that relational theory applies to NoSQL databases as it does to relational ones. Relational theory is a theory on data that matters, irrespective of whether the data is stored as tables, documents, or graphs (Hills, 2016).

When specifying the vocabulary that is used in data modeling, Hills (2016) starts from the ordinary English meanings of terms used. Namely, the technical vocabulary of data modeling typically redefines terms from everyday use, from mathematics and logics, in a subtly different, often confusing, and sometimes wrong way. Hills (2016) refines the terms in ways that they mean less, or so as to avoid ambiguity and vagueness, to make different terms overlap less, all with the aim of reducing impedance mismatch when integrating data and software. Table 2 gives an overview of meanings of basic terms in COMN in order to make understanding of this notation easier.

COMN vs. ER Model

Data Modeling in Relational Databases gives a short overview of the basic structure of the ER model, which is commonly used to model data in relational databases. It also presents definitions of basic terms such as entity, attribute, and relationship. Table 3 shows the extent to which these terms can be translated to COMN. It is important to emphasize that if there are multiple terms for a single ER term, that means the ER term has multiple meanings or, consequently, that the term is imprecise and vague (Hills, 2016).

To make it easier to compare, examples from Chapter 3 are used to present the basics of COMN. As evident in Table 3, the term entity, or the entity type from the ER model, has multiple meanings in COMN because it can be a thing, object, or concept, either real or imaginary. Figure 7 gives a parallel view of entities (entity type) as used in the ER model, which is presented in COMN as a logical record type, table of logical records, or real-world entity type.

COMN uses a slightly different presentation of relationships from the ER model. A parallel view of relationships in the ER models and COMN is given in Figure 8.

An illustration of an ER model for customer ordering is given in Figure 6 in Chapter 1. Because COMN promotes the feature of data presentation from the level of user requirement to a logical model, up to physical model, this approach is used to present the model for customer ordering using COMN.

The first step in data modeling is to understand user requirements, or what the user expects from the database and software. When it comes to the database, it is necessary to define the important things the user wants to know and about which he wants to have data stored. In terms of COMN, this means to identify and represent real-world entities, which can be objects, but also concepts. In the example of customers placing orders, a Customer is a real-world physical object, as is a Product, whereas Order is a concept (Figure 9). A Customer is the one who places the order, so this verb is used to describe the relationship between Customer and Order. A particular Customer may place many orders, provided that he becomes a Customer only when he places

Table 2. The meaning of the main COMN terms

Term	Meaning in COMN
Entity	Something that has separate and distinct existence and objective or conceptual reality (Merriam-Webster1, 2017).
Attribute	A characteristic ascribed to someone or something (Merriam-Webster2, 2017).
Data attribute	A <name, type> pair. The name gives the role of a value of the given type in the context of a tuple scheme or relational scheme.
Type	Something that designates a set, usually a set of concepts, but also possibly a set of objects.
Simple type	A type that designates a set whose members have no components.
Composite type	A type that designates a set whose members have components.
Logical record type	A composite type that is intended to be used as the type of data records stored singly or in a collection of records.
Object	Something material that may be perceived by the senses (Merriam-Webster3, 2017).
Computer object	A stateful material object whose state can be read and/or modified by the execution of computer instructions.
Hardware object	A computer object which is part of the physical composition of a computer.
Software object	An object composed of hardware objects and/or software objects by exclusively authorizing only certain routines to access the component objects.
Concept	Something conceived in the mind: thought, notion (Merriam-Webster4, 2017).
Proposition	An expression in language or signs of something that can be believed, doubted, or denied or is either true or false (Merriam-Webster5, 2017).
Relation	A relation value
Relation value	A set of tuple values, all having the same tuple scheme; informally, a table without significance to the order of or repetition of the values of its rows.
Relationship	A proposition concerning two or more entities.
Restriction relationship	A relationship between two types, where one type, called the subtype, is defined in terms of a restriction on members of the set designated by the other type, called the supertype; inverse of inclusion relationship.
Inclusion relationship	A relationship between types, where the supertype is defined as a union of its subtypes; inverse of restriction relationship.
Relationship type	A logical predicate.
Class	A description of the structural and/or behavioral characteristics of potential or actual objects.
Composite	Made up of distinct parts (Merriam-Webster6, 2017).
Component	A constituent part (Merriam-Webster7, 2017).
Aggregation	Combining two or more objects in such a way that they retain their integrity, but it is difficult or impossible to separate them again.
Assembly	Combining two or more objects in such a way that they retain their integrity and it is relatively easy to separate them again.
Collection	A set of objects having a single owner.
Array	A collection of some integral number of variables or objects of the same type or class.
Extension	The addition of components to a base class or type; its inverse is projection.

Hills, 2016.

Table 3. Mapping ER in COMN terms

ER Term	COMN Term
Entity	Logical record type, which is a kind of a composite type Table of logical records (possibly) real-world entity type
Instance	Entity
Data type	Simple type
Domain	Simple type
Data attribute	Data attribute; more generally, component of a composite type
(no equivalent)	Composite type
Conceptual	Approximate
(no equivalent)	Conceptual: relating to a concept or concepts

Hills, 2016, p. 55.

Figure 7. A comparative view of entities in the ER model and COMN

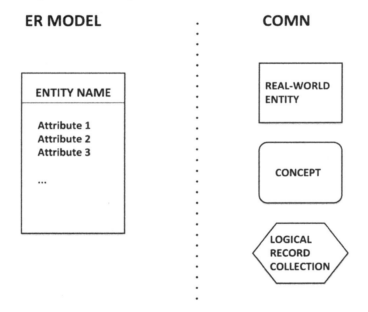

at least one Order. That is why the symbol + is used on the Order side to represent that the cardinality of the relationship from Customer to Order is 1 or more. Because every Order belongs to only one Customer, the multiplicity 1 is implied on the other side of the relationship (Figure 9).

An Order involves particular Products ordered by a Customer and must contain at least one Product to be meaningful (the relationship Order-to-

Figure 8. A comparative view of relationships in the ER model and COMN

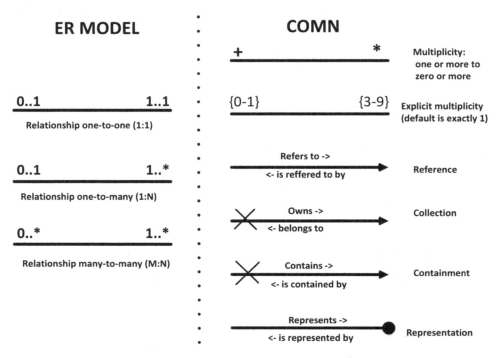

Figure 9. Real-world entities in customer ordering

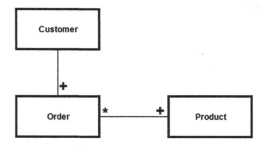

Product has a + sign at the Product end to indicate a multiplicity of one or more). An asterisk (*) sign is on the other side of the relationship (at the Order end) because every Product can be found in many Orders, but does not have to be on any (e.g., nobody wants to buy a Product, and it cannot be found on any Order).

After real-world entities and their relationships are matched with the customer, the next step in data modeling is logical data design for storage in the database. In this step, it is crucial to ensure representation of each of the real-world entities by data, as well as adequate representation of each relationship between real-world entities. A mapping of real-world entities to logical record collections is presented in Figure 10. Thus the real-world entity Customer is mapped to the Customer Record Collection (line with a solid circle at one end), and in the same way, the real-world entity Product is mapped to the Product Record Collection (line with a solid circle at one end). However, when it comes to the real-world entity Order, the situation is slightly more complex because in the real world an Order may have one or more products, and in Figure 10 it is evident that Order does not directly contain Product in the data design. The Order Record Collection consists of one or more order items, where each order item references one and only one product from the Product Record Collection. The original Order-Product cardinality is preserved in data too because one order can have one or more order items, and each order item references a product so that one order indirectly

Figure 10. COMN logical data modeling

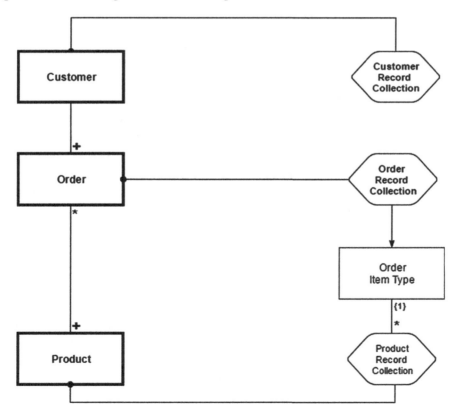

references one or more products. The relationship represented by a line from the Order data record collection to the Order Item data type indicates that an Order consists of one or more Order Items (Figure 10).

Although Figure 10 confirms that it is possible to represent the real world in a COMN model accurately, the model represented in this figure is still very global. The next step is to make a detailed model that includes information on how a customer, order, and product are identified (Figure 11). COMN allows visual presentation of the difference between composition and references (Figure 11). Namely, an order is composed of order items, but it references a customer and a product in order to have information about which customer placed the order and which products were ordered because, when defining requirements, it was established that customers, products, and orders, as real-world entities, exist independently (Figure 9). However, for an order to reference a customer or a product, there must be a value with which to accurately identify which customer and which products are involved in a particular order. It is known from relational theory that an attribute or a set of attributes that allow us to unambiguously identify a certain data record in a set is called a key, or that the value of a key is the identifier of a particular record in that set. This rule applies regardless of whether the data is stored in tables, graph nodes, documents, or some other form, because the relational theory is not limited to describing data storage in tables. Essentially, it is necessary to understand when keys for referencing data is needed before making a decision on how to store the data (Hills, 2016).

Figure 11 shows that customer and product record collections must have keys in order to make it possible for an order to reference them. Keys are noted by a suffix (PK), which is an indication of primary key (a key that uniquely identifies each data record in relation to other data records in the set). It can be seen in Figure 11 that next to the data attribute Placed by Customer in Order Record Collection there is a notation (FK), or foreign key. According to COMN terminology, a foreign key constraint defines a subtype (Hills, 2016). Namely, the type of the Placed by Customer data attribute is the set of all values that are key values of the Customer record set. The meaning of the notation (FK) for the attribute references product in the Order Item type can be explained in a similar way (Figure 11).

The COMN model presented in Figure 11 shows that this notation allows complete mapping of a real-world entity to a detailed data model. However, the model still does not show how data will be stored (physical data storage) and in what type of database, whether relational or some of the NoSQL databases.

Figure 11. COMN model with components

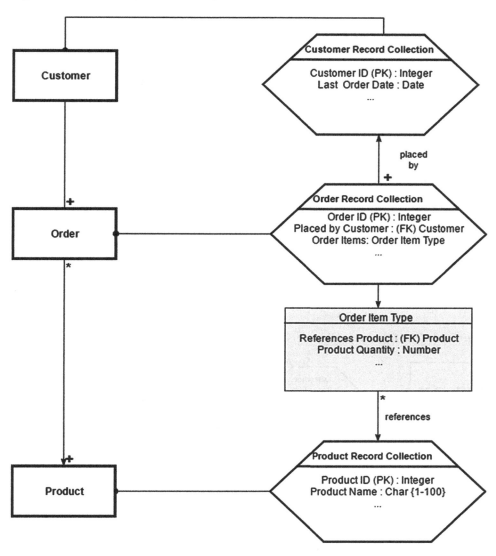

A decision on the data storage method and the database that will be used is made in the next step, and it represents the COMN physical data model.

In order to show that COMN can be used for modeling both relational and NoSQL databases, the COMN model from Figure 11 is transformed first into a COMN physical model for a relational database (Figure 12) and then to a COMN physical model for a document database (Figure 13).

Figure 12. COMN physical model of ordering for a relational database

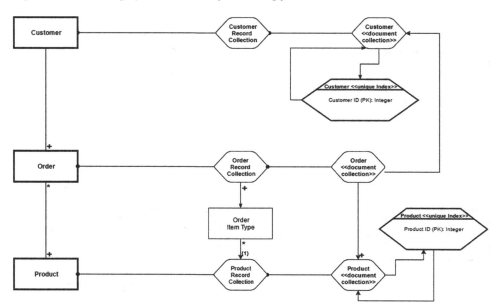

Figure 13. COMN physical model of ordering for a document database

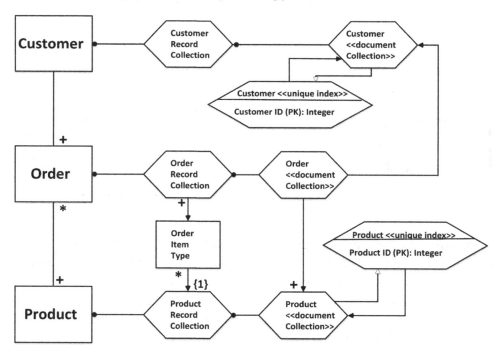

The COMN physical model for a relational database (Figure 12) clearly shows the mapping of the Customer, Order, and Product record collections to relational (SQL) tables of the same names. In addition, the Order Item type is mapped to the Order Item relational (SQL) table.

In case a document NoSQL database is selected to store data on ordering, each of the independent logical record collections (Customer, Order, Product) in Figure 11 is represented as a document collection (Figure 13). The notation Customer <<unique index>> represents an instance of a database unique index named the customer. The graphical symbol of extension, with its narrow side towards the index, visually represents the fact that the index contains a projection of the document collection (vertical slice), or that only some data attributes or a part of attributes, of each document are included in the index (Hills, 2016). In the particular example (Figure 13), the notation Customer <<unique index>> shows that only the Customer ID is included in the index. By the same analogy, the notation Product <<unique index>> shows that only the Product ID from the Product document collection is included in the index (Figure 13). Defining the unique indexes on the primary keys of the document collections ensures fast searching of these collections, or in the particular example, by customers and products.

Although the example of modeling customer orders is simple, it is sufficient to present the main features of COMN data modeling, from representing real-world entities to logical data design, to physical data design. It is important to reemphasize that COMN can be used to model relational as well as NoSQL databases, because by following this method of modeling, a decision on the data storage method or the database type is not made until the final physical data modeling, and COMN makes it possible to present a physical data model for both relational and NoSQL databases.

A COMN physical model allows such storage of details that would be sufficient for its automatic implementation in relational and/or NoSQL databases. It follows that COMN enables model-driven development, from the identification of basic (real-world) entity types to logical data modeling, all the way to multiple physical implementations of the same data (Hills, 2016).

Because data is one of the main resources in organizations today, the survival and success of most organizations depend on the extent to which they understand the data that they have collected in their databases, whether relational or NoSQL, and on the extent to which they can, using various forms of data analysis, use the data to their advantage to achieve their fundamental objectives, to improve relations with their partners (customers and/or suppliers), but also to improve internal communication and raise the level of knowledge within the organization. In this regard, data modeling should become a key step in the development of NoSQL databases. Hills's COMN approach, described in this chapter, shows that this is possible.

REFERENCES

Attribute. (2017). In *Merriam-Webster*. Retrieved July 10, 2017 from https://www.merriam-webster.com/dictionary/attribute

Chen, P. P.-S. (1976). The entity-relationship model – Toward a unified view of data. *ACM Transactions on Database Systems*, *1*(1), 9–36. doi:10.1145/320434.320440

Component. (2017). In *Merriam-Webster*. Retrieved July 10, 2017 from https://www.merriam-webster.com/dictionary/component

Composite. (2017). In *Merriam-Webster*. Retrieved July 10, 2017 from https://www.merriam-webster.com/dictionary/composite

Concept. (2017). In *Merriam-Webster*. Retrieved July 10, 2017 from https://www.merriam-webster.com/dictionary/concept

Connolly, T., & Begg, C. (2005). *Database systems: A practical approach to design, implementation and management* (4th ed.). Pearson Education Limited.

Coronel, C., Morris, S., & Rob, P. (2011). *Database systems - Design* (9th ed.). Cengage Learning.

Elmasri, R., & Navathe, S. B. (2011). *Fundamentals of database systems* (6th ed.). Addison-Wesley.

Entity. (2017). In *Merriam-Webster*. Retrieved July 10, 2017 from https://www.merriam-webster.com/dictionary/entity

Hills, T. (2016). *NoSQL and SQL data modeling – Bringing together data, semantics, and software* (1st ed.). Technics Publications.

Hoberman, S. (2009). *Data modeling made simple – A practical guide for business and IT professionals* (2nd ed.). Technics Publications, LLC.

Hoffer, J. A., Ramesh, V., & Topi, H. (2011). *Modern database management* (10th ed.). Pearson Education Limited.

Object. (2017). In *Merriam-Webster*. Retrieved July 10, 2017 from https://www.merriam-webster.com/dictionary/object

Proposition. (2017). In *Merriam-Webster*. Retrieved July 10, 2017 from https://www.merriam-webster.com/dictionary/proposition

Rumbaugh, J., Jacobsen, I., & Booch, G. (1999). *The unified modelling language reference manual*. Addison-Wesley.

Wang, A. (2016). *Unified data modeling for relational and NoSQL databases*. Retrieved January 16, 2017 from https://www.infoq.com/articles/unified-data-modeling-for-relational-and-nosql-databases

Chapter 4
How NoSQL Databases Work

ABSTRACT

The chapter explains how NoSQL databases work. Since different NoSQL databases are classified into four categories (key-value, column-family, document, and graph stores), three main features of NoSQL databases are chosen, and their practical implementation is explained using examples of one or two typical NoSQL databases from each NoSQL database category. The three chosen features are: distributed storage architecture that comprises the distributed, cluster-oriented, and horizontally scalable features; consistency model that refers to the CAP and BASE features; query execution that refers to the schemaless feature. These features are chosen because, through them, it is possible to describe most of the new and innovative approaches that NoSQL databases bring to the database world.

INTRODUCTION

The first three chapters explained the NoSQL phenomenon, the reasons for NoSQL database emergence, the main characteristics of these databases, and the types of databases. The purpose of this chapter is to explain how NoSQL databases work. Since it is beyond the scope of this book to describe NoSQL databases in detail, as there are specialized books and manuals written for that purpose, a different approach is taken here. Three main features of NoSQL

DOI: 10.4018/978-1-5225-3385-6.ch004

databases are chosen, and their practical implementation is explained using examples of one or two typical NoSQL databases from each NoSQL database category (see Chapter 2). The three chosen features are:

- Distributed storage architecture that comprises the distributed, cluster-oriented, and horizontally scalable features described in Chapter 2.
- Consistency model that refers to the CAP and BASE feature described in Chapter 2.
- Query execution that refers to the schemaless feature described in Chapter 2.

These features are chosen because, through them, it is possible to describe most of the new and innovative approaches that NoSQL databases bring to the database world.

DISTRIBUTED STORAGE ARCHITECTURES

Data distribution and use of clusters are natural features of NoSQL databases (see Chapter 2.4). Namely, it is precisely the ability to run NoSQL databases on a large cluster that has drawn attention to this type of database. As amounts of data kept increasing, it was more and more difficult and costly for the organization to scale up (to purchase larger and larger servers to run the database on), and the option to scale out (to run the database on a cluster of servers) was becoming increasingly attractive. As already explained (see Chapter), relational databases were developed primarily to run on a single server, so attempts to implement these databases in distributed and cluster environments led to many problems and disrupted the basic postulates of these databases.

Broadly, there are two styles for distributing data (Sadalage & Fowler, 2013):

- Sharding distributes data across multiple servers in a way that every server acts as the only source for the assigned data subset (see Chapter 1).

- Replication copies data across multiple servers so that each piece of data can be found in multiple places. There are two basic forms of replication:
  - Master-slave replication where one node is the authoritative copy (master) that executes writes, while slave nodes are synchronized with the master node and can run reads.
  - Peer-to-peer (masterless) replication allows writes on any node, and nodes are coordinated in order to synchronize their data copies.

Master-slave replication decreases the possibility of conflicts during updates, but peer-to-peer replication avoids assigning all writes to a single point of failure. Implementations can use either individual approach or a combination of the two.

Most NoSQL databases are designed to be operated on a high-availability file system; this is usually the Hadoop Distributed File System (HDFS). However, some NoSQL databases (e.g., Cassandra) have developed their own systems that are compatible with HDFS. Certainly, the use of a specific file system such as HDFS has both advantages and disadvantages. The advantages of using a distributed file system in NoSQL databases are (McCreary & Kelly, 2014):

- **Reuse of Reliable Components:** From the aspect of time and costs, there are significant advantages in using a prebuilt and pretested system of components. A database management NoSQL system does not need to duplicate and redesign the functionalities of a distributed file system, but it can use a solution that is already at hand.
- **Customizable Per-Folder Availability:** Most distributed file systems can be configured on a folder-by-folder basis, which allows for higher availability of the system. Namely, the same data is stored in multiple locations in distributed systems; the default is three locations. This means that a client request would only fail if all three locations fail at the same time. The probability of that happening is typically very low, so storing the same data in three locations is considered to be sufficient for most distributed systems in order to maintain an adequate level of service or response to user requests.
- **Rack and Site Awareness:** Distributed file system software must consider how computer clusters are organized. In other words, when configuring these systems, it is necessary to define which nodes are

located in which racks, and nodes within one rack are assumed to have higher bandwidth than nodes in different racks.

In addition to these advantages, the use of a distributed file system in NoSQL databases has some disadvantages, such as (McCreary & Kelly, 2014):

- **Lower Portability:** A part of distributed file systems works best on UNIX or Linux servers (HDFS). On the other hand, their transfer to another operating system—for example, Windows—is not possible, or it involves the addition of a virtual machine layer, which may lead to significantly lower performance.
- **Design and Setup Time:** Configuring a well-designed distributed system requires investing effort and time in order to understand how to establish an adequate folder structure. Namely, all files within a folder share the same properties, such as replication factor. For example, if creation dates are used as folder names, then it is important that replication can be reduced for files that are older than a certain date (e.g., 2 years or more).
- **Administrative Learning Curve:** Distributed systems are complicated to set up and maintain and require constant monitoring and data backup. This means that the organization must have staff trained to manage such a system.

As already noted, most NoSQL databases use HDFS or an HDFS-compatible distributed system. By default, most files in HDFS have the replication factor 3, which means that data blocks that make up these files are located on three different nodes. HDFS allows the replication factor to be changed for any HDFS file or folder. In addition, one of the main features of HDFS is rack awareness or the ability to logically group HDFS nodes into structures that reflect how processors are stored in physical racks and connected together using an in-rack network. This means that HDFS can be configured so as to be spread onto multiple racks, which in turn can be located in multiple data centers. Figure 1 illustrates an example in which all blocks are stored on three separate servers (the replication factor 3), and HDFS spreads the blocks over two racks (McCreary & Kelly, 2014). In the case of failure of any of the racks, there will always be a replica of both block 1 and block 2.

As explained in Chapter 2, HDFS is an integral part of the Hadoop architecture that provides high-throughput access to application data.

Figure 1. HDFS rack awareness
McCreary & Kelly, 2014.

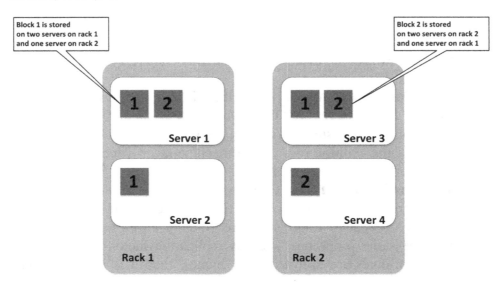

Distribution in Key-Value Stores

Most key-value stores use sharding to provide distribution and scalability. Sharding uses the value of a key to determine in which node the key will be stored. Also, key-value stores use both master-slave (e.g., Redis store) and peer-to-peer replication models (e.g., Riak store).

As it is useful to organize data into subunits (namespaces), it is also useful to organize servers in a cluster into subunits. Clusters are sets of interconnected servers or computers that coordinate their operation with one another. Key-value stores are usually loosely coupled or consist of rather independent servers that autonomously run most of their tasks with minimum coordination with other servers in the cluster.

A partitioned cluster is a group of servers in which each server, or instance of the key-value store that is run on the server, is assigned to handle a subset of the database. For example, in the case that a cluster consists of two servers, each one of them consequently runs a key-value database management system, and in an ideal case, each of the servers is loaded 50%. However, the extent to which each server will be loaded depends on the partition scheme that should ensure equal distribution of loads on servers within the cluster as possible. A partitioning scheme is based on a partition key, or the key used to determine which partition should contain a data value. In key-value stores, all keys are used to determine where the associated value will be stored. It follows that any key in a key-value store can be used as a partition key. However, it is important to stress that only the keys that distribute loads evenly on servers are considered to be good partition keys. In a situation when such keys are not available, it is normally possible to use a hash function or an algorithm that maps an input string whose size may vary to an output fixed-size string (Sullivan, 2015). The primary purpose of hash functions is to evenly distribute inputs over the set of all possible outputs, which is especially useful when hashing keys, because regardless of how similar the keys are, they will always be evenly distributed across the range of possible output values. The ranges of output values can be assigned to partitions, thus ensuring that each partition receives approximately the same amount of data.

Each node in a masterless cluster is responsible for managing a certain set of partitions. One way to organize partitions is to use a ring structure, where a ring is a logical structure for organizing partitions. A ring is a circular pattern in which each server or instance of the key-value database that is run on the server is connected with two neighboring servers or instances. Each server or instance is responsible for managing a range of data based on a partition key (Sullivan, 2015). Consequently, every time data is written to a server, the same data is also written on two servers linked with the original one. This ensures a high level of availability of key-value stores. Figure 2 shows an example of a six-server cluster configured as a ring.

The ways of implementing a ring can differ from one particular key-value store to another. Thus, for example, when it comes to the Riak key-value database, a ring represents the foundation of its masterless architecture and replication. A ring means a managed collection of partitions that share a common hash space. The hash space is called a ring because the last value in the hash space is observed as a neighbor to the first value in the space. Replications of data is stored in the next N partitions of the hash space, following the partition to which the keys hash. The Riak database uses the term *Ring State* to designate a data structure with which it is communicated and which stays synchronized among all nodes so that each node knows the state of the entire cluster. This means that, if a node receives a request for an object managed by another node, then it consults the Ring State and forwards the request to the relevant node, effectively proxying the request to the coordinating node. If a node permanently goes offline or if a new server is added, then other nodes are adjusted by balancing partitions around the cluster and then updating the Ring State. Internally, Riak calculates a 160-bit

Figure 2. A cluster of six servers configured as a ring

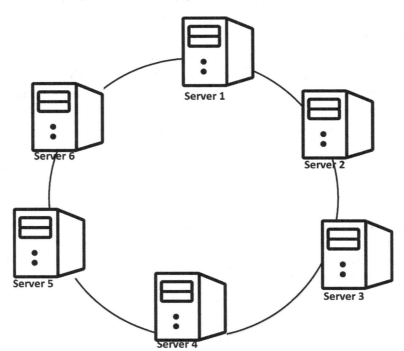

binary hash for each bucket/key pair and maps the value to a position on an ordered ring of all such values. The ring is divided into partitions, with each Riak virtual node (vnode) responsible for one such partition (Riak, 2017a).

Figure 3 presents an example of a Riak ring. Each node in a Riak cluster tries to run an approximately equal number of vnodes at any given time. This generally means that each node in a cluster is responsible for 1/(number of nodes) of the ring or (number of partitions)/(number of nodes) vnodes (see Figure 3). For example, if two nodes define a 16-partition cluster, then each node will consequently run 8 vnodes. Nodes attempt to claim their partitions at intervals around the ring such that there is an even distribution among the member nodes and that no node is responsible for more than one replica of a key (Riak, 2017a).

In key-value stores that use replication for distribution of data, it is necessary to take into account the number of replicas that need to be maintained. Namely, the more replicas that are used, the lesser the probability of data loss, but the higher the possibility of reduced system performance. The number of replicas depends on the nature of data that are stored. If data can be easily

Figure 3. Riak ring
Riak, 2017a.

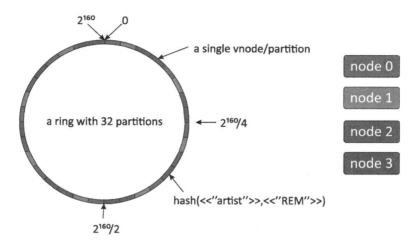

regenerated and loaded into the key-value database, then it is desirable to use less replicas. However, if data loss tolerance is low, then it is better to have more replicas. Most key-value stores allow specifying the number of replicas that must be written for the write operation to be considered completed from the perspective of the application that sent the data write request. For example, if a key-value store is configured to store three replicas, then it can be specified that information on a successful completion of writing is sent back to the application as soon as two of the three replicas are successfully written. The third replication will also be executed, but the application does not need to wait for it, and it can continue its operation.

It is also necessary to take replicas into consideration with writes. Since key-value stores normally do not enforce two-phase commits, it can happen that replicas have different versions of the same data. All versions should eventually be consistent, but sometimes, in a shorter period, they can be unsynchronized. In order to minimize the risk of reading obsolete data, it is possible to specify the number of nodes that must provide the same answer (the same data value) to a read request before the particular answer is forwarded to the application that sent the request. For example, in the case of three data replicas, it is possible to require at least two same answers from replicas before sending the answer to the program that issued the read request. On the one hand, the more same answers are required, the higher the probability that the most up-to-date answer will be sent back, but on the other hand, the longer it will take to get the answer because more replicas need to be checked. For example, Riak key-value store has a masterless architecture in which each node in a cluster is capable of serving read and write requests. All nodes are homogeneous and with no single master or point of failure. Every selected node can serve an incoming request irrespective of the location of data, providing data availability even when hardware or the network are experiencing failure conditions.

Unlike the Riak store, the Redis (REmote DIctionary Service) key-value store has a master node. The master node is responsible to receive read and write operations and to copy or replicate data to slave nodes that respond to read requests. If a master node fails, then other nodes in the cluster will elect a new master node. If a slave node fails, then other nodes in the cluster can continue responding to read requests.

Distribution in Document Stores

Document stores mainly use sharding by documents in order to provide high scalability and availability. Parts of a database called shards are stored on separate servers, or a single shard can be stored on multiple servers if the document store is configured for data replication. However, whether data is replicated or not, a server within a document store cluster can have only one shard per server. Figure 4 shows how horizontal sharding splits a database by documents or rows and distributes parts of the database, or shards, to different servers. In case that a cluster implements replication, one shard will be available on multiple servers.

For a sharding implementation to be successful, it is necessary to choose a shard key and a partitioning method properly. A shard key is one or more keys

Figure 4. Horizontal sharding
Sullivan, 2015.

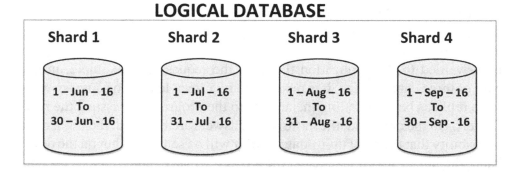

or fields that exist in all documents in a collection that are used to separate documents (Sullivan, 2015). A shard key can essentially be any individual field in a document: a unique ID of the document, name, date (e.g., creation date), type or category, geographic region, and the like. The shard key specifies the values that are used to group documents into different shards. The partitioning algorithm uses that shard key as input and determines the appropriate shard for that key.

There are three primary methods that can be used for sharding, or horizontal partitioning of data (Sullivan, 2015):

- Range
- Hash
- List

A range partition is particularly useful in a situation when a document store contains an ordered set of values of shard keys, such as dates or numbers. In this case, if, for example, all documents in a collection have the field creation date, then it can be used as the key to partition documents into monthly shards (all documents created in the period from November 1, 2016, to November 30, 2016, make one shard, and the documents created from December 1, 2016, to December 31, 2016, make another shard).

A hash partition uses a hash function to determine the shard in which to place a document. As explained earlier (see "Distribution in Key-Value Stores"), the purpose of hash functions is to generate values that are evenly distributed over the range of values of the hash function. For example, when using a five-server cluster, the hash function will generate values between 1 and 5 and ensure that approximately the same number of documents is stored on each of the five servers.

List-based partitioning uses a list, or a set of values, to determine where to place data. For example, if vehicle type designations, like a sports car, luxury car, SUV, and off-road vehicle, are used for cars, then vehicle types can be used as a shard key to allocating documents to four different servers.

For document stores, it is typical that developers can choose keys to use for sharding as well as sharding algorithms that the database management system supports.

MongoDB, one of the most frequently used document stores, supports the sharding method to distribute data on multiple servers.

A MongoDB sharded cluster consists of (MongoDB, 2017):

- **Shard**: *Each shard contains a subset of sharded data and can be deployed as a replica set.*
- **Mongos**: *Mongos act as a query router and provide an interface between client applications and the sharded cluster.*
- **Config Servers**: *Config servers store metadata and data on cluster configuration settings. (p. 2450)*

Figure 5 illustrates the interaction among these components within a sharded cluster.

MongoDB shards data at the collection level, distributing the collection data across the shards in the cluster. In order to distribute documents in a collection, MongoDB partitions the collection using the shard key. As already noted, the MongoDB shard key consists of fields that exist in each document belonging to the same collection. It is exceptionally important in MongoDB to properly choose the shard key because, once selected, the shard key cannot be changed after implementing sharding, and every sharded collection can have only one shard key.

"MongoDB partitions sharded data into chunks. Each chunk has an inclusive lower and exclusive upper range based on the shard key" (MongoDB, 2017, p. 2440). The sharded cluster balancer is used for the migration of chunks

Figure 5. MongoDB sharded cluster
MongoDB, 2017.

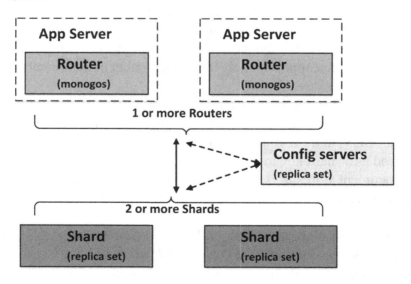

across the shards in the sharded cluster. The balancer tries to achieve an even balance of chunks across all shards in the cluster (MongoDB, 2017).

MongoDB sharding distributes data across the shards in their cluster, allowing each shard to contain a subset of the entire data in the cluster. As a number of data increases, additional shards increase the storage capacity of the cluster.

MongoDB allows a sharded cluster to continue running partial read/write operations in a situation when one or more shards are not available. Although the data subsets on unavailable shards cannot be accessed during downtime, reads or writes that are directed to available shards will be successfully completed.

In order to provide greater data availability, shards can be deployed as a replica set. Users, clients, or applications should only directly connect to a shard to perform local administrative and maintenance operations. Performing a query on a single shard returns only a subset of data. It is necessary to connect to the mongos to perform cluster-level operations, including read or write operations (MongoDB, 2017).

MongoDB allows data partitioning using a range or a hash. In the case of partitioning data in the collection using ranges of shard key values (see Figure 6), every range defines a nonoverlapping range of shard key values and is associated with a chunk (MongoDB, 2017).

MongoDB attempts to distribute chunks among shards in the cluster evenly. It is important to reemphasize that the shard key directly affects the effectiveness of chunk distribution.

Another way of partitioning data used by MongoDB is hashed sharding, which uses a hashed index of a single field as the shard key to partition data in the sharded cluster (see Figure 7).

Figure 6. MongoDB partitioning: ranges of shard key values
MongoDB, 2017.

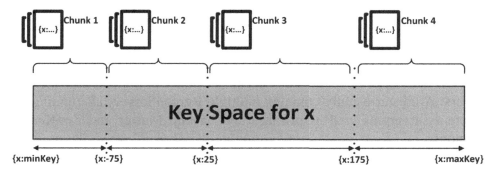

Figure 7. MongoDB partitioning: hash function
MongoDB, 2017.

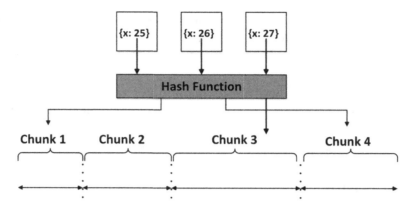

MongoDB automatically computes the hashes when resolving queries using hashed indexes, so applications are free from this part of the work—that is, they do not need to compute the hashes (MongoDB, 2017).

It is worth noting once again that the shard key and shard key values are immutable in MongoDB. This means that once a collection is sharded, it is not possible later to choose another shard key for that collection or to update values of the shard key fields.

Distribution in Column-Family Stores

Column-family stores use both master-slave (HBase) and peer-to-peer replication models (Cassandra) for improving scalability and availability.

Apache HBase column store, in keeping with the Hadoop nomenclature, supports pseudo distribution, or the distribution where all daemons, or background processes (Master, RegionServers, and ZooKeeper), run on a single node but also a fully distributed mode where all daemons are spread across all nodes in the cluster. The pseudo-distributed mode can run against the local file system, or it can run against an instance of the HDFS, while the fully distributed mode can only run on HDFS (HBase, 2017).

The cluster in HBase is configured in such a way that multiple cluster nodes enlist as RegionServers, ZooKeeper QuorumPeers, and backup HMaster servers. A cluster usually contains multiple RegionServers all running on different servers as well as primary and backup Master and ZooKeeper daemons.

The file conf/RegionServers on the master server contain a list of hosts whose RegionServers are associated with this cluster. Each host is on a separate line. All hosts listed in this file will have their RegionServer processes started and stopped when the master server starts or stops. (HBase, 2017, p. 25)

HBase uses the Hadoop (HDFS) infrastructure (see Chapter 2). As previously explained, HDFS is based on the master-slave architecture that consists of name nodes and data nodes. The name nodes manage the file system and provide centralized metadata management, while data nodes store and replicate data in accordance with configuration parameters.

ZooKeeper is a coordination service for distributed applications that provides coordination and synchronization of services within a Hadoop cluster. ZooKeeper maintains a shared hierarchical namespace. Since clients need to communicate with ZooKeeper, that potentially represents a single point of failure for HBase. Risks of failure are solved by replicating ZooKeeper data to multiple nodes.

In addition to Hadoop services, HBase also has its own server processes for the management of metadata that apply to the distribution of data from tables. RegionServers are instances that manage Regions, or storage units for HBase table data. Once a table is first created in HBase, all data is stored in a single Region, but as a number of data increases, additional Regions are created, and data is partitioned among multiple Regions (see Figure 8).

When a client device needs to read or write data from HBase, it accesses the ZooKeeper server in order to find the name of the server that stores the data on the relevant Region storage location in the cluster. Next, the client

Figure 8. HBase architecture
Sullivan, 2015.

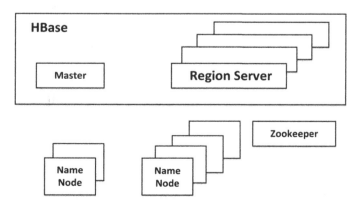

sends a request to the server with Region data to find out which server has the data for a given row key, if a read request is involved, or which server should store data associated with a row key, if a write request is involved (Sullivan, 2015).

An advantage of such architecture is that servers can be deployed and tuned for specific tasks such as managing the ZooKeeper. However, that makes the administration work somewhat harder because it is necessary to manage multiple configurations and tune each one of them. An alternative approach is to use a single type of node that can assume any role in a cluster. Column store Apache Cassandra uses this approach.

Cassandra uses a peer-to-peer distribution model, and the same software runs on all nodes. In a Cassandra store, data distribution and replication go together. Namely, data is organized into tables and identified using a primary key that also determines on which node the data is stored. Replicas are copies of rows. Replication is influenced by (Cassandra, 2017):

- **Virtual Nodes:** Assigns ownership of data to physical servers.
- **Partitioner:** Partitions data across the cluster.
- **Replication Strategy:** Determines the replicas for each row of data. The total number of replicas across the cluster is called the replication factor.
- **Snitch:** Defines the topology information used by the replication strategy for placement of replicas.

Virtual nodes (vnodes) simplify many tasks in Cassandra (Cassandra, 2017b):

- It is no longer necessary to calculate and assign tokens to each node.
- When adding or removing nodes, it is no longer necessary to rebalance a cluster.
- They improve the use of heterogeneous computers in a cluster because a proportional number of vnodes can be assigned to smaller and larger computers.
- They allow each node to own a large number of small partition ranges distributed throughout the cluster.

Within a cluster, vnodes are randomly selected and noncontinuous. The placement of a row is determined by the hash of the partition key within many smaller partition ranges belonging to each node (see Figure 9). Cassandra

Figure 9. Cassandra ring with virtual nodes
Cassandra, 2017d.

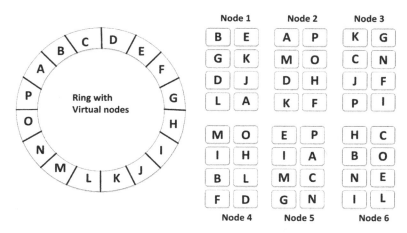

stores replicas on multiple nodes to ensure reliability and fault tolerance (Cassandra, 2017c).

Distribution in Graph Stores

Until recently, graph databases were an exception as compared to other NoSQL databases regarding scalability. The scalability problem of graph databases was stated as one of its main limitations. However, the increasing use of this type of NoSQL database, the constant increase in the number of nodes and edges, but also values of properties on nodes and edges stored in graph databases, as well as the steady growth of users, forced the producers of these databases to try to find solutions to improve scalability. Some examples are the development of the Titan graph database designed to scale horizontally, as well as the new clustering architecture of the Neo4j graph database as of version 3.1 (hereinafter: Neo4j). Neo4j offers two separate solutions for providing high availability and performance levels (Neo4j, 2017a):

- Causal clustering
- Highly available cluster

In order to meet expectations related to graph workloads, Neo4j clusters allow work to be federated across several cooperating machines. In a cluster environment, throughput goals (graph queries) can be achieved by allowing each computer to process a subset of the overall queries.

Neo4j's clustering architecture is an automated solution that allows a Neo4j database to be available at all times, provided that redundancy is deployed into the cluster so that, in the case of a failure, clusters can be masked by the remaining live instances.

Neo4j's causal clustering has two main features (Neo4j, 2017a):

1. ***Safety:*** *Core servers allow establishing a fault tolerant platform for transaction processing that will remain available while a simple majority of those Core servers are functioning.*
2. ***Scale:*** *Read replicas provide a massively scalable platform for graph queries that enable very large graph workloads to be executed in a widely distributed topology.* (p. 38)

This allows the end-user system to be fully functional in terms of read and write operations on the database, even in the case of multiple hardware and software failures.

Causal clustering assumes that a cluster has two different roles: Core and Read replica (see Figure 10).

The main responsibility of a core server is to safeguard data. Core servers fulfill this task by replicating all transactions using the Raft protocol. The Raft protocol ensures that data is safely durable before confirming transaction

Figure 10. Neo4j causal cluster architecture
Neo4j, 2017a, p. 38.

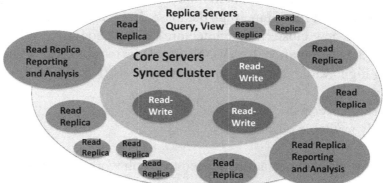

commit to the end-user application. In practical use, this means that once a majority of servers in a cluster (n/2 + 1) accept the transaction, it is safe to confirm the commit to the end-user application (Neo4j, 2017a). However, this safety requirement reflects on write latency. Implicitly, writes will be acknowledged by the fastest majority, but with the increasing number of core servers in the cluster, the size of the majority needed to acknowledge a write also increases.

The consequence is a relatively small number of computers in a typical core server cluster in order to avoid increasing write latency too much.

The primary objective of read replicas is to allow graph workloads to be scaled out. Read replicas are fully-fledged Neo4j databases capable of fulfilling arbitrary (read-only) graph queries and procedures.

Read replicas are asynchronously replicated from Core servers via transaction log shipping.

Many Read replicas can be fed data from a relatively small number of Core servers, allowing

for a large fan out of the query workload for scale. "Read replicas should be typically run in relatively large numbers and treated as disposable" (Neo4j, 2017a, p. 39).

Causal consistency allows writing to the core, where data is safe, but also reading those records from a Read replica, where graph operations are scaled out.

Another solution for providing high levels of availability and performance of Neo4j databases is a highly available cluster that consists of a single master instance and none or more slave instances. All instances in a cluster have full copies of data in their local databases. The basic highly available cluster configuration has three instances (see Figure 11).

Each instance contains the logic necessary for coordination with other cluster members in order to ensure data replication and election management. The arbiter instance contains the full Neo4j software that allows it to participate in cluster communication but does not replicate a copy of the database (arbiter mode). Each slave instance communicates with the master instance to keep its database up to date. When it comes to write operations, slaves are automatically synchronized with the master instance. If the master fails, then a new master will be elected automatically. In addition, the cluster automatically handles instances that are currently unavailable (e.g., a network failure) and accepts them as members of the cluster when they become available again (Neo4j, 2017a). In the case of failure of the master node, all write transactions being performed at that moment will be rolled back, and new transactions will be

Figure 11. Neo4j highly available cluster
Neo4j, 2017a, p. 51.

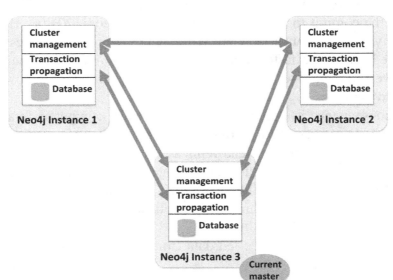

blocked or fail until a new master becomes available. Unlike write operations, read operations are highly available and able to handle read loads scales with more database instances in the cluster.

CONSISTENCY MODELS

One of the pillars of the relational databases is the ACID transaction approach. As it was explained in Chapter 1, the ACID transaction is based on an all-or-none principle, meaning that the transaction must be entirely completed or entirely aborted—that is, intermediate states are not allowed. The implementation of ACID transaction properties ensures efficient concurrency control and recovery process in case of limited scale-up and shared-something environments, which are natural environments for relational databases. Nevertheless, with the emergence of Big Data phenomenon and the urgent need for storing an enormous quantity of data across multiple database servers, the ACID approach became a serious limitation. The result was the development of the BASE (basically available, soft state, eventually consistent) approach (see Chapter 1). The BASE approach has become popular, especially with the development of NoSQL databases. NoSQL databases, distributed naturally, were designed to avoid the restrictions of strict ACID consistency and to promote themselves as databases that do not support the ACID transaction approach.

This often leads to the misconception that NoSQL databases provide only a weak, or at best eventual, consistency and that their consistency implementation mechanisms are very simple. However, NoSQL databases offer different consistency guarantees, including strict consistency, even if only at the level of an individual object. Also, owing to their departure from strict and predictable rules of ACID models, most NoSQL databases have developed complex mechanisms for establishing acceptable levels of consistency.

The most significant reduction in consistency is to limit its range to a single operation or object. Relational databases allow maintaining consistency across multiple statements (e.g., updating a row in a table and then inserting a row in another table can be a single transaction). For a set of queries accessing multiple tables, relational databases are expected to return a consistent view of data that existed when the queries were made. Most NoSQL databases do not support this level of multi-object consistency (Harrison, 2015).

However, even when single-object operations are involved, there are different consistency levels, of which the most significant are (Harrison, 2015):

- **Strict Consistency:** A read operation always returns the most up-to-date value of data.
- **Causal Consistency:** A read operation may not return the most recent value but will not return an out of sequence value either. This means that, for example, if one session created the A, B, and C updates, then another session should never be able to see the C update without having been able to see the B update.
- **Monotonic Consistency:** A session will never see a piece of data reverted to an earlier point in time—that is, once a data is read, it is not possible to see an earlier value of the data.
- **Read Your Own Write**s: This guarantees that the user will at least be able to see any of his or her executed operations.
- **Eventual Consistency:** The system may be inconsistent at any point in time, but all individual operations will eventually be consistently applied. If all updates are stopped, then the system will reach a consistent state.
- **Weak Consistency:** The system does not make any guarantee that it will ever become consistent—namely, if a server fails, then an update may be lost.

In practice, NoSQL databases implement either strict or eventual consistency, unlike relational databases that implement ACID consistency. Causal or monotonic consistency levels are not directly supported by most NoSQL databases.

Consistency in Key-Value Stores

In key-consistency value stores is applied only for operations on a single key because these operations are either a get, put, or delete on a single key. It is possible to execute optimistic writes, but their implementation is very expensive because a key-value store cannot determine a change in value.

In "Distribution in Key-Value Stores," it was explained that most key-value stores are implemented as distributed stores. Such an approach results in the use of the eventually consistent consistency model. Riak, one of the most popular key-value stores, is also based on the eventually consistent approach. More recent versions of the Riak store (as of version 2.0) claim to feature implementation of strong consistency. However, the official documentation of the Riak store (Riak, 2017b) states that strong consistency is an experimental feature and is likely to be unsupported, or removed, in the future. It also states that this feature is not commercially supported or production ready, and neither is it compatible with the primary Riak features (Multi-Datacenter Replication, Riak Search, Bitcask Expiration, LevelDB Secondary Indexes, Riak Data Types, and Commit Hooks). Therefore, it is not recommended to use strong consistency in any Riak production environment (Riak, 2017b).

Thus, the Riak store, like the Redis key-value store, implements an eventually consistent model. Since a value in a Riak store may be replicated to other nodes, Riak uses two ways to solve update conflicts (Sadalage & Fowler, 2013):

- The newer write "wins," or the older write "loses."
- Both (all) values are returned, allowing the client to solve the conflict.

Which of the two options will be used in the Riak store is determined during the bucket creation. Buckets are a way to namespace keys so that key collision can be reduced (e.g., all customer keys can be located in the customer bucket). When creating buckets, default values for consistency must be registered.

Different key-value stores have different transaction specifications. In general, there are no guarantees on writes. When implementing transactions,

Riak uses the quorum concept that requires a majority of replicas (at least a half plus one of the total replicated nodes) to respond. During the write application programming interface (API) call, Riak uses the W value (quorum) and the replication factor. For example, if a Riak cluster has a replication factor of 5 and a W value of 3 (quorum = 5/2 + 1), then the write operation is successfully recorded only when it is successfully recorded on at least three nodes. Such an approach allows the Riak store to have write tolerance, which, in this example, would mean that the cluster can tolerate two nodes (total number of nodes–quorum value, or 5–3) being down during the write operation, although this still means that some data would be lost for reads from these nodes (Sadalage & Fowler, 2013).

The Riak store does not support ACID transactions, which means that it has to rely on some other type of conflict-resolution mechanism. An advantage of Riak's eventual consistency model is that Riak does not dictate how a conflict-resolution mechanism will be implemented. Namely, although the Riak store ships with a set of defaults concerning how data is replicated and how conflicts are resolved, the user may override these defaults and choose another of the offered strategies (internal vector clocks, timestamps, special eventually consistent data types) or resolve conflicts on the application side by implementing a case-specific logic at option. Such a variety of options allows Riak's eventually consistent behavior to be managed according to the application data model(s).

In earlier Riak store versions (prior to version 2.0), all causality-based conflict resolutions, whether on the client side or in the Riak store, were implemented using vector clocks. As of version 2.0, Riak has added and recommends using the option dotted version vectors (DVVs) instead of vector clocks. Like vector clocks, DVVs are also a mechanism for monitoring object update causality in the conditions of logical time rather than in chronological time (like with timestamps) and allow Riak to decide which objects are more current than others in case of a conflict (Riak, 2017c). The main difference between vector clocks and DVVs is in the way they handle concurrent updates. Namely, vector clocks can detect concurrent updates on the same object but cannot identify which value is related to which update, the consequence of which is, depending on the sequence of update deliveries to the different replicas, possible duplication of sibling values, which can lead to a sibling explosion and thus undue latency (Riak, 2017c). Unlike vector clocks, DVVs identify each value together with the update that created it, which means that double values can always be identified and removed, thus decreasing sibling explosion (in this case, the number of sibling values is proportional to the number of concurrent updates).

However, even in a situation when the causal context is used, Riak cannot always decide which value is most causally recent, especially in the case of concurrent object updates. In that case, Riak leaves the decision to developers, except that it strongly recommends one of the following two options (Riak, 2017d):

- If data can be modeled as one of the presently available Riak data types (flags, registers, counters, sets, and maps), then it is recommended to use one of these types because each one has conflict resolution built in and thus frees applications from the need to engage in solving conflicts.
- If it is impossible to model data as one of the presently available data types, then it is recommended to allow Riak to generate siblings (they are created when Riak deals with multiple possible values for the same object, and it cannot determine which one of them is most causally recent) and develop an application that solves conflicts in a way that is most appropriate for the particular case. It is important to stress that the development of one's own resolution strategy can be a big challenge, although it may have certain advantages over other approaches.

All this indicates that the Riak store allows a mixed approach in terms of data storage and management and enables users to apply different conflict-resolution strategies within a cluster.

The Redis key-store also implements an eventually consistency model. The commands MULTI (marks the beginning of a transaction block), EXEC (executes all previously queued commands in a transaction and restores the connection state to normal), DISCARD (flushes all previously queued commands in a transaction and restores the connection state to normal), and WATCH (marks the given keys to be watched for conditional execution of a transaction) are the foundation of transaction management in the Redis store (Redis, 2017a). These commands allow a group of commands to be executed as a single step with two important guarantees (Redis, 2017b):

- All commands in a transaction are serialized and executed sequentially. It can never happen that a request issued by another client is served in the middle of the execution of a Redis transaction. This guarantees that commands are executed as a single isolated operation.

- Either all commands or none are processed, which means that a Redis transaction is atomic.

As of version 2.2, in addition to these two, Redis provides another guarantee in the form of optimistic locking (repetition of a transaction in case of a conflict, hoping that the conflict will be avoided in a new point in time).

Consistency in Document Stores

Document stores can be consistent or eventually consistent. MongoDB provides tunable consistency. By default, in a single-server implementation, data in MongoDB is consistent, meaning that all writes and reads access the primary copy of the data. In that situation, if the MongoDB document is modified, then it is locked against both reads and writes by other sessions. If MongoDB replica sets are implemented, then it is possible that read queries could be issued against secondary copies where data may be eventually consistent if the write operation has not yet been synchronized with the secondary copy.

The consistency of individual documents in MongoDB is achieved by using locks. Locking is used to ensure that two writes do not attempt to modify a document simultaneously and that the user has a consistent view of data. In terms of locking at the document level, a document update will block only those read or write operations that want to access that document.

Implementing MongoDB as a single-server configuration provides strict consistency. Strict consistency is initially provided also in the case of a multi-server configuration. In this case, all read operations are directed to the primary server that always has the latest version of a document.

However, MongoDB allows consistency to be configured using replica sets by choosing to wait for the writes to be replicated to all the slaves or a given number of slaves. Every write can specify the number of servers on which the write is to be propagated for it to be considered successful (Sadalage & Fowler, 2013).

In MongoDB, a write operation is atomic at the level of a single document, even if the write operation modifies multiple embedded documents within a single document. When one write operation modifies multiple documents, the modification of each of the documents is atomic, but the operation as a whole is not atomic, and other operations may interleave. However, the isolation operator ($isolated) can be used to isolate a single write operation that affects multiple documents. By using the isolation operation, a write operation that affects multiple documents can prevent other processes from interleaving once the write operation modifies the first document. This approach ensures that no client can see the changes until the write operation completes or returns an error. It is important to emphasize that the isolation operation does not function with sharded clusters (MongoDB, 2017).

Still, an isolated write operation does not guarantee all-or-nothing atomicity. In other words, an error that occurs during the write operation does not roll back all the changes that preceded the error. Since a single document can contain multiple embedded documents, single-document atomicity is sufficient for most cases occurring in practice. For the cases where a sequence of write operations is to be executed as a single transaction, a two-phase commit can be implemented in the application. However, a two-phase commit can only offer transaction-like semantics. Using two-phase commits ensures data consistency, but the application may return intermediate data during the two-phase commit or rollback (MongoDB, 2017).

MongoDB concurrency control allows concurrent running of multiple applications without causing data inconsistency or conflicts. One approach is to create a unique index on a field that can have only unique values. This prevents insert or update operations from creating double data. It is also recommended to create a unique index on multiple fields in order to force uniqueness on that combination of field values. Another approach involves specifying the expected current value of a field in the query predicate for the write operations. The two-phase commit allows a variation where the query predicate includes the application identifier as well as the expected state of data in the write operation (MongoDB, 2017).

MongoDB allows clients to see the results of writes before the writes are durable (MongoDB, 2017):

- Independent of write concern (the level of confirmation that MongoDB requires for write operations), other clients that use the default readConcern (the query returns the most recent data but does not guarantee that the data is written on a majority of the replica set members—that is, data rollback is possible) can see the results of a write operation before the write operation is confirmed to the issuing client.
- The client using the default readConcern may read data that may be subsequently rolled back.

For a MongoDB store configured as a stand-alone instance, a set of read and write operations to a single document is serializable. If it is configured as a replica set, then a set of read and write operations to a single document is serializable only in the case of absence of a rollback.

Consistency in Column-Family Stores

Although column-family stores are typically eventually consistent, the HBase column store provides strong consistency for individual rows. Namely, an HBase client cannot simultaneously modify a row in a way that would cause the row to become inconsistent. Such behavior is similar to the one that exists in relational databases that generally use row-level locking to prevent any simultaneous updates of a single row. However, implementing this approach is more complex when it comes to HBase because rows may contain thousands of columns in multiple column families, which may have distinct disk storage. During the update of any column or column family within a row, the entire row is locked using RegionServer in order to prevent conflicting updates to any other column. Read operations do not require locks, while write operations do not block reads. When read and write operations are run concurrently, the read will rather read an earlier version of the row than a version being updated (Harrison, 2015). Namely, all reads and writes are directed over a single region server that guarantees that all writes are executed in an order and that all reads see the most recent committed data.

In order to achieve high availability for reads, HBase provides a feature called region replication. This means that for every region of a table there will be multiple replicas that are opened in different RegionServers. Initially, the region replication is set to 1, which means that only a single region replication is implemented, and there will not be any changes from the original model.

If region replication is set to 2 or more, then the master will assign replicas of the region of the table. The Load Balancer ensures that the region replicas are not cohosted in the same region servers and also in the same rack, if possible. (HBase, 2017, p. 291)

Region replicas were introduced to improve the availability of the HBase store. Namely, a failure of a RegionServer should not result in data loss, or it can lead to a slight reduction in performance because it takes a while to establish a new RegionServer. Region replicas allow immediate failover to a backup RegionServer that keeps a copy of region data. By default, all reads in HBase are directed to the primary RegionServer, which has strictly consistent behavior as a result. However, if consistency for read is configured as timeline consistency, then a read request will be first sent to the primary RegionServer but will soon be followed by a double request directed to the secondary RegionServer. The first server that returns a result ends the request. Since the primary RegionServer starts first, it will usually be the first to return the result, if available. This feature is called timeline consistency because the secondary RegionServer always receives region updates in the same sequence as the primary. However, that does not guarantee that a secondary RegionServer will have up-to-date data. If there are multiple secondary RegionServers, then it is possible that reads will return writes out of order, as there may be race conditions occurring among the multiple secondary servers and the primary (Harrison, 2015).

Owing to the feature timeline consistency, HBase introduces a consistency definition per read operation (get or scan). Timeline consistency, as implemented by HBase, differs from pure eventual consistency considering the followingg (HBase, 2017):

- Single homed and ordered updates. Whether a region replication is involved or not, on the write side, there is still only one defined replica (primary) that can accept writes. This replica is responsible for ordering the edits and preventing conflicts. This guarantees that two different writes will not be committed simultaneously by different replicas and that data will not be different. With this kind of approach, there is no need to do read-repair or last-timestamp-wins kind of conflict resolution.
- The secondaries also apply the edits in the order that the primary committed them. In this way, the secondaries will hold a snapshot of the primary data at any point in time. This kind of approach is similar to replication in relational databases and even HBase's own multi-datacenter replication but in a single cluster.
- On the read side, the client can detect whether a read comes from up-to-date or outdated data. In addition, the client can issue a read with different consistency requirements on a per-operation basis in order to ensure its own semantic guarantees.
- The client can still observe edits out of order. It means that client has the ability to go back in time if it observes reads from one secondary replica first, then another secondary replica. The client is not obligatory to stick to region replicas or a transaction ID-based guarantee. If necessary, this restriction can be implemented later.

Figure 12 illustrates how timeline consistency works on the example of two clients, where client 1 first writes x = 1, then x = 2, and later x = 3. In Figure 12, it is visible that all write operations are handled by the primary region replica in a way that all writes are stored in the write-ahead log and then asynchronously replicated to other replicas. In the example in Figure 12, one replica (replica_id = 1) received two updates and showed that x = 2, while the other replica (replica_id = 2) only received a single update and shows that x = 1. In a situation when a client reads with strong consistency, it will only talk with the primary replica (replica_id = 0), and this guarantees that it will always read the most up-to-date value, in this case, x = 3. However, in a situation when a client issuing timeline consistency reads, the read request goes to the master, or if the master does not respond, then it goes to all other replicas, and the result from the one that responds first will be returned to the client. Consequently, the client can see either of the values 1, 2, or 3 as x. In the example in Figure 12, if the primary region fails and the client executes multiple read operations with timeline consistency, then it can first read that the value is x = 2 and then x = 1.

Cassandra column store supports a per-operation trade-off between consistency and availability using consistency levels. An operation's consistency level specifies how many replicas need to respond to the request

Figure 12. Timeline consistency
HBase, 2017.

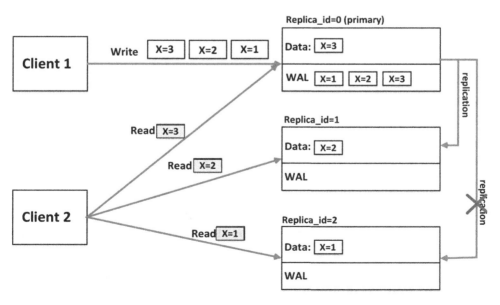

(read/write) toward the coordinator for the operation to be considered successfully completed. Cassandra provides the following consistency levels (Cassandra, 2017e):

- **One:** Only a single replica must respond.
- **Two:** Two replicas must respond.
- **Three:** Three replicas must respond.
- **Quorum:** A majority (n/2 + 1) of the replicas must respond.
- **All:** All replicas must respond.
- **Local Quorum:** A majority of replicas in the local datacenter (whichever datacenter the coordinator is in) must respond.
- **Each Quorum:** A majority of replicas in each datacenter must respond.
- **Local One:** Only a single replica must respond. In a multi-datacenter cluster, this guarantees that read requests will not be sent to replicas in a remote datacenter.
- **Any:** A single replica must respond, or the coordinator may store a hint. If the hint is stored, then the coordinator will attempt later to replay the hint and to deliver the mutation to the replicas. This consistency level is accepted only for write operations. (p. 1)

In the Cassandra store, write operations are always sent to all replicas regardless of consistency level. Consistency level only controls how many responses the coordinator waits for before responding to the client. For read operations, the coordinator usually only issues read commands to a sufficient number of replicas in order to meet the consistency level. There are two basic exceptions from this behavior (Cassandra, 2017e):

- If the other replicas have not responded within a specified time frame, the speculative retry may issue a redundant read request to an extra replica.
- In order to repair potentially inconsistent data, read requests may be randomly sent to all replicas.

Cassandra does not have transactions in the sense of the transactions in relational databases (where a single transaction may consist of multiple writes). In the Cassandra store, a write is atomic at the level of a row, which means that adding or updating columns for a given row key will be treated as a single write and may either be completed in success or fail. Writes are first written to commit logs and memtables and are considered to be successful only in a situation when the write to commit log and memTable were successful (Sadalage & Fowler, 2013). If a node fails, then a commit log is used to apply changes to the node. To synchronize writes and reads, external transaction libraries, like ZooKeeper (part of the Hadoop ecosystem), are often used with Cassandra.

Consistency in Graph Stores

Consistency in graph stores is ensured through transactions. They do not allow dangling relationships.

The main rule is that the start and end node always have to exist. Deleting of nodes is allowed only if they don't have any relationships attached to them (Sadalage & Fowler, 2013).

In single-server configurations, data is always consistent, especially in the Neo4j graph store, which is fully ACID compliant. When Neo4j uses a cluster configuration, write to the master is eventually synchronized to the slaves, while slaves are always available for reads. Writes to slaves are allowed, and they are immediately synchronized with the master. However, other slaves are not synchronized right away because they have to wait for the data to propagate from the master.

Since Neo4j is an ACID-compliant graph store, a transaction has to be started before changing any node or adding relationships to existing nodes. If operations are not wrapped in transactions, then the system returns an error message. Unlike write operations, read operations can be executed without initiating a transaction. A transaction must be marked as successful, or Neo4j assumes that there was an error and rolls back the transaction when the finish is issued. Unlike relational databases, setting success without issuing finish does not commit data to the database. Neo4j transactions are all-or-nothing operations. When a transaction starts, every following operation will succeed or fail as an atomic unit—failure of one means failure of all.

Neo4j (enterprise version) enables a configurable consistency model in order to balance performance and durability. In order for the Neo4j store to be able to benefit from all the advantages of the high-availability operation mode, it is necessary to configure the store as a cluster. In that case, write to one slave is not immediately synchronized with all other slaves so that there is a danger of consistency loss for a brief moment, which makes Neo4j eventually consistent. In addition, this leads to loss of pure ACID-compliant transactions. Servers in a cluster will elect a master that is the gold copy of data, except that slaves accept writes and synchronize them with the master node, which then propagates the changes to other slaves (Redmond & Wilson, 2012).

Neo4j uses ZooKeeper as an external cluster coordinator service whose primary purpose is to provide the service of coordinating distributed applications. In addition, each Neo4j server has its own related coordinator in charge of managing its place in the cluster.

Using clusters allows configuring very read-heavy systems to deal with replicating a graph across multiple servers and thus sharing the load (Redmond & Wilson, 2012). Although in this case, the cluster as a whole is only eventually consistent, there are ways to reduce the chance of reading stale data, such as assigning a session to a single server. However, in the case of need for data distribution, Neo4j is available and partition tolerant (AP) at the expense of consistency. In other words, each slave will return only what it has at the moment, although that can be temporarily out of synchrony with the master node. This is one of the reasons why the cluster option of the Neo4j store is recommended primarily for the situations when most requests are oriented to reads rather than to writes.

QUERY EXECUTION

One of the key reasons for the long dominance of relational databases is the almost universal adoption of the SQL language as the primary language to search, enter, and update data. SQL proved to be flexible enough to meet the requirements of both professional developers and database users who are not programming oriented. This is because SQL is a very simple and yet powerful domain-specific language. On the one hand, a limited vocabulary, unambiguous grammar, and simple syntax make SQL very easy to learn. On the other hand, SQL allows powerful manipulation (inputting, updating, deleting, querying, grouping, aggregating, etc.) of structured data stored in relational databases (see Chapter 1). It is based on the relational model or relational tables as the basic data structures is exactly what caused the new generation of databases to be specifically declared as ones that do not use SQL (see Chapter 2). While at first NoSQL databases were promoted as databases that do not use SQL, they still had a need to search, input, update, and delete data, so they too had to find their own ways to search and manipulate data. NoSQL databases essentially started to solve what had already been solved in SQL, and the remainder of this chapter will present the extent to which they managed to do so when it comes to data querying.

As already explained (see Chapter 2), the term NoSQL is an umbrella term that applies to very different types of NoSQL databases, developed to solve various real-life problems (one size does not fit all), which is reflected in their approach to solving data searches or the way they execute queries.

Query Execution in Key-Value Stores

The main property of all key-value stores is the possibility to search by keys, not values, and the searching is restricted to exact matches (see Chapter 2). This means that a requirement for a different type of search (i.e., search by an attribute of the column value) has to be resolved using an application code because key-value stores do not support it.

Key-value stores are intended for simple lookup operations, so there is not a standard query language for these stores. However, some key-value stores understand commonly used structures, such as XML and JSON, while most programming languages have libraries that support constructing and parsing XML and JSON. Search applications, such as Solr (Solr, 2017) and Lucene (Lucene, 2017), also have mechanisms for parsing XML and JSON. Although this combination of structured formats and programming libraries is not equivalent to a standard query language like SQL, these combinations do provide some of the features typical of query languages (Sullivan, 2015).

Consequently, despite inherent limitations of key-value stores, there are more and more different programming libraries and applications offering additional features to provide an implementation of different query requirements.

Queries that are usually in relational databases, like range queries (e.g., selecting data with names in some range of the alphabet, such as names that start with "Ma") are not directly supported in key-value stores and are solved by using additional programming libraries and applications. In the event that a key-value store supports secondary indexes, then range queries can be executed but only on indexed values (Sullivan, 2015).

Queries based on keys have some side effects. Thus, there may be a problem if a key is unknown, like during ad hoc querying in debugging, because most key-value stores do not provide a list of all primary keys. And even if a key-value store provides a list of primary keys, retrieving this list and then querying for the value can be very cumbersome (Sadalage & Fowler, 2013).

The Riak key-value store implements a pure key-value system. Objects in a Riak store are found through object keys, and an object retrieved by the key is a binary object whose content is invisible to the database.

Most interactions with a Riak store are reduced to setting or finding the value of a key. Riak HTTP API or Riak's Protocol Buffers Client API interface can be used for this purpose. In addition, Riak supports client libraries for Erlang, Java, PHP, Python, Ruby, and C/C++ as well as community-supported projects for NET, Node.js, Python (and Twisted), Griffon, Small Talk, Perl, Scala, Clojure, and many others (Riak, 2017e).

Sending a request to a Riak store over HTTP is explained through basic examples of reading, storing, and deleting objects and keys. The examples are presented in curl, a command-line tool for data transfer to and from a server using different protocols. In curl, all HTTP methods are prefixed with –X.

All updates to existing objects should include the X-Riak-Vclock header that was retrieved from Riak, along with the object. Also, Riak understands many HTTP-defined headers, like Accept for content-type negotiation (Riak, 2017d).

Reading an object is one of the main commands that allows retrieval of a key from a bucket (Riak, 2017f):

```
GET /riak/bucket/key
```

Example 1

```
curl -XGET "$RIAK/types/items/buckets/car/keys/favorite"
suv
```

Example 1 illustrates a GET command that reads the value suv under the type/bucket/key items/car/favorite. It should be noted that Riak holds much more information that can be accessed if reading the entire response, including the HTTP header.

A GET command returns the content of an object, if one exists. A Riak GET command may have multiple parameters whose explanations go beyond the scope of this book and can be found in the Riak documentation (Riak, 2017g). The parameter r for setting the R-value for a GET request describes the number of replicas that must agree when retrieving an existing object in order to return a successful response, and it is interesting from the viewpoint of data consistency.

There are two approaches that can be used to store objects in a Riak store: storing an object with an existing or user-defined key, or storing a new object and assigning a random key (Riak, 2017h).

In the case of storing an object with an existing or user-defined key, the following command is used (Riak, 2017h):

```
PUT /riak/bucket/key
```

Example 2

```
        curl -XPUT "$RIAK/types/items/buckets/car/keys/
favorite" \
-H "Content-Type:text/plain" \
-d "suv"
```

Example 2 shows the PUT command that puts the value suv into the key favorite under the car bucket. The mark –d denotes that the next string will be the value, declaring it as text with the proceeding line –H "Content-Type:text/plain." This defines the HTTP MIME type of this value as plain text. However, instead of plain text, it is possible to set any value at all, be it XML or JSON—even an image or a video—because Riak does not care what data is uploaded so long as the object size doesn't get much larger than 4MB (Redmond & Daily, 2015, p.27).

It is important to note that buckets are created automatically when keys are assigned to them, so there is no need to create buckets explicitly. Like GET, the PUT command supports multiple parameters, and the following are interesting from the aspect of consistency (Riak, 2017g):

- r: How many replicas need to agree when retrieving an existing object before the write.
- w: How many replicas to write before returning a successful response.
- dw: How many replicas to commit to durable storage before returning a successful response.
- returnbody: Whether to return the contents of the stored object.

When the approach based on storing a new object and assigning a random key is used to store an object in a Riak store, it is necessary to use the POST command or to send a POST request to the bucket URL instead of a PUT to a bucket/key pair (Riak, 2017h):

```
POST /riak/bucket
```

Example 3

```
    curl -i -XPOST "$RIAK/types/json/buckets/car/keys"
\
  -H "Content-Type:application/json" \
  -d '{"name":"rav4"}'
```

Example 3 illustrates a POST command that adds a JSON value to represent a car under the json/car type/bucket. The response header is where a POST will return the key it generated. Namely, if the Riak store does not receive a key name after the bucket, then Riak knows that one is to be created.

The command used to delete keys in a Riak store is (Riak, 2017i):

```
DELETE /riak/bucket/key
```

Example 4

```
curl -XDELETE "$RIAK/types/json/buckets/car/keys/
DNQGJYOKtcHMirkidasA066yj5V"
```

A deleted object in Riak is internally marked as deleted by writing a marker known as a tombstone. Unless configured otherwise, another process called a reaper will later finish deleting the marked objects. (Redmond & Daily, 2015, p. 29)

A Riak key-value store supports secondary indexes, which means that it can execute range queries but only on indexed values. Secondary indexes in Riak enable tagging objects stored in Riak, at write time, with one or more queryable values. Those values can then be used to find multiple objects in Riak. For example, if data on cars are stored, then it is possible to tag each object associated with that car with a car identifier or other unique marker (Riak, 2017j).

Since Riak has no real knowledge of the data it stores (they're just binary values), the user must define exactly what attribute to index on and what its index value should be via key/value metadata.

Secondary indexes have the following features (Riak, 2017j):

- They allow two types of secondary attributes: integers and strings (i.e., binary).
- They allow querying by exact match or range on one index.
- Query results can be used as input to a MapReduce query.

It is recommended to use secondary indexes in Riak store in the following cases (Riak, 2017j):

- When it is desired to search data on terms other than an object's bucket/key pair.
- When a value that is stored is an opaque blob, like a binary file, and needs to be indexed via added attributes.
- When there is a need for an easy-to-use search mechanism because secondary indexing does not require a schema to be present and has a basic query interface.

Secondary indexes use document-based partitioning, or a local index, where the indexes reside with each document, local to the vnode. Secondary indexes essentially represent a list of key/value pairs that are similar to HTTP headers. At write time, objects are tagged with index entries consisting of key/value metadata. This metadata can be queried to get the matching keys. The object's value and its indexes should be thought of as a single unit. There is no way to alter the indexes of an object independently from the value of an object and vice versa. Indexing is atomic and is updated in real time when writing an object. This means that an object will be present in future index queries as soon as the write operation completes (Riak, 2017j).

Example 5 illustrates insertion of objects with secondary indexes.

Example 5

```
curl -i -XPUT $RIAK/types/shopping/buckets/people/keys/casey \
-H "Content-Type:application/json" \
-H "X-Riak-Index-age_int:45" \
-H "X-Riak-Index-computer_bin:2345" \
-d '{"work":"programmer"}'
```

This example shows an entry for a customer aged 45 who purchased a computer with the code 2345 for the type computer and who works as a programmer. In this example, querying can be performed in two ways: exact match and range. If several other customers who purchased a computer of the same type—that is, with the code 2345 (e.g., Ana, aged 39; Petar, aged 28)—are added to the Riak store, then a query that answers the question which customers purchased the computer of the type 2345 is in fact a quick lookup to get the keys that have matching index values:

```
        curl "$RIAK/types/shopping/buckets/people/index/
computer_bin/2345"
{"keys":["ana","petar"]}
```

The other way of querying is an inclusive ranged match. For example, all customers younger than 30 years of age in the preceding case are found with:

```
curl "$RIAK/types/shopping/buckets/people/index/age_int/0/30"
{"keys":["petar"]}
```

This kind of put/get model can be sufficient for some types of applications. However, it is not adequate for modifying and querying complex data types. In such situations, it is necessary to use Riak API. Application code does not need to provide a full copy of the new object that is to be inserted. Instead, the application specifies only a change vector that should be applied to the existing object (Harrison, 2015). For example, if an object is a list of employees, then a new employee can be added just by specifying the new employee's name, without having to retrieve and reinsert all existing employees.

Query Execution in Document Stores

Unlike key-value stores that can search data only by key, document stores provide APIs or query languages that enable retrieving of documents based on attribute values. As explained earlier (see Chapter 2), document stores are very flexible. They make it possible to store different types of documents and their variations in document collections.

Document stores also offer different data search options that are very similar to what SQL provides (e.g., it is possible to find documents created on a specific date, documents of a particular type, or documents that contain a particular string—"tablet" in the description of the product—or it can be any combination thereof). Since document stores allow execution of complex queries, they must consequently be capable of finding a way for the optimal execution of these queries. That is why document stores implement query processors to find the optimal sequence of steps to retrieve data specified by a query. The query takes as input queries and data about the documents and collections in the database and produces a sequence of operations that retrieve the selected data (Sullivan, 2015).

A good property of document stores is that, unlike key-value stores, they do not need to retrieve the whole document by its keys in order to query data inside the document. This feature brings these stores closer to the relational database query model (Sadalage & Fowler, 2013).

Unlike relatively simple APIs using key-value stores (see "Query Execution in Key-Value Stores") that require explicit navigation to the desired value and do not provide any direct support for complex queries, document stores, such as MongoDB, try to overcome these limitations by providing rich query languages, very similar to SQL by their properties.

MongoDB stores data as BSON documents. BSON is a binary representation of JSON documents and contains more data types than JSON. To preserve type information, MongoDB adds the following extensions to the JSON format (MongoDB, 2017):

- Strict mode. Strict mode representations of BSON types conform to the JSON RFC. Any JSON parser can parse these strict mode representations as key/value pairs; however, only the MongoDB internal JSON parser recognizes the type of information conveyed by the format.
- Shell mode. The MongoDB internal JSON parser and the mongo shell can parse this mode. (p. 86)

The MongoDB store provides different query features, from simple to highly complex ones such as a query on embedded/nested documents, query an array, query an array of embedded documents, and the like.

Collection objects within MongoDB include a find() method that allows fairly complex queries to be constructed. But for queries that have to aggregate across documents, it is necessary to use the aggregate() method, which is a logical equivalent of the SQL GROUP BY clause (Harrison, 2015, p. 173). Table 1 gives a comparative view of examples of queries in MongoDB and their SQL equivalents.

Generally, the query for MongoDB is simpler because the objects are embedded inside a single document, meaning that the query can be based on the embedded child documents (Sadalage & Fowler, 2013).

MongoDB uses the $elemMatch operator for specifying multiple criteria on an array of embedded documents such that at least one embedded document satisfies all the specified criteria (MongoDB, 2017). Example 6 illustrates

Table 1. MongoDB query versus SQL statements

MongoDB Statements	SQL Statements	Description
db.vehicles.find()	select * from vehicles	View of all vehicles from the collection vehicles, or in SQL, from the table vehicles.
db.vehicles.find({ carType: "suv", fuelType: "diesel"})	select id, car_name from vehicles where car_type="suv" and fuel_type="diesel"	View of all vehicles from the collection vehicles, or in SQL, from the table vehicles, which satisfies the condition that carType is suv and that fuelType is diesel.
db.orders.agregate([{$match: {status:"ordered"}}, {$group: {_id: "$_vehicle_id", total: {$sum: "$quantity"}}}]	select vechicle_id, sum(quantity) from orders where status="ordered" group by vechicle_id	View by vehicle of the total number of ordered vehicles for all orders with the status "ordered."

a query that looks through all documents to find the documents where the in-stock array has at least one embedded document that contains the field quantity that is less than or equal to 100 and greater than 50:

Example 6

```
db.inventory.find({"instock": {$elemMatch: {quantity:
{$lte:100, $gt:50}}}})
```

When specifying conditions on multiple fields nested in an array of documents, it is possible to specify

the query such that either a single document meets these conditions or any combination of documents (including a single document) in the array meets the conditions.

Query Execution in Column-Family Stores

The main property of column-family stores is that they are denormalized stores or that they are structured in such a way that all important information on an object is contained in a single, mainly very wide, row. In this way, column-family stores avoid joins and subqueries, which are extensively used in relational databases. Instead, column-family stores use denormalization to maintain related information using a common row identifier (Sullivan, 2015).

Query languages that use column-family stores may look similar to SQL because they support SQL-like terms such as select, insert, update, and delete.

However, these languages also support operations specific to column-family stores (for example, create columnfamily).

Column-family stores support different types of querying that allow selection of data subsets available in a row.

The HBase column store is based on Apache Drill, a low-latency distributed query engine for large-scale datasets, including structured and semistructured/ nested data. But Drill is also useful for short, interactive ad hoc queries on large-scale datasets. Drill is capable of querying nested data in formats like JSON and Parquet and performing dynamic schema discovery (Drill, 2017a).

It is important to note that Apache Drill queries do not require prior knowledge of the data in queries. Knowledge of data is not required by its source system or its schema and data types. The powerful feature of Apache Drill is an SQL query workload against complex data: data made up of various types of records and fields rather than data in a recognizable relational form (discrete rows and columns). Drill is capable of discovering the form of the data when the query is submitted. Not only are nested data formats such as JSON files and Parquet files accessible, but Drill provides special operators and functions that can be used to drill down into these files. These operators and functions include (Drill, 2017b):

- References to nested data values
- Access to repeating values in arrays and arrays within arrays (array indexes)

Example 7 illustrates a very simple HBase query that shows data from the HBase table employees.

Example 7

```
SELECT * FROM employees;
```

The query looks identical to an SQL query that has the same purpose, to show all employees stored in the relational table (SELECT * FROM employees): The difference is that the query from Example 7 will return data that are unusable because data is stored as byte arrays. To make the data readable, it is necessary to convert them from byte arrays to UTF8 (character encoding capable of encoding all possible characters, defined by Unicode) types (see Example 8).

Example 8

```
SELECT CONVERT_FROM(row_key, 'UTF8') AS employeeid,
CONVERT_FROM(employees.account.name, 'UTF8') AS name,
CONVERT_FROM(employees.address.country, 'UTF8') AS country,
CONVERT_FROM(employees.address.town, 'UTF8') AS town,
CONVERT_FROM(employees.address.street, 'UTF8') AS street
         FROM employees;
```

Results of the query from Example 8 are readable now (see Figure 13).

As already noted, the HBase column store allows for the execution of very complex queries, which is covered in depth in the HBase documentation (HBase, 2017).

Relational databases require a good knowledge of data in order to write necessary queries, which is not the case with HBase. Namely, although some data is not manifested as columns in a source database, Drill will return them in the result set as if they had the predictable form of columns in a table (Drill, 2017b).

The Cassandra column store uses an SQL-like language called Cassandra Query Language (CQL) that uses the familiar SELECT statement for data definition, manipulation, and querying. It is now the preferred method for interacting with Cassandra databases from query tools or within programs.

Figure 13. The query output (Example 8)

employeeid	name	country	town	street
employee1	Ana	BH	Mostar	K.Tvrtka 11
employee2	Mark	Croatia	Split	Zrinski 34
employee3	Carol	BH	Mostar	Stari grad 23
employee4	Peter	BH	Mostar	Balinovac 18
employee5	Maria	Croatia	Split	Frankopan 54

One of the most significant and likely also controversial features of CQL is that it abstracts the underlying wide column BigTable-style data model in favor of a more relational-like tabular scheme.

The consequence is that it is possible to write functional Cassandra CQL without understanding the underlying Cassandra data model, which, on the one hand, is an advantage for users who are more proficient in SQL, but on the other hand, can pose a risk because, in order to properly use CQL features, it is necessary to know both CQL and Cassandra column structures (Harrison, 2015).

Although familiar SQL-like statements provide the possibility to perform updates and deletes, create indexes, or issue queries, the CQL SELECT statement has limited capabilities when compared to standard SQL (Harrison, 2015):

- Joins are not supported.
- Ordering and range queries are limited to clustering columns within a specific partition key. (p. 176)

At first impression, these limitations may seem confusing if CQL tables are to be thought of as relational structures. However, wide column structures in CQL are defined by using composite primary keys, where the first part of the key defines partitioning or the row key, and the second part of the key defines the clustering columns that become dynamic column names in the wide column family. A consequence of such a structure is that row key is consistently hashed across the cluster, and the limitations become more understandable. Namely, Cassandra can neither effectively perform a range scan across hashed row key values nor can it allow access to the partition columns without accessing a specific row, since every row could have entirely distinct column values (Harrison, 2015).

CQL consists of statements that can be divided into the following categories (Cassandra, 2017f):

- Data Definition statements, to define and change how the data is stored (keyspaces and tables).
- Data Manipulation statements, for selecting, inserting, and deleting data.
- Secondary Indexes statements.
- Materialized Views statements.
- Database Roles statements.

- Permissions statements.
- User-Defined Functions statements.
- User-Defined Types statements.
- Triggers statements.

Readers who are familiar with SQL will recognize most of the SQL features in the listed categories, once again confirming the extent to which CQL is similar to SQL.

CQL is a typed language that supports a rich set of data types, including native types, collection types (maps, sets, lists), user-defined types, tuple types, and custom types.

Like SQL, for data search, CQL offers a SELECT statement with the following syntax (Cassandra, 2017g):

```
SELECT [ JSON | DISTINCT ] (select_clause | '*')
FROM table_name
[ WHERE where_clause ]
[ GROUP BY group_by_clause ]
[ ORDER BY ordering_clause ]
[ PER PARTITION LIMIT (integer | bind_marker) ]
[ LIMIT (integer | bind_marker) ]
[ ALLOW FILTERING ]
```

Examples 9, 10, 11, and 12 present some of the main possibilities of CQL.

Example 9:

SELECT name, job_description, date_of_employment
FROM employees
WHERE id_employee IN (154, 287, 334, 398);

The query shows the name, job_description, and date_of_employment for employees with id specified in the list (154, 287, 334, 398).

Example 10:

SELECT JSON name, job_description, date_of_employment
FROM employees
WHERE id_employee = 334;

The query shows the name, job_description, and date_of_employment from the JSON document for the employee with id 334.

Example 11:

SELECT name, professional_qualification
FROM employees
WHERE job_description = 'programmer' AND
        date_of_employment > '2015-01-01';

The query shows the name and professional_qualification for all employees whose job_description='programmer' and date_of_employment is greater than 2015-01-01.

Example 12:

SELECT COUNT(*) AS number_of_employees
FROM employees;

The query shows the total number of employees

As evident in these examples, since CQL does not support joins or subqueries, the SELECT statement applies only to a single table.

A detailed overview of CQL query features goes beyond the scope of this book and can be found, among others, in the Cassandra documentation (Cassandra, 2017h).

It is also worth noting here that the use of the GROUP BY option is possible only for grouping rows at the partition key level or at a clustering column level. By consequence, the GROUP BY option only accepts as arguments primary key column names in the primary key order. If a primary key column is restricted by an equality restriction, then it is not required to be present in the GROUP BY clause (Cassandra, 2017).

CQL supports two main categories of functions (Cassandra, 2017i):

- The scalar functions, which simply take a number of values and produce an output with it.
- The aggregate functions (count, max, min, sum, avg), which are used to aggregate multiple rows results from a SELECT statement.

In both cases, CQL provides several native "hard-coded" functions as well as the ability to create new user-defined functions.

In addition, CQL supports creating secondary indexes on tables, allowing queries on the table to use those indexes.

Since version 2.2, Cassandra introduces JSON support to SELECT and INSERT statements (see Example 10). This feature does not fundamentally alter the CQL API (e.g., the schema is still enforced); it simply provides a convenient way to work with JSON documents.

Query Execution in Graph Stores

The main feature of all graph stores is enabling an application to walk through a set of connected nodes based on the relationships among these nodes. The programming interface that allows this varies from vendor to vendor, ranging from the simple imperative approach to more declarative mechanisms. When using the simple imperative approach, the process is first to select a node that will be the starting point, examine relationships with other nodes, and then traverse each relationship to find related nodes; the process is repeated for each related node until all requested data is found or there are no more data to search. Using the more declarative approach involves selecting a starting point, specifying the criteria that filter the relationships to traverse and nodes to match, and then letting the database server implement its own graph-traversal algorithm in order to return a collection of matching nodes. The declarative approach makes it possible to avoid tying the code structure too close to the structure of the database (McMurtry, Oakley, Subramanian, Zhang, & Sharp, 2013).

Finding nodes and their immediate relations is simple, but this is nothing new as compared to relational databases because they provide this possibility themselves. The real power of graph stores comes into play when it is necessary to traverse the graphs at any depth and to specify a starting node for the traversal.

The possibility of traversing the graphs is particularly useful when trying to find nodes that are related to the starting node at more than one level down.

Another useful feature of graph stores is finding paths between two nodes, or determining if there are multiple paths and finding all the paths or the shortest path. This feature is most commonly used in social networks to present relationships between any two nodes. To find all paths and the distance between nodes for each path, it is necessary first to create a list of distinct paths between the two nodes. The length of each path is the number of hops on the graph needed to reach the destination node from the start node (Sadalage & Fowler, 2013).

Graph stores support the following query methods (Sullivan, 2015):

- Declarative
- Traversal based

Languages based on the declarative query method, like Cypher, are well suited to handle the problems requiring selection of nodes based on their properties. Declarative languages are also useful when it is necessary to apply aggregate operations of the type grouping or summing the values from node properties. Thus, for instance, the Cypher language provides a declarative SQL-like language for building queries. It is used with Neo4j graph store.

Traversal-based languages, like Gremlin, provide a higher level of control over the execution of queries because, for example, they offer the possibility to select between searching by depth-first or breadth-first methods. Traverse means to travel across or through. Graph traversal is the process of logically moving from one node to another over an edge (Sullivan, 2015).

Neo4J provides the Cypher—declarative query language to query and update of the graph. Cypher is inspired by several different approaches and builds on established practices for expressive querying. Most of the keywords like WHERE and ORDER BY are inspired by SQL. Pattern matching borrows expression approaches from SPARQL (RDF query language). Some of the collection semantics have been borrowed from languages such as Haskell and Python (Neo4j, 2017b).

The basic structure of the Cypher language is borrowed from SQL. Namely, queries are built up using various clauses that are chained together, and they feed intermediate result sets among one another (matching variables from one MATCH clause can be the context that the next clause exists in).

The flow of data within a Cypher query is an unordered sequence of maps with key-value pairs—a set of possible bindings among the variables in the query and values derived from the database. This set is refined and augmented by subsequent parts of the query (Neo4j, 2017b).

Table 2 gives an overview of Cypher clauses dedicated to read data from the graph store.

Table 3 gives an overview of general Cypher clauses that are used in combination with read and other clauses.

The MATCH clause is the primary way of getting data into the current set of bindings. It allows specifying the patterns Neo4j will search for in the database. As a rule, MATCH comes paired with the WHERE clause, which adds restrictions or predicates to the MATCH patterns. Example 13 illustrates a simple MATCH clause that only specifies a pattern with a single node and no labels. The result of this query is a view of all nodes in the graph store.

Table 2. The Cypher read data clauses

Clause	Description
MATCH	Specify the patterns to search for in the database.
OPTIONAL MATCH	Specify the patterns to search for in the database while using nulls for missing parts of the pattern.
WHERE	Add constraints to the patterns in a MATCH or OPTIONAL MATCH clause or filter the results of a WITH clause.
START	Find starting points through legacy indexes.
AGGREGATION	Aggregation functions including count(), sum(), avg(), max(), min(), collect(), and others. Includes DISTINCT.
LOAD CSV	Use when importing data from CSV files.

Neo4j, 2017c.

Table 3. General Cypher clauses

Clause	Description
RETURN	Defines what to include in the query result set.
ORDER BY	A subclause following RETURN or WITH, specifying that the output should be sorted in a particular way.
LIMIT	Constraints the number of rows in the output.
SKIP	Defines from which row to start including the rows in the output.
WITH	Allows query parts to be chained together, piping the results from one to be used as starting or criteria in the next.
UNWIND	Expands a list into a sequence of rows.
UNION	Combines the result of multiple queries.
CALL	Invokes a procedure deployed in the database.

Neo4j, 2017c.

Example 13

```
MATCH (n)
RETURN n
```

A view of the query showing all nodes with a particular label (book) on them is given in Example 14. The query returns all books from the database.

Example 14

```
MATCH (book:Book)
RETURN book.title
```

Example 15 shows the query that uses the symbol "- -" which means related to, without regard to type or direction of the relationship. In this case, the query returns all books written by 'Ernest Hemingway' as a result.

Example 15

```
                        MATCH (writer { name: 'Ernest Hemingway' }}-
-(book)
                RETURN book.title
```

When the direction of a relationship is interesting, it is shown by using the symbol - -> or <- -, like in Example 16, which shows the query when the type of relationship on which to match is known. It is specified by using a colon together with the relationship type. This query returns all actors who ACTED_IN "The Old Man and the Sea."

Example 16

```
  MATCH (oldmanandsea:Movie { title: 'The Old Man and the Sea'
}) < -[:ACTED_IN]-(actor)
  RETURN actor.name
```

As stated earlier, the MATCH clause is usually paired with the WHERE clause. Example 17 illustrates a query that uses a combination of MATCH and WHERE clauses, and for a given list of user names, it should find all nodes with names from this list, match their friends, and return only those followed users who have a 'name' property starting with 'M' (Neo4j, 2017d).

Example 17

```
MATCH (user)-[:friend]->(follower)
WHERE user.name IN ['Mario', 'Paul', 'Sara', 'Mitchell', 'Ana']
AND follower.name =~'M.*'
RETURN user.name, follower.name
```

All values that are handled by Cypher have a distinct type. The supported types of values are (Neo4j, 2017e):

- Numeric values
- String values
- Boolean values

- Nodes
- Relationships
- Paths
- Maps from Strings to other values
- Lists of any other type of value

To calculate aggregated data, Cypher, similar to SQL, offers aggregate functions (see Table 2).

Aggregation can be done over all the matching subgraphs, or it can be further divided by introducing key values. These are nonaggregate expressions that are used to group the values going into the aggregate functions.

Example 18 illustrates a query intended to find all friends of friends and to count them. In the aggregation function, count(DISTINCT friend_of_friend), DISTINCT removes the duplicates, meaning that friend_of_friend will be counted only once.

Example 18

```
                 MATCH (me:Person)- ->(friend:Person)-
->(friend_of_friend:Person)
                 WHERE me.name = 'A'
                 RETURN count(DISTINCT friend_of_friend)
```

The previous examples show that all queries against a graph database require a node (or a collection of nodes) as a starting point. Instead of referencing nodes by their identity numbers, nodes are usually selected by specifying values for one or more properties. Graph stores allow creating indexes over each of the properties used to specify the starting graph search criterion and thus enable the database server to quickly locate a node based on the values of these properties.

REFERENCES

Cassandra. (2017a). *Data distribution and replication.* Retrieved July 7, 2017 from http://docs.datastax.com/en/cassandra/2.1/cassandra/architecture/archi tectureDataDistributeAbout_c.html

Cassandra. (2017b). *Virtual nodes*. Retrieved July 7, 2017 from http://docs. datastax.com/en/cassandra/2.1/cassandra/architecture/architectureDataDist ributeVnodesUsing_c.html

Cassandra. (2017c). *Data replication*. Retrieved July 7, 2017 from http:// docs.datastax.com/en/cassandra/2.1/cassandra/architecture/architectureDat aDistributeReplication_c.html

Cassandra. (2017d). *How data is distributed across a cluster (using virtual nodes)*. Retrieved July 7, 2017 from http://docs.datastax.com/en/cassandra/2.1/ cassandra/architecture/architectureDataDistribute Distribute_c.html

Cassandra. (2017e). *Tunable consistency*. Retrieved July 7, 2017 from http://cassandra.apache.org/doc/latest/architecture/dynamo.html#tunable-consistency

Cassandra. (2017f). *Statements*. Retrieved July 8, 2017 from http://cassandra. apache.org/doc/latest/cql/definitions.html#statements

Cassandra. (2017g). *Data manipulation*. Retrieved July 8, 2017 from http:// cassandra.apache.org/doc/latest/cql/dml.html#data-manipulation

Cassandra. (2017h). *The Cassandra query language (CQL)*. Retrieved July 8, 2017 from http://cassandra.apache.org/doc/latest/cql/index.html

Cassandra. (2017i). *Functions*. Retrieved July 8, 2017 from http://cassandra. apache.org/doc/latest/cql/functions.html

Drill. (2017a). *Architecture introduction*. Retrieved July 8 17, 2017 from https://drill.apache.org/docs/architecture-introduction/

Drill. (2017b). *Querying complex data introduction*. Retrieved July 8 17, 2017 from https://drill.apache.org/docs/querying-complex-data-introduction/

Harrison, G. (2015). *Next generation databases: NoSQL, NewSQL, and big data. Apress*. doi:10.1007/978-1-4842-1329-2

HBase. (2017). *HBase manual*. Retrieved February 3, 2017 from http://hbase. apache.org/apache_h base_reference_guide.pdf

Lucene. (2017). Retrieved February 4, 2017 from http://lucene.apache.org/

McCreary, D., & Kelly, A. (2014). *Making sense of NoSQL: A guide for managers and the rest of us*. Manning Publications Co.

McMurtry, D., Oakley, A., Subramanian, M., Zhang, H., & Sharp, J. (2013). *Data access for highly-scalable solutions: Using SQL, NoSQL, and polyglot persistence. Microsoft.*

MongoDB. (2017). *MongoDB manual 3.4.* Retrieved June 23, 2017 from https://docs.mongodb.com/manual/meta/pdfs/

Neo4j. (2017a). *The Neo4j operations manual v3.1.* Retrieved February 3, 2017 from https://neo4j.com/docs/pdf/neo4j-operations-manual-3.1.pdf

Neo4j. (2017b). *Developer manual - Chapter 3. Cypher.* Retrieved July 6, 2017 from http://neo4j.com/docs/developer-manual/current/cypher/

Neo4j. (2017c). *Developer manual - 3.3. Clauses.* Retrieved July 6, 2017 from http://neo4j.com/docs/developer-manual/current/cypher/clauses/#header-reading-clauses

Neo4j. (2017d). *Developer manual - 3.3.1. MATCH.* Retrieved July 6, 2017 from http://neo4j.com/docs/developer-manual/current/cypher/clauses/match/

Neo4j. (2017e). *Developer manual - 3.2.1. Values.* Retrieved July 6, 2017 from http://neo4j.com/docs/developer-manual/current/cypher/syntax/values/

Redis. (2017a). *Commands.* Retrieved February 3, 2017 from https://redis.io/commands

Redis. (2017b). *Transactions.* Retrieved February 3, 2017 from, https://redis.io/topics/transactions

Redmond, E., & Daily, J. (2015). *A little Riak book for Lisp flavoured Erlang.* Retrieved June 20, 2017 from https://www.gitbook.com/book/billo/lfe-little-riak-book/details

Redmond, E., & Wilson, J. (2012). *Seven databases in seven weeks: A guide to modern databases and the NoSQL movement.* Pragmatic Bookshelf.

Riak. (2017a). *Clusters.* Retrieved July 5, 2017 from https://docs.basho.com/riak/kv/2.2.3/learn/concepts/clusters/

Riak. (2017b). *Strong consistency.* Retrieved July 5, 2017 from, http://docs.basho.com/riak/kv/2.2.3/developing/app-guide/strong-consistency/

Riak. (2017c). *Causal context.* Retrieved July 5, 2017 from http://docs.basho.com/riak/kv/2.2.3/learn/concepts/causal-context/#dotted-version-vectors

Riak. (2017d). *Conflict resolution.* Retrieved July 5, 2017 from, http://docs.basho.com/riak/kv/2.2.3/developing/usage/conflict-resolution/

Riak. (2017e). *Client libraries.* Retrieved July 5, 2017 from, http://docs.basho.com/riak/kv/2.2.3/developing/client-libraries/

Riak. (2017f). *HTTP get bucket properties.* Retrieved July 5, 2017 from, http://docs.basho.com/riak/kv/2.2.3/developing/api/http/get-bucket-props/

Riak. (2017g). *Replication properties.* Retrieved July 5, 2017 from, http://docs.basho.com/riak/kv/2.2.3/developing/app-guide/replication-properties/#available-parameters

Riak. (2017h). *HTTP store object.* Retrieved July 5, 2017 from, http://docs.basho.com/riak/kv/2.2.3/developing/api/http/store-object/

Riak. (2017i). *HTTP delete object.* Retrieved July 5, 2017 from, http://docs.basho.com/riak/kv/2.2.3/developing/api/http/delete-object/

Riak. (2017j). *Using secondary indexes (2i).*, Retrieved July 5, 2017 from, http://docs.basho.com/riak/kv/2.2.3/developing/usage/secondary-indexes/

Sadalage, P. J., & Fowler, M. (2013). *NoSQL distilled - A brief guide to the emerging world of polyglot persistence.* Pearson Education, Inc.

Solr. (2017). Retrieved February 4, 2017 from http://lucene.apache.org/solr/

Sullivan, D. (2015). *NoSQL for mere mortals.* Pearson Education, Inc.

Section 2
Bringing Together Relational and NoSQL Databases

Chapter 5
Bridging Relational and NoSQL Worlds

ABSTRACT

The chapter discusses the fact that the development and use of NoSQL databases showed that neither everything was good in NoSQL nor everything was so bad in relational databases. Namely, when operating with data, NoSQL databases have identical requirements for entering, updating, deleting or searching data, or for the data manipulation that SQL already resolved long ago. Therefore, it is not surprising that further development of many NoSQL databases shifted towards supporting SQL, which is one of the topics of this chapter. Namely, database users are generally not concerned with details about how data is stored. Rather, they want to have the possibility to view and analyze data together, regardless of whether the data is stored in relational or NoSQL databases. Therefore, vendors of relational databases were forced to look for solutions that would allow them to work with data stored in NoSQL databases as well.

INTRODUCTION

The first part of the book (Chapters 1, 2, 3, and 4) describes the reasons behind the appearance of NoSQL databases, as well as their main characteristics. When developing the first NoSQL databases, it was imperative to depart from relational databases as much as possible (elimination of ACID transactions,

DOI: 10.4018/978-1-5225-3385-6.ch005

SQL, etc.). First NoSQL databases were promoted as databases developed for coders, with one of the primary goals being to avoid the eternal impedance mismatch between the object-oriented approach to programming and relational databases. That is why SQL was avoided, and the focus was on the development of specific APIs and programming languages. However, such an approach soon turned out to be a limiting factor of wider implementation of NoSQL databases because it lacked the critical mass of well-trained developers (see Chapter 2), and a plethora of different APIs and programming languages was not beneficial for their faster training. On the other hand, the advent of many unstandardized APIs and abandonment of SQL were not welcomed with open arms by the SQL community that consisted of a large number of well-trained developers.

Further development and use of NoSQL databases showed that neither everything was good in NoSQL nor everything was so bad in relational databases. Namely, when operating with data, NoSQL databases have identical requirements for entering, updating, deleting, or searching data, or for the data manipulation that SQL already resolved long ago. Therefore, it is not surprising that further development of many NoSQL databases shifted toward supporting SQL, which is the topic of "From NoSQL Toward SQL."

As already emphasized, the first NoSQL databases were created out of necessity because it was not possible to resolve Big Data challenges using relational databases (see Chapter 2). Also, one of the basic postulates in the development of NoSQL databases is that there is not just one solution for all (data) problems. Practice shows that transaction-oriented requirements can be better solved using relational databases (ACID, SQL), whereas NoSQL databases are better suited to specific Big Data demands. However, these problems are not always clearly separated, and in everyday life they are often intertwined. Database users are generally not concerned with details about how data is stored: they want to have the possibility to view and analyze data together, regardless of whether the data is stored in relational or NoSQL databases. Therefore, producers of relational databases were forced, partly for the sake of solving customers' requirements, partly for the sake of keeping market share, to look for solutions within relational databases that would allow them to work with data stored in NoSQL databases as well. "Extending Relational Databases" describes how that was accomplished by the three largest database vendors: Oracle, Microsoft, and IBM.

FROM NoSQL TOWARD SQL

Development of databases showed that NoSQL moved away from relational databases because of the structural relational constraints it imposed, especially those related to the ACID transactions, which became a serious limitation to scaling and dealing with large data sets. Although the umbrella name for the new generation of databases is NoSQL, the recent development of those databases is showing that they are not necessarily opposed to SQL (i.e., that NoSQL means not just SQL). Today it is generally accepted that the aim of NoSQL databases is not to abandon SQL, but to find solutions to overcome technical limitations of the relational databases, especially when it comes to working with Big Data. It seems that NoSQL should really have been NonRel, implying nonrelational (Tiwari, 2011). Namely, every day more and more NoSQL databases provide support for SQL or create query languages in a syntax very similar to SQL. One of the reasons for the shift to SQL probably lies in the fact that, when it comes to data manipulation and search, NoSQL databases have requirements almost identical to those of relational databases. Namely, both the databases must allow entering, updating, deleting, and searching for data, except that all this was already solved long ago in SQL—the query language that was mainly associated with relational databases until now. After the initial enthusiasm regarding various NoSQL programming languages and APIs, SQL turned out to have significant advantages. It is a language with a high-level abstraction that simplifies access to and manipulation of data. In addition, it is a language in which literally millions of database users are conversant, and there are hundreds of popular business intelligence and analytic tools that use it under the hood as the means for getting at data (Harrison, 2015).

Chapter 4 briefly describes query languages that are similar to SQL (Drill, CQL, and Cypher) and that are used, among other things, to execute queries on NoSQL databases (HBase, Cassandra, and Neo4j).

This chapter gives an overview of two SQL-like query languages: Hive Query Language and Couchbase N1QL, both of which are designed to make it possible to use SQL features in NoSQL databases.

Hive

Hive Query Language (HQL) is a SQL-based language used on Hadoop. It is Hive that made Hadoop more accessible for many users, especially those familiar with SQL. The main purpose of Hive is to allow searching of Hadoop data, although Hive supports data manipulation (insert, update, delete) and other SQL-like operations.

Hive was developed by Facebook, but later the Apache Software Foundation company took it over and continued developing it as an open-source product under the name Apache Hive. Different companies presently use Hive, for example, Amazon in its Amazon Elastic MapReduce.

The main features of Hive are (Hive, 2014):

- Stores schema in a database and processed data into HDFS.
- Intended for OLAP (OnLine Analytical Processing).
- Provides SQL-like language for querying called HiveQL or HQL.
- It is familiar, fast, scalable, and extensible.

Figure 1 provides a view of the basic Hive architecture, consisting of a user interface, meta-store, HiveQL process engine, execution engine, and HDFS or HBase.

Figure 1. The architecture of Hive
Hive, 2014.

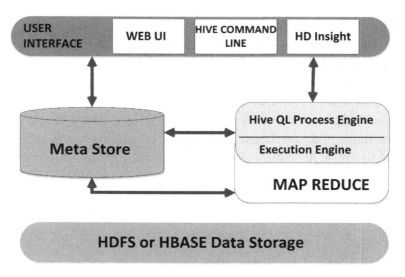

The user interface (Figure 1) provides interaction between the user and HDFS. The Hive interface supports the Hive Web UI (user interface), Hive command line, and Hive HD Insight (in Windows server).

The purpose of metastore (Figure 1) is to provide selection of a database server for storing the various objects (schema of tables, metadata, databases, table columns and their data types, and HDFS mapping).

Hive QL process engine (Figure 1) enables support for Hive query language (HQL). HQL provides querying on schema information on the metastore. Essentially, it is a replacement for the traditional approach of MapReduce, because instead of writing a MapReduce program in the Java programming language, it is possible to write a SQL-like query for a MapReduce job and process it (Hive, 2014).

The execution engine (Figure 1) links the HiveQL process engine and MapReduce in order to processes the query and generates results the same as MapReduce results (Hive, 2014).

HDFS (Hadoop distributed file system) or HBase (Figure 1) are the data storage systems for storing data into a file system (see Chapter 2).

Hive provides the basic SQL operations that work on tables or partitions. These operations are (Hive, 2017):

- Filtering rows from a table using a WHERE clause
- Selecting particular columns from the table using a SELECT clause
- Executing equijoins between two tables
- Evaluating aggregations on multiple "group by" columns for the data stored in a table
- Storing the results of a query into another table
- Downloading the contents of a table to a local (for example, NFS) directory
- Storing the results of a query in a Hadoop DFS directory
- Managing tables and partitions (create, drop, and alter)
- Plugging in custom scripts in the language of choice for custom map/ reduce jobs.

Like SQL, Hive distinguishes between DDL (Data Definition Language) and DML (Data Manipulation Language) statements. Hive provides the following DDL statements (Hive, 2017):

- CREATE DATABASE/SCHEMA, TABLE, VIEW, FUNCTION, INDEX
- DROP DATABASE/SCHEMA, TABLE, VIEW, INDEX
- TRUNCATE TABLE
- ALTER DATABASE/SCHEMA, TABLE, VIEW
- MSCK REPAIR TABLE (or ALTER TABLE RECOVER PARTITIONS)
- SHOW DATABASES/SCHEMAS, TABLES, TBLPROPERTIES, VIEWS, PARTITIONS, FUNCTIONS, INDEX[ES], COLUMNS, CREATE TABLE
- DESCRIBE DATABASE/SCHEMA, table_name, view_name

Table 1 provides a comparative view of the main DDL commands in Hive and SQL.

Hive provides following DML statements:

- LOAD
- INSERT
- UPDATE
- DELETE
- IMPORT/EXPORT
- SELECT

Table 1. Comparison of DDL commands in Hive and SQL

Hive Statement	SQL Statement	Description
CREATE DATABASE vehicledb; OR CREATE SCHEMA vehicledb;	CREATE DATABASE vehicledb;	Creating a database with name vehicledb
CREATE TABLE vehicle (vehicleid int, description String, type String) COMMENT 'Vehicle details' ROW FORMAT DELIMITED FIELDS TERMINATED BY '\t' LINES TERMINATED BY '\n' STORED AS TEXTFILE;	CREATE TABLE vehicle (vehicleid int NOT NULL, description VARCHAR(50) NOT NULL, type VARCHAR(20) NOT NULL);	Creating a table with name vehicle and columns vehicleid, description and type.
ALTER TABLE vehicle ADD COLUMNS (manufacturer String COMMENT 'Vehicle manufacturer')	ALTER TABLE vehicle ADD manufacturer VARCHAR(50);	Adding a new column – manufacturer- to table vehicle
DROP TABLE vehicle;	DROP TABLE vehicle;	Deleting table vehicle with all its data.

Table 2 provides a comparative view of the main DML commands in Hive and SQL.

Hive, like SQL, supports all basic aggregate functions (count, sum, avg, min, max), but also supports additional aggregate functions like variance, stdev (standard deviation), covar (covariance), corr (correlation), percentile, and the like. Table 2 illustrates the use of the aggregate function count().

Also, like SQL, Hive supports JOINS, which are used to combine some fields from two tables using the values common to these tables. This allows linking and simultaneous viewing of data stored for easier maintenance in different database tables.

Hive supports only equi-joins (i.e., equality-based joins), specifically:

- JOIN
- LEFT OUTER JOIN
- RIGHT OUTER JOIN
- FULL OUTER JOIN

Table 3 provides an overview of Hive commands for these types of joins. The examples illustrate execution of joins on tables VEHICLE and MANUFACTURER, where the table VEHICLE has the field manufacturerid that records producer codes, which is compared to value with the field id representing the code in the table MANUFACTURER.

The Hive LEFT OUTER JOIN returns all the rows from the left table, even if there are no matches in the right table. This means that if the ON clause matches 0 (zero) records in the right table, the JOIN still returns a row in the result, but with NULL in each column from the right table (Hive, 2014).

Table 2. Comparison of DML commands in Hive and SQL

Hive Statement	SQL Statement	Description
INSERT INTO TABLE vehicle VALUES (5, 'Rav 4', 'SUV');	INSERT INTO TABLE vehicle VALUES (5, 'Rav 4', 'SUV');	Inserting into table vehicle
UPDATE vehicle SET type = 'Jeep' WHERE vehicleid=5;	UPDATE vehicle SET type = 'Jeep' WHERE vehicleid=5;	Updating value of type for table vehicle
DELETE FROM vehicle WHERE vehicleid=5;	DELETE FROM vehicle WHERE vehicleid=5;	Deleting from table vehicle, vehicle with vehicleid=5
SELECT type, COUNT(*) FROM vehicle GROUP BY type HAVING COUNT(*)>5	SELECT type, COUNT(*) FROM vehicle GROUP BY type HAVING COUNT(*)>5	Finding a total number of vehicles by types, for those types of vehicles that have more than 5 cars.

Table 3. Examples of JOINS statements in Hive

Hive Query Statement	Type of Join	Description
SELECT v.vehicleid, v.description, m.name FROM vehicle v JOIN manufacturer m ON (v.manufacturerid = m.id)	JOIN	JOIN links tables vehicle and manufacturer, and for each vehicleid and description shows the name of manufacturer from table manufacturer
SELECT v.vehicleid, v.description, m.name FROM manufacturer m LEFT OUTER JOIN vehicle v ON (m.id = v.manufacturerid)	LEFT OUTER JOIN	LEFT OUTER JOIN returns all the values (name) from the left table (manufacturer), plus the matched values (vehicleid, description) from the right table (vehicle), or NULL in the case of no matching JOIN predicate. So, if the table manufacturer has an id, or producer whose value for id does not exist as a value for the field manufacturerid in the table vehicle (the table vehicle does not have a single vehicle of that producer), the SELECT statement will return NULL for vehicleid and description.
SELECT v.vehicleid, v.description, m.name FROM manufacturer m RIGHT OUTER JOIN vehicle v ON (m.id = v.manufacturerid)	RIGHT OUTER JOIN	RIGHT OUTER JOIN returns all the values (vehicleid, description) from the right table (vehicle), plus the matched values (name) from the right table (manufacturer), or NULL in the case of no matching JOIN predicate. Because the field manufacturerid in table vehicle is a foreign key, it has to have a corresponding value for id in the table manufacturer, which means that it will not be a null value for m.name.
SELECT v.vehicleid, v.description, m.name FROM manufacturer m FULL OUTER JOIN vehicle v ON (m.id = v.manufacturerid)	FULL OUTER JOIN	FULL OUTER JOIN is a combination of the previous two examples, which means that it returns all values for both tables (vehicle and manufacturer), and in case a producer in the table vehicle is not assigned to any vehicle (LEFT OUTER JOIN), a null value will be returned for vehicleid and description).

The Hive RIGHT OUTER JOIN returns all the rows from the right table, even if there are no matches in the left table. If the ON clause matches 0 (zero) records in the left table, the JOIN still returns a row in the result, but with NULL in each column from the left table (Hive, 2014).

The Hive FULL OUTER JOIN combines the records of both the left and the right outer tables that fulfill the JOIN condition. The joined table contains either all the records from both the table, or fills in NULL values for missing matches on either side (Hive, 2014).

It is important to note that, unlike SQL, Hive always inserts the results of select statements into a table.

Hive supports different built-in and custom-developed storage formats. Some of the built-in storage formats are (Hive, 2017):

- STORED AS TEXTFILE: Stored as plain-text files.
- STORED AS SEQUENCEFILE: Stored as a compressed sequence file.
- STORED AS ORC: Stored as ORC (Optimized Row Columnar) format, which supports ACID transactions and cost-based optimizer.
- STORED AS PARQUET: Stored as Parquet format. Apache Parquet is a columnar storage format available to any project in the Hadoop ecosystem, regardless of the choice of data processing framework, data model, or programming language (Parquet, 2017).
- STORED AS AVRO: Stored as Avro format. Avro is a data serialization system that relies on *schemas*. Avro schemas are defined with JSON, and this facilitates implementation in languages that already have JSON libraries (Avro, 2012).
- STORED AS RCFILE: Stored as Record Columnar File format. RCFile is a data placement structure designed for MapReduce-based data warehouse systems. RCFile stores table data in a flat file consisting of binary key/value pairs. It first partitions rows horizontally into row splits and then it vertically partitions each row split in a columnar way. RCFile combines the advantages of both row-store and column-store to satisfy the need for fast data loading and query processing, efficient use of storage space, and adaptability to highly dynamic workload patterns (Leverenz, 2015).

Hive makes it possible to organize tables into partitions or to divide one table into related parts based on values of partitioned columns such as vehicle type and producer (type and manufacturerid from table vehicle). Thanks to partitions, it is easier to search parts of data. Tables or partitions are subdivided into buckets, which provide an additional data structure that can be used for more efficient searching. Bucketing is based on the value of the hash function of some column of a table (Chapter 2).

Unlike the logical partitioning in RDBMS, partitioning in Hive is physical—for each partition, a different directory is created. Now while querying, if a partitioned column is specified, then only the data of the specified partition will be processed (Data-flair, 2016).

Partitioned tables are created using the PARTITIONED BY statement. A table can have one or more partition columns, and separate data directories are created for each distinct value combination in the partition columns (Hive, 2017).

Partitioning of the table vehicle and its data is described in Example 1.

Example 1

Table vehicle has fields vehicleid (vehicle code), description, type, and year of production (prodyear), with rows presented in Table 4.

If table vehicle (Table 4) is searched by vehicle production year, or if it needs to find all vehicles manufactured in 2016, it is necessary to search the entire table, generally with many more rows than shown in Table 4. However, if table vehicle is partitioned by production year (prodyear) and data about vehicles is stored in separate tables, that reduces query processing time.

```
CREATE TABLE vehicle(vehicleid INT, description STRING, type
STRING, prodyear INT) PARTITIONED BY (year STRING);
LOAD DATA LOCAL INPATH 'record/vehicledata/2016/file2'
OVERWRITE INTO TABLE vehicle PARTITION (year='2014');
LOAD DATA LOCAL INPATH 'record/vehicledata/2016/file3'
OVERWRITE INTO TABLE vehicle PARTITION (year='2016');
```

In the case of the table vehicle (Table 4), this would mean creating two partitions with the following data:

```
         - partition 1 - file2 (year 2014) contains the data
                143, Audi Q7, SUV, 2014
                187, Passat, sedan, 2014
              - partition 2 - file3 (year 2016) contains
the data
                234, Rav4, SUV, 2016
                211, Skoda Superb, sedan, 2016
```

Table 4. Example of table vehicle

Vehicleid	Description	Type	Prodyear
234	Rav4	SUV	2016
143	Audi Q7	SUV	2014
187	Passat	sedan	2014
211	Skoda Superb	sedan	2016

Partitions can be added by altering the table:

```
ALTER TABLE vehicle
  ADD PARTITION (year = '2014')
  Location '/2014/part2014';
```

The partition can be deleted (dropped) by using the following statement:

```
ALTER TABLE vehicle DROP
      PARTITION (year='2014')
```

It is important to notice that what partitions to use in a query is determined automatically by the system on the basis of WHERE clause conditions on partition columns.

HQL is compiled to MapReduce, i.e. in later releases to more sophisticated MapReduce 2.0 (MRv2) or YARN-based DAG algorithms (see Chapter 2).

The described examples (Table 4) show that Hive statements look and operate like SQL statements. However, there are some substantial differences between Hive and SQL (Harrison, 2015):

- Hive supports numerous table-generating functions that can be used to return multiple rows from an embedded field that can contain an array of values or a map of name:value pairs. The function Explode() returns a single row for each element in an array or map, and json_tuple() explodes an embedded JSON document.
- Hive supports the SORT BY statement that requires output to be sorted only within each reducer within the MapReduce pipeline. If compared to SQL ORDER BY clause, SORT BY avoids a large sort in the final reduce stage, which can have as a consequence results not being returned in a sorted order.
- The DISTRIBUTE BY clause provides control of the distribution of mappers'output to reducers. Instead of distributing values to reducers based on hashing of key values, it is possible to insist that each reducer receives a contiguous range of specific columns. DISTRIBUTE BY can be used together with SORT BY for ordering the results without a need to use an expensive sort operation. CLUSTER BY merges the semantics of DISTRIBUTE BY and SORT BY operations that defined the same column list.

As already explained, Hive can query data in HBase tables and data held in HDFS, and although support for Spark is available, its development is still in progress.

Couchbase N1QL

N1QL (pronounced "nickel") is query language developed for querying the JSON data in Couchbase. The name was derived from the non-first normal form, which is a superset and generalization of the relational first normal form: 1NF (Couchbase, 2017a). N1QL is a declarative query language that extends the possibility of using SQL to JSON documents. N1QL allows querying of JSON documents, just as SQL allows querying of relational tables, and JOIN in N1QL allows combining data from multiple JSON documents.

The main purpose of N1QL is to meet the query needs of a distributed document database, meaning Couchbase.

Similar to SQL, N1QL statements are divided into two groups (Couchbase, 2017a):

- **Data Definition Language (DDL):** The statements to create, modify, and delete indexes.
- **Data Manipulation Language (DML):** Statements are SELECT, INSERT, UPDATE, DELETE, and UPSERT (to insert rows into a database table if they do not already exist, or to update them if they do). The specified statements for adding(INSERT/UPSERT), modifying (UPDATE/UPSERT), and deleting (DELETE) JSON documents are in the experimental stage and are not recommended in production Couchbase (Couchbase, 2017a).

Like SQL, N1QL supports nested subqueries. Because N1QL queries are executed on JSON documents, searching over multiple documents is performed using the JOIN clause, and suitable operators and functions that enable navigation through nested arrays are also available. Like in SQL, conditions on data is set in the WHERE clause, and it is also possible to use standard SQL clauses GROUP BY, ORDER BY, aggregate, and other functions for data transformation, as required.

A N1QL query returns a set of documents as the result. The document set being returned does not necessarily need to be uniform, although it may be. A SELECT statement in which a fixed set of columns (attributes) is specified results in a uniform set of documents, whereas a SELECT statement in which a wildcard (*) is specified results in a nonuniform result set (Table 5).

Like with SQL, a simple query in N1QL has three basic parts (Couchbase, 2017a):

- **Select:** Parts of document to return
- **From:** The data bucket or data store to work with
- **Where:** Conditions the document must satisfy.

Table 6 gives a comparative view of N1SQL and SQL statements.

It is important to note there is NO SCHEMA in Couchbase.

N1QL provides paths in order to enable support for nested data. Paths use dot notations syntax to identify the logical location of attributes within a document. For example, the path manufacturer.address.street is used to obtain

Table 5. Examples of N1QL statements and results

N1QL Statement	Result

SELECT *
FROM users
WHERE family_name = 'Gaspar'
	{
	"results": [
	{
	"users": {
	"first_name": "Drazena",
	"age": 57,
	"children": [
	{
	"age": 27,
	"first_name": "Petra",
	"gender": "f"
	},
	],
	"email": "drazena.gaspar@gmail.com",
	"family_name": "Gaspar",
	"profession": [
	"professor"
	],
	"family_name": "Tomic",
	"relation": "sister",
	"title": "Ms.",
	"type": "contact"
	} }] }

SELECT children FROM users WHERE family_name = 'Gaspar'	{ "results": [{ "children": [{ "age": 27, "first_name": "Petra", "gender": "f" }] }] }

Table 6. Comparison of N1SQL and SQL statements

N1QL Statement	SQL Statement	Description
SELECT family_name, age FROM users WHERE age < 25	SELECT family_name, age FROM users WHERE age < 25	The results of this query are documents where the user's age is less than 25.
SELECT family_name, children FROM users WHERE children IS NULL	SELECT family_name, children FROM users WHERE children IS NULL	The results of this query are users who have the children field explicitly set to NULL.
SELECT COUNT(*) AS count FROM users	SELECT COUNT(*) AS count FROM users	Aggregate function COUNT(*) gives the number of documents in the bucket.
SELECT relation, COUNT(*) AS count FROM users GROUP BY relation	SELECT relation, COUNT(*) AS count FROM users GROUP BY relation	GROUP BY clause forms groups based on relation (for example: friend, parent, cousin) to the user.
SELECT u.relation, COUNT(*) AS count, AVG(c. age) AS avg_age FROM users u UNNEST u.children c WHERE c.age > 10 GROUP BY u.relation HAVING COUNT(*) > 1 ORDER BY avg_age DESC	SELECT u.relation, COUNT(*) AS count, AVG(c. age) AS avg_age FROM users u, children c WHERE c.user_id=u.id c.age > 10 GROUP BY u.relation HAVING COUNT(*) > 1 ORDER BY avg_age DESC	The UNNEST step is used to access the nested content of an array by joining it with its parent, as per the N1QL specs. This is used in the query in order to have access to all the nested entries for children as well. The WHERE clause eliminates children 10 years old or younger. The GROUP BY forms groups according to each relation (for example: friend, parent, cousin). The HAVING clause removes groups with less than one member. Finally, the groups are ordered by the average age of the group members in descending order.

the street from a producer's address. A path is predominantly used with arrays or nested objects to get the attributes within the data structure (Couchbase, 2017a). Paths provide a way to find data in document structures without having to retrieve the entire document or handle it within an application.

The command-line shell that can be used to issue N1QL queries on Couchbase Server directly is named cbq (Couchbase query).

N1QL supports various data types: Boolean values, numeric values, string values, arrays, objects, NULL, and MISSING. Although N1QL does not support the Date data type, it provides a robust set of functions to work with dates (Couchbase, 2017a).

N1QL distinguishes the following function categories (Couchbase, 2017a):

- Aggregate functions (SUM, AVG, COUNT, MIN, MAX)
- Array functions (ARRAY_SUM, ARRAY_AVG, ARRAY_COUNT, ARRAY_MIN, ARRAY_MAX, ARRAY_LENGTH, ARRAY_POSITION, etc.)
- Comparison functions (GREATEST, LEAST)

- Conditional functions for unknowns (IFMISSING, IFMISSINGORNULL, IFNULL, MISSINGIF, NULLIF)
- Conditional functions for numbers (IFINF, IFNAN, IFNANORINF, NANIF, NEGINFIF, POSINFIF)
- Date functions (CLOCK_LOCAL, CLOCK_TZ, CLOCK_STR, DATE_ADD_MILLIS, DATE_ADD_STR, DATE_FORMAT_STR, etc.)
- JSON functions (DECODE_JSON, ENCODE_JSON, ENCODED_SIZE, POLY_LENGTH)
- Meta and UUID functions (BASE64, BASE64_ENCODE, BASE64_DECODE, META, UUID)
- Number functions (ABS, ACOS, ASIN, EXP, LOG, POWER, SIGN, RANDOM, ROUND, etc.)
- Object functions (OBJECT_LENGTH, OBJECT_NAMES, OBJECT_VALUES, OBJECT_PUT, OBJECT_PAIRS, etc.)
- Pattern-matching functions (REGEXP_CONTAINS, REGEXP_LIKE, REGEXP_POSITION, REGEXP_REPLACE)
- String functions (CONTAINS, LENGTH, LOWER, UPPER, LTRIM, RTRIM, TRIM, POSITION, REPEAT, REPLACE, SUBSTR, etc.)
- Type functions (ISARRAY, ISNUMBER, ISOBJECT, ISSTRING, TOARRAY, TONUMBER, TOOBJECT, TOSTRING, etc.).

The N1QL SELECT statement queries a keyspace and returns a JSON array that contains zero or more objects. Figure 2 shows the query execution workflow at a high level, which illustrates the interaction with the query, index, and data services (Couchbase, 2017b).

A N1QL SELECT statement is executed as a sequence of steps. Every step in this process results in objects that are used as inputs in the next step, and so on until the process ends. The workflow diagram (Figure 2) shows all possible phases through which a query goes before returning the result. The clauses and predicates in the query decide the phases and the number of times that the query goes through—for example, the sorting stage can be skipped if there is no ORDER BY clause in the SELECT statement (Couchbase, 2017b).

Figure 3 shows the possible elements and operations during execution of a query.

As shown in Figure 3, the possible elements and operations in a query include (Couchbase, 2017b):

Figure 2. Couchbase the query execution flow
Couchbase, 2017b.

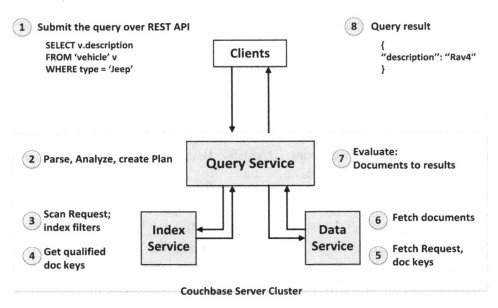

Figure 3. Query execution phases
Couchbase, 2017b.

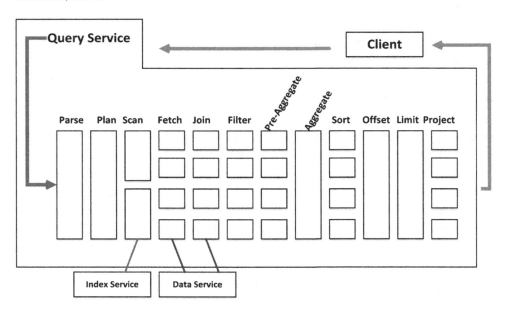

- Specifying the keyspace that is queried
- Specifying the document keys or using indexes to access the documents
- Fetching the data from the data service
- Filtering the result objects by specifying conditions in the WHERE clause
- Removing duplicate result objects from the result set by using the DISTINCT clause
- Grouping and aggregating the result objects
- Ordering (sorting) items in the result set in the order specified by the ORDER BY expression list
- Skipping the first *n* items in the result object as specified by the OFFSET clause
- Limiting the number of results returned using the LIMIT clause

N1QL supports the following types of JOIN clauses that make it possible to create new input objects based on a combination of two or more source objects:

- JOIN
- LEFT OUTER JOIN
- NEST
- UNNEST
- Chaining JOINs

It is important to stress that joins must use the ON KEYS clause. By default, JOIN is an INNER join, meaning that for each joined object produced, both the left and right source objects must be nonmissing and non-null (Couchbase, 2017). Example 2 illustrates the use of the JOIN clause.

Example 2

DESCRIPTION: The assumption is that there are two buckets: users_orders and orders_by_users, where the bucket users_orders contains user profiles and IDs of orders created by these users (order ID). The bucket orders_by_users contains the description of a particular order created by a particular user, in this case "Drazena." In order to see a user profile together with the orders created by the user, it is necessary to use the JOIN clause to execute it. JOIN combines a user profile document referenced by the key "Drazena_1807960155" with the description of the orders that the user has placed.

```
N1QL:
          SELECT u.personal_details, orders
           FROM users_orders u
           USE KEYS "Drazena_1807960155"
                          JOIN orders_by_users orders
                          ON KEYS ARRAY s.order_id FOR s IN
u.shipped_order END
```

The specified N1QL statement provides a list of orders by unrolling the shipped_order and uses that as input to the JOIN clause to combine the user's personal details with the order descriptions.

LEFT OUTER JOIN means that at least one joined object is produced for each source object on the left. If the source object on the right is NULL or MISSING, then the joined object's right-hand side value is also NULL or MISSING (omitted), respectively (Couchbase, 2017). Example 3 illustrates the use of the LEFT OUTER JOIN clause.

Example 3

```
          SELECT u.personal_details, orders
          FROM users_orders u
          USE KEYS "Drazena_1807960155"
          LEFT JOIN orders_by_users orders
          ON KEYS ARRAY s.order_id FOR s IN
u.shipped_order END
```

In this query user "Drazena_1807960155" has no orders, so running the query without the LEFT clause will produce an empty result.

The NEST clause performs a join across two buckets, but instead of producing a cross-product of the left and right inputs, a single result is produced for each left input, and the corresponding inputs on the right are collected into an array and nested as a single array-valued field in the result object. Similar to the JOIN clause, the NEST clause also supports LEFT joins. Example 4 illustrates the use of the NEST clause.

Example 4

```
SELECT u.personal_details, orders
FROM users_orders u
USE KEYS "Drazena_1807960155"
NEST orders_by_users orders
ON KEYS ARRAY s.order_id FOR s IN
u.shipped_order END
```

The query on the right nests a user's order descriptions in the result.

The UNNEST clause allows taking the contents of nested arrays and joining them with the parent object. Example 5 illustrates the use of the UNNEST clause.

Example 5

```
SELECT *
FROM user AS contact
UNNEST contact.children
WHERE contact.family_name = 'Gaspar'
```

This query joins user with family_name 'Gaspar' with each of her children.

Chaining JOINs refers to situations where JOINS can be chained and combined with UNNEST as many times as desired. Example 6 illustrates the use of chaining JOINS.

Example 6

```
SELECT u.personal_details.display_name name, s
AS order_no, o.product_details
FROM users_orders u USE KEYS
"Drazena_1807960155"
UNNEST u.shipped_order s
JOIN users_orders o ON KEYS s.order_id
```

In the example an in-document join is performed on the right to generate a complete order that contains the order IDs along with the user's details. This is then JOINED with the order descriptions from the users_orders bucket.

Like SQL, N1QL supports a subquery, that is, an expression that is evaluated by executing an inner SELECT query. In the case of a subquery expression, the inner SELECT is executed once for each input document to the outer statement. A subquery expression returns an array every time it is evaluated; the array contains the results of the inner SELECT query. A subquery can refer to variables in the outer statement (Couchbase, 2017). Example 7 illustrates the use of a subquery in N1QL.

Example 7

```
SELECT orders.orderId, 1.product
        FROM orders UNNEST orders.lineItems 1
        WHERE DATE_PART_STR(orders.purchsedAt, "month") = 12
                    AND DATE_PART_STR(orders.purchasedAt,
"year") = 2016
                    AND EXISTS (SELECT product.productId
FROM product
                    USE KEYS 1.product WHERE product.
initPrice > 200);
```

In this example, the intention is to find orders from December 2016 that contain at least one product with the price higher than 200 monetary units. The query can be divided into two parts (queries):

- Which products were ordered in December 2016?
- Which of these products have a price higher than 200 monetary units?

Each query builds on the results of the previous one. The first query finds the products ordered in December 2016. The second query is a subquery. It takes the result set from the first query and finds the products that cost more than 200 monetary units.

The final result set contains those products purchased in December 2016 with a price over 200 monetary units.

These examples show that the N1QL SELECT statement provides a variety of data-processing capabilities such as filtering, querying across relationships using JOINs or subqueries, deep traversal of nested documents, aggregation, combining result sets using operators, grouping, sorting, and more. A detailed description of all the possibilities of N1QL goes beyond the scope of this book, and interested readers can find information on https://www.couchbase.com/n1ql.

Although there is a significant similarity between N1QL and SQL, still there are some differences too. The most significant differences are (Couchbase, 2017c):

- Data modeling
- Projection, selection, and filtering of data.

In relational SQL-oriented databases, the foundation of the data model is a table (relation) composed of a set of named columns (attributes) and an arbitrary number of rows (tuples), where each tuple contains only one value per attribute (Chapter 1). In document databases, specifically Couchbase that supports N1QL, the data exists as freeform documents, gathered as large collections called *keyspaces*. There is no uniformity, and there is no logical proximity of objects of the same data shape in a keyspace (Couchbase, 2017c). Table 7 gives a comparative view of these two models on the example of a record of online courses passed by a user.

Data projection refers to situations when a SELECT statement returns a subset of the set of all columns found in a table. In SQL, a header can be retrieved to obtain metadata about each column, and in relational databases it is not possible to get a result set where each row has a different set of columns (Example 8.)

Example 8

```
        SELECT u.FName, u.LName, c.Description
  FROM   users u, courses c
         WHERE u.course_id=c.id
```

Unlike SQL, N1QL allows reshaping of data by embedding the attributes of the statement in the desired result object shape (Couchbase, 2017), which is shown in Example 9.

Example 9

```
        SELECT fName, lName, course, {"Finished":
true} AS "Status"
         FROM user_courses
```

In SQL (relational databases), data selection refers to the selection of data FROM tables, whereas in N1QL the FROM clause is used to select between data sources (keyspaces). This means that, for the keyspace "user_courses" (Table 7), the SELECT statement in Example 10 selects the fName attribute from all documents in that keyspace that have an fName attribute defined.

Table 7. Comparison of relational (SQL) and N1QL data model

Relational (SQL) Data Model				Document (Couchbase) N1QL Data modDocument (Couchbase) N1QL Data Model
Table: USERS				Keyspace: User_courses
Id	Fname	LName	Course_id	{ "id": "124",
124	Petra	Petric	33	"fName": "Petra", "lName": "Petric",
125	Ana	Anic	33	"course":
126	Mario	Matic	42	{"Id": "33", "description": "Oracle SQL",
Table:COURSES				"start": "15.10.16.", "end": "15.12.16."
Id	Description	Start	End	} "id": "125",
33	Oracle SQL	15.10.16.	15.12.16.	"fName": "Ana", "lName": "Anic",
42	Couchbase N1QL	01.10.16.	01.12.16.	"course": {"Id": "33", "description": "Oracle SQL",
				"start": "15.10.16.", "end": "15.12.16."
				} "id": "126", "fName": "Mario", "lName": "Matic", "course": {"Id": "42", "description": "Couchbase N1QL", "start": "01.10.16.", "end": "01.12.16." }

Example 10

```
SELECT fName FROM user_courses
```

In addition, N1QL makes it possible for each document to regard itself as a data source and run a query over its nested elements. Such nested elements are addressed using the dot (.) operator to descend a level and the square bracket ([ ]) operator to index into an array element (Couchbase, 2017), which is shown in Example 11.

Example 11

```
SELECT Finished FROM user_course.Status
```

In both SQL and N1QL, data filtering is performed using the WHERE clause, but with some slight differences. Namely, N1QL data can be irregularly shaped, and hence undefined values are recognized as distinct from null. N1QL provides a complementary set of operators like IS MISSING in addition to standard operators like IS NULL. New conversions—for example, from nonzero integer values to Boolean value true—are also supported.

In addition to the standard filtering predicates, N1QL provides new operators to work with arrays in documents: ANY, SOME, and EVERY. ANY and SOME evaluate a condition for each element and return true if any element meets the condition. EVERY also evaluates a condition for each element, except it returns true only if all elements match the condition.

EXTENDING RELATIONAL DATABASES

All the information about NoSQL and relational databases can be reduced to a single and simple requirement, which is to enable decision makers to use Big Data as a powerful tool to make better decisions based on its analysis. Because of the enormous importance of data for organizations, storing and managing data is financially an exceptionally valuable business, which is also corroborated by Gartner's report (Adrian, 2015) that the value of the DBMS market amounted to $35.9 billion in 2015 (an 8.7 percent jump from 2014). However, it is noteworthy that relational databases, or Oracle, Microsoft, and IBM as three major vendors alone, keep 77.5 percent of the market. One thing is for sure: these three definitively want to keep their leading position in the database world. Like other producers of relational databases, they realized early on that NoSQL databases bring some innovative and good solutions to the problems they had been facing for years (Big Data, data distribution, high availability, etc.). Oracle and Microsoft even went a step further and developed their own versions of NoSQL databases (Oracle NoSQL Database, MS Azure DocumentDB).

This section describes how the three largest DBMS vendors, Oracle, Microsoft, and IBM, innovated and extended their relational databases and thus brought them closer to NoSQL databases. These extensions primarily involved manipulating unstructured data (e.g., JSON documents), providing sharding, improved possibilities of SQL, and high availability.

Oracle Database Convergence Toward NoSQL

Since 1979 when the company Relational Software, Inc. (RSI), renamed Oracle Systems Corporation in 1982, launched its first commercial relational database Oracle (release 2), Oracle database has been the leader in the world of relational databases, with over 40 percent market share in 2015 (Adrian, 2015). One of the reasons for the long leadership is the strenuous work to enhance the possibilities of the Oracle database. With each of its new versions, the Oracle database has strived to bring new or improved solutions to requirements such as storage of Big Data, continuous growth in the number of users of the database, increased demands for high availability and data distribution, and all with the objective of providing its users successful data storage and manipulation. For example, as of version 9i (2001), Oracle provides the possibility of operating XML documents and the integration of relational and multidimensional databases. The Oracle Company took up the NoSQL challenge very early and seriously, and in 2006 purchased the company Sleepycat Software, which had developed the open-source Berkeley DB, key-value storage, and in 2011 the Oracle NoSQL Database, based on Berkeley DB technology, appeared on the market. A part of the knowledge of the NoSQL world was used to improve the core Oracle database—more precisely the latest version Oracle 12c, where c stands for cloud. Thus, Oracle made efforts to bridge the gap between the two worlds, relational and NoSQL, and help users capitalize on the benefits of both of them.

Oracle database 12c release 2 (hereinafter Oracle database) brought many innovations, not necessarily related to the NoSQL approach, and their explanation largely exceeds the purpose of this book (interested readers are referred to the Oracle documentation for details). This section presents a part of the new Oracle 12c features that bring it closer to the NoSQL databases, such as:

- JSON support
- SQL and PL/SQL improvements
- Oracle Big Data SQL
- Sharding
- High availability

Oracle JSON Support

The Oracle database supports JavaScript Object Notation (JSON) in two ways:

- API support through a family of Simple Oracle Document Access (SODA) APIs for access to JSON data stored in the database.
- Native support, meaning that it is possible to use JSON documents with relational database features, including transactions, indexing, declarative querying, and views. It means that the Oracle database can declaratively generate JSON documents from relational data using SQL and the ability to manipulate JSON documents as PL/SQL objects (Oracle, 2017).

The purpose of SODA is to enable development of schema-less applications, without a need to know relational database features or languages such as SQL and PL/SQL. SODA allows creating and storing document collections in an Oracle database, as well as their finding and searching without a need to know how documents are stored in the database.

Oracle implements SODA as (Oracle_JSON_DG, 2017):

- **SODA for Java:** Java classes that represent databases, collections, and documents.
- **SODA for REST:** SODA operations as representational state transfer (REST) requests, using any language capable of making HTTP calls.

Unlike the API approach (SODA), which is an upgraded interface for operating JSON documents on NoSQL principles, native support makes it possible to work with JSON data in a similar manner as with other objects in an Oracle database (e.g. tables), that is, it enables the use of most relational features when working with these documents, including transactions, indexing, declarative querying, and views. Namely, Oracle database provides the possibility to use SQL to join JSON data with relational data, making JSON data available for relational processes and tools. Also, it is possible to query from within the database JSON data that is stored outside Oracle Database in an external table (Oracle_JSON_DG, 2017).

JSON data is stored in Oracle databases as the common SQL data types VARCHAR2, CLOB, and BLOB. Oracle recommends that an is_json check constraint always be used to ensure that column values are valid JSON instances (Oracle_JSON, 2017). Example 12 shows SQL commands for creating and inserting a JSON document for an order.

Example 12

```
a)          Creating the table order
                  CREATE TABLE order
(order_id VARCHAR2 (32) NOT NULL PRIMARY KEY,
date TIMESTAMP (6) WITH TIME ZONE,
po_document VARCHAR2 (32767)
CONSTRAINT ensure_json CHECK (po_document IS JSON));
b)          Entering a JSON document into the table order
                  INSERT INTO order
    VALUES (SYS_GUID(),
to_date('15-JAN-2017'),
'{"PONumber": 1245,
   "Contract": "HERA-2016",
   "ContactPerson": "Mario Matic",
   "Vendor": "HERA",
   "ContractDetails": {…},
   "AdditionalInstructions": {...},
   "TransactionItems": [...]}');
```

Oracle database does not impose any restrictions on tables that can be used for the storage of JSON documents. A column that contains JSON documents can coexist with any other data type in the Oracle database, and a table can have multiple columns that contain JSON documents.

Oracle tables that contain JSON columns usually have several non-JSON housekeeping columns that track metadata about the JSON documents (Oracle_JSON, 2017).

Oracle SQL and PL/SQL Improvements

Although Oracle strives to follow industry-accepted standards (both ANSI and the ISO/IEC), Oracle SQL includes many extensions to those standards. The latest Oracle SQL extensions related to enhanced support for NoSQL features are (Oracle, 2017):

- Join groups for optimization of join queries for table columns that are stored in the In-Memory Column Store (CREATE INMEMORY JOIN GROUP, ALTER INMEMORY JOIN GROUP, DROP INMEMORY JOIN GROUP)
- SQL support for Oracle sharding (CREATE TABLESPACE SET, ALTER TABLESPACE SET, DROP TABLESPACE SET, clauses SHARDED and DUPLICATED of CREATE TABLE)
- SQL for JSON documents (JSON_EXISTS, IS JSON, JSON_TEXTCONTAINS, JSON_QUERY, JSON_TABLE, JSON_VALUE, JSON_ARRAY, JSON_ARRAYAGG, JSON_DATAGUIDE, JSON_OBJECT, JSON_OBJECTAGG, JSON_QUERY, JSON_VALUE)
- Approximate query processing functions (APPROX_MEDIAN, APPROX_PERCENTILE, APPROX_COUNT_DISTINCT_DETAIL, APPROX_COUNT_DISTINCT_AGG, TO_APPROX_COUNT_DISTINCT, APPROX_PERCENTILE_DETAIL, APPROX_PERCENTILE_AGG, TO_APPROX_PERCENTILE)

Example 13 illustrates the use of the SQL statement CREATE TABLESPACE SET to create a tablespace set that can be used in a sharded database as a logical storage unit for one or more sharded tables and indexes.

Example 13 (Oracle, 2017)

```
CREATE TABLESPACE SET tablespaceset1
IN SHARDSPACE shardgroup5
USING TEMPLATE
(DATAFILE SIZE 200m
   EXTENT MANAGEMENT LOCAL
   SEGMENT SPACE MANAGEMENT AUTO
);
```

In Oracle database, if JSON data is queried, the return value is always of a VARCHAR2 data type and represents a JSON value. JSON data stored in Oracle database can be accessed in two ways:

- Using specialized functions and conditions
- Using a simple dot notation

The majority of the SQL functions and conditions are SQL/JSON standard functions, but a few of them are specific to Oracle (Oracle, 2017):

- SQL/JSON *generation* functions json_object, json_array, json_objectagg, and json_arrayagg collect SQL data in order to produce JSON data (as a SQL value).
- Oracle SQL aggregate function json_dataguide produces JSON data that is a *guide to data*. These can be used to find information on the content and structure of other JSON data in the database.
- SQL/JSON *query* functions json_value, json_query, and json_table and SQL/JSON query conditions json_exists, is json, is not json, and json_textcontains evaluate SQL/JSON path expressions against JSON data to produce SQL values.

Dot notation works in a similar manner as a combination of the query functions json_value and json_query and looks like a SQL object access expression, that is, attribute dot notation for an abstract data type (ADT). It represents the *easiest* way for querying JSON data in the database (Oracle_JSON_DG, 2017).

Example 14 shows a dot notation of a query of the documents stored in JSON column po_document of the table order (aliased here as o). It obtains all order requestors (JSON field Requestor).

Example 14

```
SELECT o.o_document.Requestor FROM order o;
```

Table 8 presents some simple examples of SQL used for querying JSON documents.

In the same way as standard SQL commands are used within PL/SQL code, SQL commands can also be used to work with JSON documents, with the restriction that it is not possible to use an empty JSON field name in any SQL code used in PL/SQL.

The following SQL/JSON functions and conditions are also available as built-in PL/SQL functions: json_value, json_query, json_object, json_array, and json_exists. In PL/SQL, the SQL condition json_exists is a Boolean function (Oracle, 2017).

Table 8. Examples of using SQL for querying JSON documents

SQL Statement	Description
SELECT o.o_document.PONumber FROM order o	The following query extracts from each document in JSON column o_document, a *scalar* value, the JSON number that is the value of the field PONumber from the objects in JSON column o_document.
SELECT o.o_document.Shipping.Address FROM order o	The following query extracts from each document an *array* of JSON address objects, which is the value of field Address of the object that is the value of field Shipping.
SELECT o.o_document.Address.City FROM order o	The following query extracts from each document *multiple* values as an array: the value of field City for each object in array Address. The returned array is not part of the stored data, but it is constructed automatically by the query.
SELECT o.o_document FROM order o WHERE json_exists(o.o_document'˜$.Items.Part.Code')	This example selects order documents that have an item whose part description contains a code entry.
SELECT o.o_document FROM order o WHERE json_exists(o.o_document, '$?(@Items.Part.Code==222222222)')	Select documents that have an item whose part contains a code with a value of 222222222. The scope of the filter is the context item, that is, an entire order. @ refers to the context item.
SELECT o.o_document FROM order o WHERE json_exists(o.o_document, '$.Items?@Part.Code==222222222)')	The filter scope is an Items array (and each of its elements implicitly). @ refers to an element of that array.
SELECT o.o_document FROM order o WHERE json_exists(o.o_document, '$Items.Part?@.Code==222222222)')	The filter scope is a Part field of an element in a Items array. @ refers to a Part field.
SELECT json_query(*column, json_path* RETURNING *data_type array_wrapper error_hander* ON ERROR) FROM table OR SELECT *jt.column_alias* FROM table, json_table(*column,*'$' *error_handler* ON ERROR COLUMNS ("COLUMN_ALIAS" *data_type* FORMAT JSON *array_wrapper* PATH *json_path*)) AS "JT"	SQL/JSON function json_query can be viewed as a special case of function json_table. The two SQL statements are equivalent; both have the same effect.

Oracle Big Data SQL

Oracle Big Data SQL is a data virtualization innovation from Oracle that makes it possible to search nonrelational data stored in different Big Data storages like Apache Hive, HDFS, Oracle NoSQL Database, Apache HBase, and other NoSQL databases. It enables unified queries for distributed data, as well as the possibility to view and analyze data from different disparate data stores in a way as if all were stored in the Oracle database. This is possible because Oracle Big Data SQL fully supports Oracle SQL syntax.

Oracle Big Data SQL makes it possible to (Oracle, 2016):

- Combine data from Oracle database, Apache Hadoop, and NoSQL within a single SQL query
- Perform very complex SQL SELECT statements on data in the Hadoop ecosystem, whether manually or through already existing user applications
- Maximize performance of queries on all data using advanced techniques such as smart scan, partition pruning, storage indexes, bloom filters, and predicate push-down in a distributed architecture
- Extend security and access policies from Oracle Database to data stored in Apache Hadoop and NoSQL
- Improve external tables functionality

Figure 4 provides a graphical view of Oracle Big Data SQL.

Big Data SQL has added new external types of tables to Oracle database 12c. An external table is an Oracle database object that identifies and describes the location of data outside of a database (Oracle, 2016). Oracle guarantees querying of an external table by using the same SQL SELECT syntax as for any other database tables.

Figure 4. Oracle Big Data SQL
Oracle, 2016.

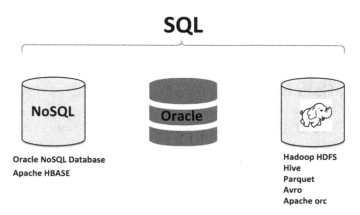

Big Data SQL monitors the metadata on external data sources—both clusters and the tables within them—without moving or copying data. External tables for Big Data SQL provide (Oracle_BD, 2017):

- Smooth integration of metadata and queries that join data from Oracle Database with data from Hadoop and NoSQL databases
- Automatic mappings from metadata stored in HCatalog (or the Hive Metastore) to Oracle tables
- Support for multiple clusters to make it possible for an Oracle Database to query multiple Hadoop clusters
- Improved parameters for access so that database administrators have the flexibility to control mapping of columns and data accessing behaviors

External tables use *access drivers* to parse the data outside of the database. A unique access driver is necessary for each type of external data. Oracle Big Data SQL has two drivers for accessing Big Data with metadata, specified only by an Oracle administrator (Oracle_BD, 2017):

- **ORACLE_HIVE:** Driver for data that has metadata defined in Apache Hive. It enables creation of Oracle external tables over Apache Hive data sources. Also it has a possibility of accessing data stored in other locations (for instance, HBase) if there are Hive tables defined for them.
- **ORACLE_HDFS:** Driver for accessing data stored in the Hadoop Distributed File System. It enables creating of Oracle external tables directly over files stored in HDFS. This driver uses Hive syntax for describing a data source, and it assigns default column names of COL_1, COL_2, etc. The ORACLE_HDFS access parameters are necessary for specifying the metadata and are stored within the definition of the external table in Oracle Database.

As already stated, Oracle allows searching external tables or data stored in HDFS and Hive tables in the same way as if this data was stored in tables in Oracle database. Oracle database accesses these data by using metadata provided when the external table was created.

Example 15 shows the syntax for creating an external table in Oracle Database that can access the HBase data through a Hive external table.

Example 15 (Oracle_BD, 2017)

```
            CREATE TABLE tablename (colname colType [, colname
colType …])
               ORGANIZATION EXTERNAL
                 (TYPE ORACLE_HIVE DEFAULT DIRECTORY
DEFAULT_DIR
                    ACCESS PARAMETERS (access parameters)
                 )
               REJECT LIMIT UNLIMITED;
```

Example 16 illustrates the syntax for creating a table named ORDER to access the data in all files stored in the /usr/cust/summary directory in HDFS.

Example 16 (Oracle_BD, 2017)

```
CREATE TABLE order (cust_num VARCHAR2 (15),
                                       order_num VARCHAR2
(20)
                             order_total NUMBER (15,2))
ORGANIZATION EXTERNAL
   (TYPE oracle_hdfs
     DEFAULT DIRECTORY DEFAULT_DIR
   )
   LOCATION ('hdfs:/usr/cust/summary/*');
```

In the Oracle statement in Example 16 no access parameters are set, so the ORACLE_HDFS access driver will use the default settings to connect to the default Hadoop cluster and read data.

Oracle Sharding

One of the NoSQL features offered by Oracle is sharding, a technique for database scaling by horizontally partitioning data across multiple Oracle databases. Shards in Oracle are normally hosted on dedicated servers. These servers can be commodity hardware or engineered systems. The shards can run on single-instance or Oracle RAC databases. They can be placed on premises, in a cloud, or in a hybrid on-premises and cloud configuration (Oracle_CNCPT, 2017).

Applications see the set of all shards as a single logical database, which allows simple scaling of data, transactions, and users to any level, on any platform, by adding databases (shards) to the pool. It is important to note that Oracle database has limited scaling, or it supports scaling up to 1,000 shards.

Figure 5 shows the basic elements of the Oracle sharding architecture (Oracle_CNCPT, 2017):

- **Sharded Database (SDB):** A single logical Oracle Database partitioned horizontally across a pool of physical Oracle Databases (shards) that share no hardware or software.
- **Shards:** Independent physical Oracle databases that host a subset of the sharded database.
- **Global Service:** Different database services that enable access to data in an SDB.
- **Shard Catalog:** An Oracle Database for supporting automated shard deployment, centralized management of a sharded database, and multishard queries.

Figure 5. Oracle sharding architecture
Oracle_CNCPT, 2017.

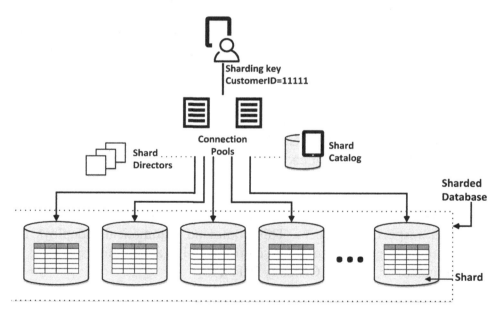

- **Shard Directors:** Network listeners that provide high-performance connection routing based on a sharding key.
- **Connection Pools:** Shard directors that at runtime enable routing database requests across pooled connections.
- **Management Interfaces:** GDSCTL (command-line utility) and Oracle Enterprise.

What is evident in Figure 5 is that shards are independent Oracle databases that are hosted on database servers that have their own local resources: CPU, memory, and disk. No shared storage is required across the shards.

A sharded database represents a collection of shards. Placement of shards can be organized either by placing all shards in a single region, or by placing shards in different regions. In Oracle sharding, a region is a data center or multiple data centers that are in close network proximity. Oracle Data Guard replication technology is used for shards replication in order to ensure high availability and efficient disaster recovery. For example, for the purposes of providing high availability, Data Guard will place the standby shards in the same region where the primary shards are placed, whereas in the case where efficient data recovery is the priority, Data Guard will place the standby shards in another region.

It is possible to deploy, manage, and monitor Oracle sharded databases using the GDSCTL command-line interface, which offers a simple declarative way to specify the configuration of a sharded database and automate its deployment. It takes just a few GDSCTL commands to create a sharded database (Oracle, 2017):

- CREATE SHARDCATALOG
- ADD GSM and START GSM (create and start shard directors)
- CREATE SHARD (for each shard)
- DEPLOY

The GDSCTL DEPLOY command automatically creates the shards and their respective listeners. This command automatically deploys the replication configuration used for shard-level high availability specified by the administrator (Oracle_CNCPT, 2017).

Oracle High Availability

Oracle offers different possibilities to achieve high availability (sharding, Data Guard, etc.). Some of the new features (Oracle database 12c release 2) that support Oracle maximum availability architecture (MAA) are:

- Sharding MAA
- Multientant
- Data Guard enhancements
- GoldenGate
- Recovery Manager (RMAN) enhancements.

As already explained in previous chapters (see Chapter 1), sharding is used to ensure linear scalability and fault isolation. The potential problems with scalability of a single physical database can be avoided by using a sharded database. Also, the sharded database eliminates the possibility of a one single point of failure for an application in situations of unplanned outages or planned maintenance. The Oracle sharding architecture uses the standard bronze, silver, gold, and platinum reference architectures as building blocks to provide shard-level high availability where each shard is a standalone Oracle Database (Oracle_CNCPT, 2017).

Oracle Multitenant is the method for consolidation of databases (from Oracle database 12c) that makes it possible for a container database (CDB) to hold a number of pluggable databases (PDBs). From the application side, the PDBs are standalone databases. It means that there is no need to change the application in order to be able to access the PDB. By providing the consolidation of multiple PDBs into a single CDB, Oracle enables that users can manage "many as one". Oracle Multitenant feature is fully compatible with Oracle Real Application Clusters, Oracle Data Guard, and Oracle GoldenGate, just like any non-container database (non-CDB). This feature can be used in any of the Oracle MAA reference architectures. By grouping multiple PDBs that have the same high-availability requirements into the same CDB, Oracle ensures that all of those PDBs and their applications are managed and protected with the same technologies and configurations (Oracle_CNCPT, 2017).

Data Guard replication technology was already mentioned in the section on sharding. Data Guard comprises a full set of services for creating, managing, maintaining, and monitoring one or more standby databases. These features enable that Oracle databases can survive all types of blackouts (natural disasters and data corruptions). A Data Guard standby database is an exact replica of the production database, so it can be transparently used in conventional backup, restoration, flashback, and cluster techniques in order to provide the highest possible level of data protection and data availability (Oracle_HA, 2017).

Oracle GoldenGate is logical replication solution for data distribution and data integration. It provides capture, routing, transformation, and delivery of transactional data across heterogeneous databases in real time based on a real-time, log-based change data capture and replication software platform.

Oracle Maximum Availability Architecture (MAA) represents a set of best practices for the integrated use of Oracle High Availability technologies (Figure 6).

The Oracle Maximum Availability Architecture offers a selection of architecture patterns for high availability and scalability (Oracle_MAA, 2017):

- Four standard reference architectures (bronze, silver, gold, and platinum), that provides application-transparent scalability (with Oracle RAC), data protection, high availability, and disaster recovery for the Oracle Database.

Figure 6. Oracle's HA technologies and the Oracle maximum availability architecture Oracle_MAA, 2016.

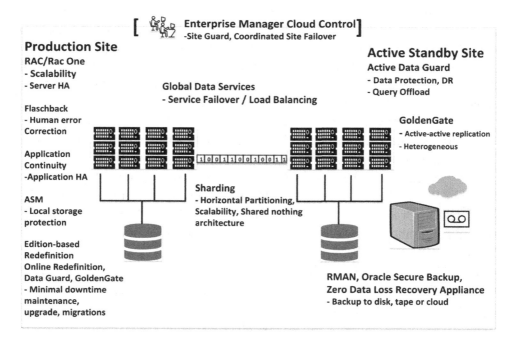

- A special-purpose reference architecture based on Oracle Sharding for linear scalability with complete fault isolation. The Oracle Sharding MAA reference architecture, introduced in Oracle Database 12c Release 2, is a separate MAA reference architecture that is only applicable to shard-ready applications.

Oracle MAA architecture defines four standard high-availability reference architectures that cover the full range of availability and data protection required by enterprises of all sizes and lines of business (Oracle_HA, 2014):

- Bronze Architecture is based upon a single-instance Oracle Database with MAA, and offers automated restart and restore from backup. Bronze architecture contains many data protection and high availability features covered with Oracle Enterprise Edition license. Oracle-optimized backups using Oracle Recovery Manager (RMAN) provide data protection and are used for restoring availability if an outage prevents the database from restarting.
- Silver architecture adds clustering technology, either Oracle RAC or Oracle RAC One Node. If the cluster cannot be restarted because of blackout, RMAN provides database-optimized backups for protecting data and restoring availability.
- Gold architecture adds the database-aware replication technologies Oracle Active Data Guard and Oracle GoldenGate. They are able to synchronize one or more replicas of the production database to provide real-time data protection and availability.
- Platinum architecture adds applications: Oracle Active Data Guard Far Sync that ensures zero data loss protection at any distance; Oracle GoldenGate extensions for zero downtime upgrades and migrations; and Global Data Services for automated service management and workload balancing in replicated database environments. These applications ensure continuity for reliable replay of in-flight transactions that masks blackouts from users.

MS SQL Server Convergence Towards NoSQL

In the period from 2010 to 2015, out of the major database producers (Oracle, Microsoft, and IBM), only Microsoft succeeded in increasing its share on the database market by about 1 percent and reached a 19.4 percent share (Adrian, 2015). The first version of the Microsoft SQL Server database appeared on the market in 1988 (almost 10 years after the Oracle database) and was developed in collaboration with Sybase. This collaboration was ended in 1994, and since then Microsoft took over full responsibility for developing SQL Server databases. SQL Server database very soon became the second most popular relational database and has kept the position up to now, at least when it comes to market share. Like Oracle, in 2014 Microsoft launched on the market its NoSQL database, MS Azure DocumentDB, managed as a service within Azure cloud framework. Experiences gained in the development of Azure DocumentDB were used to improve and extend the functionalities of the SQL Server database.

The latest version, SQL Server 2016, was announced by Microsoft as the biggest step forward in the development of their database, primarily because of new features related to gaining real-time insights across transactional and analytical data with a scalable database platform that has everything built in, from unparalleled in-memory performance, new security innovations, and high availability, to advanced analytics that make mission-critical applications intelligent (Microsoft, 2017).

This section summarizes new SQL Server 2016 (hereinafter SQL Server) features that bring that database closer to NoSQL databases, such as:

- Built-in JSON support
- Transact-SQL (T-SQL) improvements
- PolyBase for querying data in Hadoop or Azure Blob Storage
- High availability
- MS Azure SQL Database elastic features (sharding)

MS SQL Server Built-In JSON Support

The version of SQL Server 2016 brought built-in support for import and export of JSON documents and the possibility to operate with JSON strings. The built-in support contains the following statements and functions (Microsoft, 2017):

- **FOR JSON Clause:** Added in the SELECT statement to enable the format of query results as JSON or export of JSON.
- **OPENJSON Function:** Allows conversion of JSON data into rows and columns, or import of JSON data into SQL Server, or conversion of JSON data into rows or columns for applications or services that cannot operate with JSON documents directly.

- **ISJSON Function:** Tests whether a string contains a valid JSON.
- **JSON_VALUE Function:** Extracts a scalar value from a JSON string.
- **JSON_QUERY Function:** Extracts an object or an array from a JSON string.
- **JSON_MODIFY Function:** Updates the value of a property in a JSON string and returns the updated JSON string.

The FOR JSON clause either allows the output structure to be explicitly specified or allows the structure SELECT statement to define the output. Two modes that are used with the FOR JSON clause are defined for this purpose (Microsoft, 2017):

- **PATH Mode:** Used to maintain full control over the JSON output format in a way that the user can create wrapper objects and nest complex properties.
- **AUTO Mode:** Used for automatic formatting of JSON output based on the structure of the SELECT statement.

Example 17 shows the SELECT statement with a FOR JSON clause and its output when PATH mode is used.

Example 17

Input Table Data

See Table 9.

Query With FOR JSON Clause

```
SELECT Id AS [Order.Id], Date AS [Order.Date], Vendor AS
Account,
            Price AS 'Item.UnitPrice', Quantity AS 'Item.
Quantity'
```

Table 9.

ID	Date	Vendor	Price	Quantity
1234	2016-09-27T00:00:00	Hera	152.88	11
4321	2016-11-11T00:00:00	Microsoft	562.55	5

```
FROM VendorOrder
FOR JSON PATH, ROOT('Orders')
```

JSON Output

```
{
    "Orders":
        [
          { "Order": {
                        "Id":"1234",
                        "Date:" 2016-09-27T00:00:00"
                            },
            "Account":"Hera",
            "Item": {
                        "Price": 152.88,
                        "Quantity":11
                  }
                        },
                        { "Order": {
                                        "Id":"4321"
                                        "Date:" 2016-
11-11T00:00:00"
                                            },
                                "Account":"Microsoft",
                                "Item": {
"Price":532.55,

"Quantity":5
                                                  }
                        }}}
```

In PATH mode it is possible to use the dot syntax, for example, 'Item.Price' (Example 17), to format nested output.

Example 18 shows the SELECT statement with the FOR JSON clause and its output when AUTO mode is used. By default, null values are not included in the output. The INCLUDE_NULL_VALUES can be used to change this behavior.

Example 18

Query in Transact-SQL

```
SELECT id, vendor
FROM VendorOrder
FOR JSON AUTO
```

Result in JSON

```
[{
        "id": "1234",
                "vendor": "Hera",
        },
        {
        "id": "4321",
            "vendor": "Microsoft"
            }]
```

Control of the output of the FOR JSON clause can be made by using the following options (Microsoft, 2017):

- If it is desired to add one top-level element to the JSON output, it is necessary to specify the ROOT option. If the ROOT option is not specified, the JSON output will not have a root element.
- If it is wanted to include null values in JSON output, the INCLUDE_ NULL_VALUES option should be specified. If the INCLUDE_ NULL_VALUES option is not specified, the output will not contain JSON properties for NULL values in the query results.
- If it is desired to remove the initially placed square brackets that surround the JSON output of the FOR JSON clause, it is necessary to specify the WITHOUT_ARRAY_WRAPPER option. This option is used to generate a single JSON object as output. If the WITHOUT_ ARRAY_WRAPPER option is not specified, the JSON output is enclosed within square brackets.

MS SQL Server T-SQL Improvements

SQL Server uses Transact-SQL (T-SQL) language. It is Microsoft SQL version used to administer instances of the SQL Server database, to create and manage database objects and to insert, retrieve, modify, and delete data. Transact-SQL is an extension of the language defined in the SQL standards published by the International Standards Organization (ISO) and the American National Standards Institute (ANSI).

The new version of SQL Server (2016) brings the following enhancements to T-SQL (Microsoft, 2017):

- T-SQL improvements for memory-optimized tables
- T-SQL improvements for natively compiled modules

T-SQL improvements for memory-optimized tables include support for (Microsoft, 2017):

- UNIQUE constraints and indexes
- FOREIGN KEY references between memory-optimized tables
- CHECK constraints
- AFTER TRIGGERs on memory-optimized tables
- All SQL Server code pages and collations with indexes and other artifacts in memory-optimized tables and natively compiled T-SQL modules
- Altering memory-optimized tables, meaning ADD and DROP indexes, change bucket_count of hash indexes, schema changes, add/drop/alter columns, and add/drop constraint
- LOB (large object) types varbinary(max), nvarchar(max), and varchar(max) in memory-optimized tables

T-SQL improvements for natively compiled modules include (Microsoft, 2017):

- **Support for Query Constructs:** UNION and UNION ALL, SELECT DISTINCT, OUTER JOIN, and subqueries in SELECT
- Expanded INSERT, UPDATE, and DELETE statements that can include the OUTPUT clause
- LOBs used in a native procedure

- Inline—meaning single-statement—table-valued functions (TVFs) natively compiled
- Scalar user-defined functions (UDFs) natively compiled
- Support for EXECUTE AS CALLER, which means the EXECUTE AS clause is no longer required when a natively compiled T-SQL module is creating

MS SQL Server Polybase

As of version 2014, SQL Server offers the possibility to work with PolyBase, an exclusive interface for Microsoft Analytics Platform System (APS) that makes it possible to access data stored in HDFS by using SQL syntax in queries. SQL Server 2016 also expanded the possibilities of PolyBase so that it can be used to query data in Hadoop or Azure Blob Storage and combine the results with relational data stored in SQL Server. In order to achieve optimal performance, PolyBase is capable of dynamically creating columnstore tables, parallelizing data extraction from Hadoop and Azure sources, or pushing computations on Hadoop-based data to Hadoop clusters where necessary. After the PolyBase service is installed and PolyBase data objects configured, users and applications have the possibility of accessing data from nonrelational sources without having a particular knowledge about Hadoop or blob storage (Varga, Cherry & D'Antoni, 2016).

PolyBase allows data scaling by creating PolyBase scale-out groups, as shown in Figure 7. A PolyBase scale-out group consists of one head node and one or more compute nodes. The head node is made up of the SQL Server database engine, the PolyBase engine service, and the PolyBase data movement service, and each compute node is made up of a database engine and data movement service. The head node receives the PolyBase queries, distributes the work related to external tables to the data movement service on the available compute nodes, receives the results from each compute node, finalizes the results in the database engine, and then returns the results to the requesting client. The head and compute nodes have data movement service for transferring data between the external data sources and SQL Server and between the SQL Server instances on the head and compute nodes (Varga, Cherry & D'Antoni, 2016).

SQL Server 2016 provides the possibility to work with external data sources that tell PolyBase where to find data.

Figure 7. PolyBase scale-out groups
Varga, Cherry, & D'Antoni, 2016.

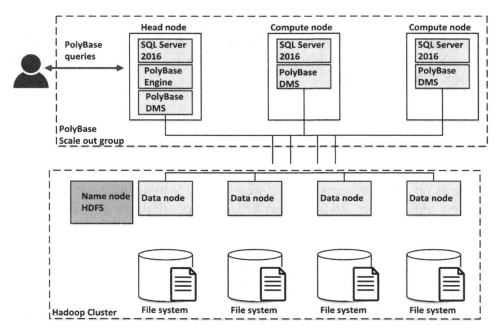

If blob storage is used, it is necessary to specify the name of the blob container and the storage account in the LOCATION argument of the CREATE EXTERNAL DATA SOURCE statement, as shown in Example 19. The CREDENTIAL argument uses the database-scoped credential created for accessing blob storage.

Example 19 (Microsoft, 2017)

```
                    CREATE EXTERNAL DATA SOURCE AzureBlobStorage
with
        (TYPE = HADOOP,             LOCATION='wasbs://<datacontai
ner>@<azure_storage_account_name>
              .blob.core.windows.net/',
              CREDENTIAL = AzureBlobStorageCredential);
```

In order to create an external data source for Hadoop storage, it is necessary to specify the Uniform Resource Indicator (URI) for Hadoop in the LOCATION argument of the CREATE EXTERNAL DATA SOURCE statement, as shown in Example 20.

In Hadoop storage, it is possible optionally to include the RESOURCE_ MANAGER_LOCATION argument and provide the address and port for the Hadoop Name Node. If pushdown computations for PolyBase is enabled, SQL Server's query optimizer can send data to the Name Node for preprocessing to reduce the volume of data transferred between SQL Server and Hadoop.

Example 20 (Microsoft, 2017)

```
                 CREATE EXTERNAL DATA SOURCE HadoopStorage
WITH
           (TYPE = HADOOP, LOCATION ='hdfs://10.10.10.10
:8020',                 RESOURCE_MANAGER_LOCATION =
'10.10.10.10:8032',
   CREDENTIAL = HadoopCredential);
```

After creating external tables, data can be accessed by using standard T-SQL queries. Any application or reporting tool that can access SQL Server can use PolyBase in a way that it references an external table in the same way as it would reference any relational table stored in SQL Server, without requiring special configuration in the tool or special knowledge from users. Example 21 shows that not only is it possible to perform queries on external tables, but it is also possible to join the unstructured data with structured data stored in SQL server (i.e., to join a PolyBase external table with a SQL Server table).

Example 21 (Microsoft, 2017)

```
SELECT CustomerLastName, CustomerFirstName, CustomerEmail,
cs.TirePressure
FROM Customer c INNER JOIN CarSensorData cs ON c.VIN = cs.VIN
WHERE cs.TirePressure < 20
```

If data stored in Hadoop is used, it is possible to add OPTION (FORCE EXTERNALPUSHDOWN) or OPTION (DISABLE EXTERNALPUSHDOWN) at the end of the statement as a query hint to force or disable pushdown computations, respectively.

MS SQL Server High Availability

The feature AlwaysOn Availability Groups first became available in SQL Server 2012 Enterprise Edition, with the basic purpose to enable data protection by sending transactions from the transaction log on the primary replica to one or more secondary replicas, a process that is conceptually similar to database mirroring. Each new version of SQL Server brought new improvements and functionality extensions, and SQL Server 2016 brought the following new possibilities (Varga, Cherry & D'Antoni, 2016):

- AlwaysOn Basic Availability Groups
- Support for group Managed Service Accounts (gMSAs)
- Database-level failover
- Distributed Transaction Coordinator (DTC) support
- Load balancing for readable secondary replicas
- Up to three automatic failover targets
- Improved log transport performance

SQL Server 2016 allows simpler and more flexible data protection as compared to earlier versions with greater throughput to support modern storage systems and CPUs. AlwaysOn Availability Groups and AlwaysOn Failover Cluster Instances have better security, reliability, and scalability. Operation of SQL Server 2016 clearly provides more options to better manage clusters and storage.

High availability of SQL Server is closely related to Microsoft Azure SQL Database, the cloud services that provide a secure, robust, and flexible database platform for hosting all types of applications. Since the version V12 that brings new features like elastic database pools, SQL Database has become an enterprise-class platform-as-a-service (PaaS) offering. In addition, its rapid cycle in development is favorable for SQL Database as well as its on-premises counterpart. SQL Database has greater parity with on-premises SQL Server. This parity enables users to more easily port present on-premises applications to Azure, and it comes with improved support for corporate and DevOps requirements in the cloud, thus highly increasing the number of potential use cases for SQL Database. Specifically, Azure SQL Database provides the following features for databases used in the cloud (Varga, Cherry & D'Antoni, 2016):

- Parallel queries
- Table partitioning
- Online reindexing
- XML indexes
- CLR (common language runtime) integration
- Change tracking for data changes
- Columnstore indexes
- T-SQL windowing functions
- Over 100 new DMVs (dynamic management views)
- Striped backups to Microsoft Azure Blob storage (maximum backup size of 12.8 TB)
- File-snapshot backups to Microsoft Azure Blob Storage where all database files are stored using the Microsoft Azure Blob storage service

MS AZURE SQL Database Elastic Features: Sharding

Microsoft offers two approaches when using sharding. One approach involves writing custom code and additional complexity of the application layer, which in that case needs to provide adequate implementation and maintenance of sharding. Example 22 shows a part of code written in the programming language C#, which ensures that SQL Server acts as a shard, or code, for a situation where each database holds a subset of the data used by an application. The application extracts data distributed across the shards using its own sharding logic. A method called GetShards returns the details of the data that is located in each shard. This method returns an enumerable list of ShardInformation objects, where the ShardInformation type contains an identifier for each shard and the SQL Server connection string that an application should use for connecting to the shard (Varga, Cherry & D'Antoni, 2016).

Example 22 (Varga, Cherry, & D'Antoni, 2016)

```
                private IEnumerable<ShardInformation>
GetShards()
                {
                    // This retrieves the connection
information from a shard store
                    // (commonly a root database).
                    return new[]
```

```
                {
                   new ShardInformation
                    {
                        Id = 1,
                        ConnectionString = ...
                    },
                   new ShardInformation   {
                        Id = 2,
                        ConnectionString = ...
                    }
                };
        }
```

The other approach in creating and implementing sharding involves the use of the MS Azure SQL Database (hereinafter SQL Database) elastic feature. The main purpose of the SQL Database elastic feature is to simplify implementation and management of software-as-a-service (SaaS) solutions, as well as to simplify creating and managing sharded applications. One or more of the following features are used for that purpose (Varga, Cherry & D'Antoni, 2016):

- **Elastic Scale:** With this feature, database capacity can be grown or shrunk in order to meet different application requirements. One way to manage elasticity is to partition data across multiple databases that are identically structured through the use of sharding.
- **Elastic Database Pool:** This feature makes it possible to allocate a common pool of DTUs (Database Transaction Units) resources and to share them in multiple databases. This approach provides support to multiple types of workloads on demand without monitoring databases individually for changes in performance requirements that necessitate intervention.
- **Elastic Database Jobs:** This feature allows a T-SQL script to be executed on all databases in an elastic database pool in order to streamline administration for repetitive tasks such as rebuilding of indexes. SQL Database automatically scales script and applies built-in retry logic as necessary.
- **Elastic Query:** This feature is used in situations requiring combinations of data from multiple databases, and it allows creating a single connection string and executing a single query. SQL Database then aggregates the data into one result set.

SQL Database provides elastic database tools for simplifying the creation and management of sharded applications in a database through the use of an elastic database client library or the split-merge service. These tools are useful if the database is distributed across multiple shards or if the database implements one shard per end customer, as shown in Figure 8.

An elastic query is capable to execute a T-SQL query across multiple SQL Databases by using a single connection, without need that those databases coexist in a single elastic database pool. Elastic query is especially useful when combined results from multiple databases need to be returned to reporting or data integration tools. Because Azure SQL database transparently handles the distributed query processing, users and applications see only one database, using any driver compatible with SQL Database, as shown in Figure 9 (Varga, Cherry, & D'Antoni, 2016).

In order to be able to use elastic queries, it is necessary to create a database-scoped master key and credentials to connect to the shard map manager and the shards and then create an external data source and external tables.

With data storage costs on a steady decline and the number of data formats used by applications continuously changing, it is necessary to have the ability to manage access to historical data relationally, as well as to smoothly integrate relational data with semistructured and unstructured data. SQL Server 2016 comes with several new features that support this changing environment by

Figure 8. Elastic database tools in managing sharding
Varga, Cherry, & D'Antoni, 2016.

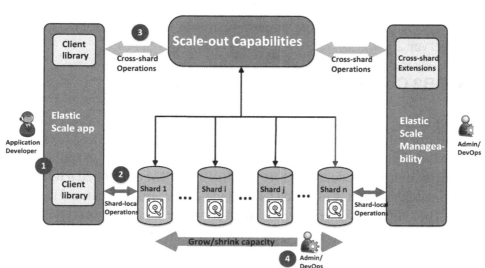

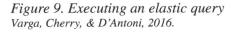

Figure 9. Executing an elastic query
Varga, Cherry, & D'Antoni, 2016.

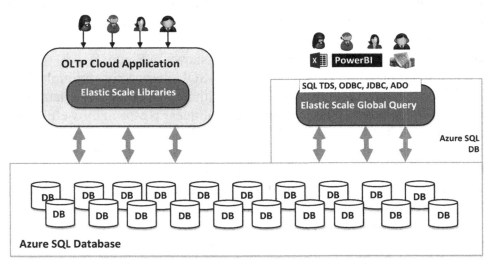

enabling access to a wider range of data. The newly introduced temporal tables provide the possibilities of maintaining historical data in the database, transparently managing changes of data, and easily retrieving data values at a particular point in time. SQL Server also allows importing JSON data into relational storage; exporting relational data as JSON structures; and even parsing, aggregating, or filtering JSON data. For scalable integration of relational data with semistructured data in Hadoop or Azure storage, it is possible to use SQL Server PolyBase, which is no longer limited to the massively parallel computing environment that it was when introduced in SQL Server 2014.

IBM DB2 Convergence Toward NoSQL

The beginning of development of the IBM database DB2 can be related to the work of Edgar F. Codd in the early 1970s, who, working as a researcher for IBM, described the theory of relational databases and in 1970 published a data manipulation model (Codd, 1970). In 1974, IBM developed a relational DBMS called System R in which Codd's ideas were implemented. However, IBM's first commercial relational database on the market appeared in 1981 under the name SQL/DS and was intended for DOS/VE and VM/CMS operating systems. IBM named the first release of its database development system DB2 (Database 2) in 1983, and the name has been kept up to now. According to 2015 data (Adrian 2015), IBM DB2 is the third most popular database with 16.5 percent, after Oracle and Microsoft SQL Server, when it comes to share on the total database market.

This section briefly presents some of the new features for IBM DB2 12 for z/OS, where z/OS refers to IBM's mainframe operating system, which brings this database closer to NoSQL databases, such as:

- JSON support
- SQL enhancements for JSON
- IBM solutions for ensuring high availability

IBM DB2 JSON Support

IBM DB2 12 for z/OS (hereinafter DB2) provides three ways to manipulate JSON documents (IBM_JSON, 2017):

- **JSON Capability for Java API:** This is a set of methods to store, search, or manipulate JSON documents. These methods can be called using Java applications directly through an API that works with documents in the database. Because DB2 database is the data store for JSON documents, this component translates operations that are requested in the method invocations into SQL statements.
- **JSON Command-Line Interface (CLI):** This is the command shell for issuing administrative commands for collections of JSON documents, as well as for performing queries and update operations on JSON collections.
- **JSON Wire Listener:** This is a server application that intercepts the MongoDB wire protocol. This wire listener acts as the midtier gateway server between MongoDB applications and DB2. It uses the NoSQL for JSON API to interface with the DB2 database server, either by allowing execution of MongoDB applications written in programming languages such as Java NodeJS, PHP, and Ruby, or by using the MongoDB CLI to communicate with the DB2 server.

JSON documents are stored in DB2 in binary format (extended BSON). The Java API supports the JSON-oriented query language, which is derived from the MongoDB query language. This Java API is the basis for additional application interfaces, such as the command-line interface and the wire listener. Figure 10 provides an illustration of JSON components in DB2.

In order to provide support for basic features of the MongoDB query language, the DB2 database, within its JSON capabilities, offers extensions that can be used to apply some DB2 database features to JSON documents, such as transaction control for grouping of multiple operations into one commit scope and batch processing for multirow insert operations.

It was already stated that the Java API contains a set of methods for storing, searching, and manipulating JSON documents.

Storing of JSON documents can be performed in two ways. One way is to manually construct objects that represent JSON documents (DBObject instances of the interface). The other way is to use the BasicDBObjectBuilder class, which is more user friendly.

In order to be able to insert a JSON document into a DB2 database, it is necessary first to obtain DBCollection from a database instance, because

Figure 10. JSON components in DB2
IBM_JSON, 2017.

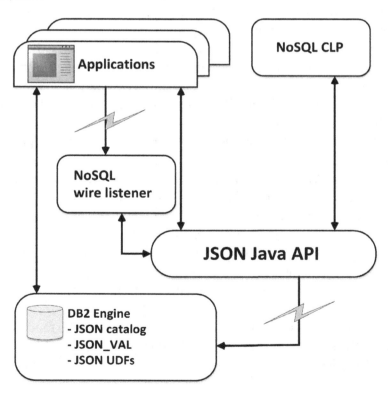

collection is represented using the DBCollection class. Example 23 gives the part of a Java program that shows how to get a collection, as well as the part of the code related to storage of a JSON document.

Example 23

Get Collection Employees

```
                            DBCollection empColl =
db.getCollection("employees");
                              BasicDBObject obj = new
BasicDBObject();
                        obj.put ("name", "Joe");
                        obj.put ("age", 50);
                        obj.put ("salary", 60000);
                     empColl.insert(obj);
```

Insert

```
  DBCollection empColl = db.getCollection("employees");
     for(int i=0; i<100; i++)
          { // queues the object to be inserted
             empColl.insert(dbObject[i], com.ibm.nosql.json.
api.WriteConcern.NORMAL);
             }
     // waits until all work sent from this thread on this
database instance is processed
     Db.waitQueue();
```

It is important to note that the insert operation by default waits for confirmation of successful completion by the database. If it is desired to increase throughput at the expense of write safety, it is possible to use the option WriteConcern. NONE or WriteConcern.NORMAL, in which case inserts are queued, batched, and inserted with less frequent commits, drastically increasing speed, but also increasing transaction log space requirements on the DB2 server side. In any case, the DB2 server is providing atomicity, consistency, isolation, and durability (ACID). It is the API that is relaxing the rules for speed (IBM_JSON, 2017).

When selecting JSON documents one of several overloaded DBCollection. find() methods can be used. Example 24 illustrates Java programming code that shows how to search a JSON document.

Example 24

```
                DBCollection empColl =
db.getCollection("employees");
                // looking for employees that are named 'Joe'
                DBCursor cursor = empColl.find(new
BasicDBObject("name", "Joe"));
                try {
                    while(cursor.hasNext()) {
                        DBObject obj = cursor.next();
                        doSomething(obj);
                    }
                }
                finally {
                        // close the cursor no
matter what
                        Cursor.close();
                }
```

The CLI interface is used for dynamic interaction with JSON collections and requires a Java runtime environment (JRE) of Version 1.5 or later. There are three ways to interact with the command line (IBM_JSON, 2017):

- Start an interactive shell by specifying the URL, user ID, and password.
- Run a .js file. The command line runs the .js file instead of through a shell. The application ends after all the commands are completed.
- Evaluate a command by using the eval command. The command line runs a one-line command, and then the applications ends.

The wire listener leverages the JSON API to interface with the DB2 database. It makes it possible to use a Mongo application written in some of the supported application languages (such as Java, NodeJS, or pymongo), or to use the Mongo command-line interface to communicate with the DB2 database.

IBM DB2 SQL Enhancements for JSON

SQL can be used to directly store and retrieve JSON data. JSON values can be stored in DB2 columns without parsing or indexing on specific fields inside the JSON document. The CLOB or VARCHAR type column can be used to hold the value and query and update based on another key column in the table.

The next extensions of DB2 SQL allow direct manipulation of JSON data (IBM_JSON, 2017):

- **JSON_VAL Function:** Ensures SQL interface for extracting and retrieving JSON data into SQL data types from BSON objects. It can also searches data within a JSON document.
- **JSON_LEN Function:** Returns the number of array elements inside a JSON document. If an element is not an array then NULL is returned.
- **JSON_TYPE Function:** Returns the BSON type for a given element.
- **JSON_TABLE Function:** Returns a two-column table where the first column is the BSON type and the second is a string value.
- **JSON2BSON Function:** Converts the specified JSON document in string format to an equivalent binary representation in BSON format. It can also be used as part of an INSERT command to add JSON data in table or as part of an UPDATE command to update JSON data in a table.
- **BSON2JSON Function:** Converts a JSON document in binary format (extended BSON) into a readable JSON text format.

Example 25 shows a SQL statement that creates a table for storage of a JSON document where CALL_RECORDS is the column to store JSON data.

Example 25

```
        CREATE TABLE CLAIMS (CLAIM_ID
VARCHAR(10),

POLICY_NUM                              VARCHAR(12),

CUSTOMER_ID             VARCHAR(8),

STATUS                  VARCHAR(20),

CALL_RECORDS            BLOB);
```

Example 26 shows a SELECT statement that uses the JSON_VAL function to find a value within a JSON document.

Example 26

```
SELECT C.CUSTOMER_ID, C.CLAIM_ID, C.CALL_RECORDS, A.NAME,
A.ASSOC_ID
FROM CLAIMS C, ASSOCIATES A
WHERE JSON_VAL(C.CALL_RECORDS,'satisfactionSurveyResult', s:25)
= 'poor' AND
                JSON_VAL(C.CALL_RECORDS, 'associate', s:40) =
A.NAME;
```

IBM Solutions for High Availability

IBM DB2 12 for z/OS provides several innovative solutions for enabling high data availability, massive scalability, breakthrough in-memory performance, deployment flexibility, and continuous data availability (Quintero, Bolinches, Sutandyo, Joly & Katahira, 2016):

- IBM Data Engine for Hadoop and Spark
- IBM Spectrum Scale file system
- IBM Spectrum Conductor for Spark
- IBM Spectrum Symphony
- IBM Platform Cluster Manager
- IBM Cloudant

The IBM Data Engine for Hadoop and Spark is a fully integrated architecture that contains integrated cluster management and analytics software that is optimized for Hadoop-based and Apache Spark–based workloads. It combines the power of OpenPOWER Linux servers designed for Big Data and analytical processing with an open-source Apache Hadoop and Spark distribution along with advanced analytics capabilities. This architecture comprises the following elements (Quintero, Bolinches, Sutandyo, Joly & Katahira, 2016):

- **Complete Cluster:** It is a comprehensive and tightly integrated cluster, and it is intended to be easily obtained, deployed, and operated. It contains all the necessary components for Big Data applications, including servers, network, operating system (OS), management software, Hadoop- and Apache Spark–compatible software, and runtime libraries.

- **Scale-Out Architecture:** It is designed to run with a traditional Hadoop architecture. Each data node in the system includes locally attached disks that are used to create the Hadoop Distributed File System (HDFS) or IBM Spectrum Scale file system for the cluster. As a protection against loss of data, the data is replicated three times between different nodes. Compute and file system capacities are together scaled with the addition of more data nodes.

- **Open Software With Optional Value-Added Components:** The Open Data Platform initiative (ODPi) is a shared endeavor of the industry to promote and advance the state of Apache Hadoop and Big Data technologies. The ODPi Core is a set of common open-source software components, including Apache Hadoop and Apache Ambari. IBM Open Platform with Apache Hadoop is a distribution supported by IBM that includes open-source components that are harmonized with the Open Data Platform (ODPi) consortium. It includes Apache Spark, which provides exceptionally fast in-memory analytics. IBM BigInsights V4 provides a choice of value-added services that provide important improvements that exceed the capabilities of the open-source stack:

  ○ BigInsights Analyst supports modernization of data centers with capabilities to run massively parallel SQL queries directly on the Hadoop cluster, including federation with external data sources, and to perform analytics using intuitive browser-based tools.

  ○ BigInsights Data Scientist provides advanced analytics capabilities such as BigR for statistical analysis and modeling.

- **Open Hardware With POWER8 Processors:** IBM Power Systems provides a range of solutions for Big Data, from standard configurations for dedicated Hadoop or Spark infrastructures with the IBM Data Engine for Hadoop and Spark – Power Systems Edition to petabyte-scale, mixed analytics solutions with the IBM Data Engine for Analytics – Power Systems Edition. Data Engine for Hadoop and Spark offers a series of configurations based on the new storage-dense, analytics-optimized S812LC line of IBM POWER8 servers. These servers offer up to 14 large form-factor disk drives or solid-state drives and up to 1 TB of memory.

The IBM Spectrum Scale file system is an alternative to Hadoop File System. It provides a nonforked, open-source Hadoop version and enhances it with capabilities, such as enterprise-class storage by using an IBM Spectrum

Scale File System, security by reducing the surface area and securing access to administrative interfaces and key Hadoop services, and workload optimization by using the Adaptive MapReduce algorithm that optimizes execution time of multiple small and large jobs. IBM Spectrum Scale also functions as a Portable Operating System Interface (POSIX) compliant file system enabling that other computers that do not belong to the Hadoop cluster can access these files in a normal manner. The IBM Spectrum Scale approach leverages kernel-level metadata and facilities and provides file system block-level granularity (Quintero, Bolinches, Sutandyo, Joly & Katahira, 2016).

IBM Spectrum Conductor for Spark is a complete enterprise-grade multitenant solution for Apache Spark. It is designed to meet the demands of users who need to adopt the Apache Spark technology and integrate it into their environment. To address Apache Spark challenges, IBM Spectrum Conductor for Spark makes it possible for Apache Spark to run natively on a shared infrastructure without the dependency of Hadoop (Quintero, Bolinches, Sutandyo, Joly & Katahira, 2016).

IBM Spectrum Symphony is a resource scheduler for grid environments. It works with applications enabled for grid and has the ability to provide high-resource utilization rates along with low latency for certain kinds of jobs. It is possible to use IBM Spectrum Symphony as a job scheduler for MapReduce tasks in an IBM Open Platform environment. IBM Spectrum Symphony can replace the open-source YARN scheduler in a framework based on MapReduce and provide benefits such as improved performance by providing lower latency for certain MapReduce-based jobs. Also, it is compatible with both HDFS and IBM Spectrum Scale and can be integrated with IBM Open Platform (Quintero, Bolinches, Sutandyo, Joly & Katahira, 2016).

IBM Platform Cluster (PCM) is software for management of clusters that can perform bare-metal or virtualized systems deployment and can create cluster configurations on the deployed systems. PCM can be used for managing IBM POWER server hardware, installing a specific operating system (OS) image on them, and using a couple of these servers to create an IBM Open Platform cluster (Quintero, Bolinches, Sutandyo, Joly & Katahira, 2016).

IBM Cloudant is a hosted and fully managed database-as-a-service (DBaaS) built to make sure that the data flow between an application and its database stays without interruptions and with high performance. It can handle a wide range of data types like JSON, full text, and geospatial. Cloudant is an operational data store optimized for dealing with simultaneous reads and writes and enables high availability and data durability. It provides an HTTP API for working with JSON data and 24-hour operational support and maintenance. Cloudant is based on Apache CouchDB and is delivered as various multitenant, dedicated, and installed services.

All requests to Cloudant go through the Web. This means that any system that can speak to the Web can speak to Cloudant. All language-specific libraries for Cloudant are actually only wrappers that provide some convenience and linguistics to help in working with a simple API. Cloudant supports the following HTTP request methods (IBM_Cloudant, 2017):

- **GET:** Requests the specified item, meaning static items, database documents, and configuration and statistical information. In most cases the information is returned in the form of a JSON document.
- **HEAD:** This method is used to get the HTTP header of a GET request without the body of the response.
- **POST:** Upload data. Within Cloudant's API, this method is used to set values, upload documents, set document values, and start some administration commands.
- **PUT:** It is used to create new objects, including databases, documents, views, and design documents.
- **DELETE:** It deletes the specified resource, including documents, views, and design documents.
- **COPY:** It can be used to copy documents and objects.

Cloudant stores documents using JSON encoding so that it is possible to store anything encoded into JSON as a document. Files that contain media, such as images, audio, and videos, are called BLOBs (Binary Large OBjects), and they can be stored as attachments associated with documents.

Cloudant's API enables interaction with a collaboration of numerous machines (i.e., a cluster). It is necessary that the machines of a cluster be located in the same data center, but they can be within different subclusters, or "pods," in the particular data center. Through the use of pods, it is possible to improve the high-availability features of Cloudant.

REFERENCES

Adrian, M. (2015). *DBMS 2015 numbers paint a picture of slow but steady change*. Retrieved December 8, 2016 from http://blogs.gartner.com/merv-adrian/2016/04/12/dbms-2015-numbers-paint-a-picture-of-slow-but-steady-change/

Codd, E. F. (1970). A relational model of data for large shared data banks. *Commun. ACM, 13*(6), 377-387. DOI:10.1145/362384.362685

Couchbase. (2017a). *Couchbase server/N1QL language reference*. Retrieved February 8, 2017 from https://developer.couchbase.com/documentation/server/current/n1ql/n1ql-language-reference/index.html

Couchbase. (2017b). *Couchbase server overview: SELECT statement processing*. Retrieved February 8, 2017 from https://developer.couchbase.com/documentation/server/4.6/n1ql/n1ql-language-reference/selectintro.html

Couchbase. (2017c). *Couchbase server/N1QL and SQL differences*. Retrieved February 8, 2017 from https://developer.couchbase.com/documentation/server/4.6/n1ql/n1ql-intro/n1ql-sql-differences.html

Data-flair. (2016). *Data partitioning – An optimization technique in Apache Hive*. Retrieved December 17, 2016 from http://data-flair.training/blogs/data-partitioning-optimization-technique-apache-hive

Harrison, G. (2015). *Next generation databases: NoSQL, NewSQL, and big data*. Apress. doi:10.1007/978-1-4842-1329-2

Hive. (2014). *Hive query language*. Retrieved February, 9, 2017 from https://www.tutorialspoint.com/hive/hive_tutorial.pdf

Hive. (2017). *Language manual DDL*. Retrieved February 5, 2017 from https://cwiki.apache.org/confluence/display/Hive/LanguageManual+DDL

IBM_Cloudant. (2017). *Cloudant basic*. Retrieved February 6, 2017 from https://console.ng.bluemix.net/docs/services/Cloudant/basics/index.html#cloudant-basics

IBM_JSON. (2017). *Working with JSON documents version 12.0.0.* Retrieved February 5, 2017 from https://www.ibm.com/support/knowledgecenter/en/SSEPEK_12.0.0/json/src/tpc/db2z_jsonworkingwithdocs.html

Microsoft. (2017). *What's new in SQL server 2016 (database engine).* Retrieved February 5, 2017 from https://msdn.microsoft.com/en-us/library/bb510411.aspx

Oracle. (2016). *Oracle big data SQL release 3.1. Oracle data.* Retrieved February 5, 2017 from http://www.oracle.com/technetwork/database/bigdata-appliance/overview/bigdatasql-datasheet-2934203.pdf

Oracle_BD. (2017). *Big data SQL user's guide.* Retrieved February 5, 2017 from http://docs.oracle.com/bigdata/bds31/BDSUG/toc.htm

Oracle_CNCPT. (2017). *Oracle database concepts: 12c release 2 (12.2).* Retrieved February 5, 2017 from https://docs.oracle.com/database/122/CNCPT/CNCPT.pdf

Oracle_HA. (2014). *Oracle database high availability overview 12c release 1 (12.1).* Retrieved February 5, 2017 from https://docs.oracle.com/database/121/HAOVW/toc.htm

Oracle_HA. (2017). *Oracle database high availability overview12c release 2 (12.2).* Retrieved February 5, 2017 from https://docs.oracle.com/database/122/HAOVW/toc.htm

Oracle_JSON. (2017). *JSON in Oracle database.* Retrieved February 5, 2017 from http://docs.oracle.com/database/122/ADJSN/json-in-oracle-database.htm#ADXDB6246)

Oracle_JSON_DG. (2017). *Database JSON developer's guide.* Retrieved February 5, 2017 from http://docs.oracle.com/database/122/ADJSN/function-JSON_QUERY.htm#ADXDB6384

Oracle_MAA. (2017). *Maximize availability with Oracle database 12c release 2*. Oracle White Paper. Retrieved February 5, 2017 from http://www.oracle.com/technetwork/database/availability/maximum-availability-wp-12c-1896116.pdf

Quintero, D., Bolinches, L., Sutandyo, A. G., Joly, N., & Katahira, R. T. (2016). *IBM data engine for Hadoop and Spark*. IBM Redbooks.

Tiwari, S. (2011). *Professional NoSQL*. John Wiley & Sons, Inc.

Varga, S., Cherry, D., & D'Antoni, J. (2016). *Introducing Microsoft SQL server 2016 - Mission-critical applications, deeper insights, hyperscale cloud*. Retrieved February 5, 2017 from https://blogs.msdn.microsoft.com/microsoft_press/2016/02/02/free-ebook-introducing-microsoft-sql-server-2016-mission-critical-applications-deeper-insights-hyperscale-cloud-preview-2/

Chapter 6
Integration of Relational and NoSQL Databases

ABSTRACT

The chapter proposes three ways of integration of the two different worlds of relational and NoSQL databases: native, hybrid, and reducing to one option, either relational or NoSQL. The native solution includes using vendors' standard APIs and integration on the business layer. In a relational environment, APIs are based on SQL standards, while the NoSQL world has its own, unstandardized solutions. The native solution means using the APIs of the individual systems that need to be connected, leaving to the business-layer coding the task of linking and separating data in extraction and storage operations. A hybrid solution introduces an additional layer that provides SQL communication between the business layer and the data layer. The third integration solution includes vendors' effort to foresee functionalities of "opposite" side, thus convincing developers' community that their solution is sufficient.

INTRODUCTION

Starting any information technology project that will result in new software almost certainly involves selecting an appropriate database. The market is big, so making a choice is not easy and requires examining features. Though all databases have the same or similar purpose of storing and extracting data,

DOI: 10.4018/978-1-5225-3385-6.ch006

there are many differences among them. Selecting a programming language plays a significant role in achieving the ultimate goal of a project; choosing the appropriate database is important as well. What is important when selecting a database? Project objectives drive the answer to this question, along with some global expectations of modern information systems. These expectations include a large number of users, high availability, and throughput of the system with huge amounts and consistency of data.

In the present world of software development, the dominant solution for high scalability and throughput requirements is NoSQL databases. However, this selection imposes upon business-layer programmers the task of solving a number of deficiencies that the world of relational databases had previously solved and standardized. Integrity and consistency of the data based on ACID transactions are the foremost of these problems. Developers spend huge amounts of time developing complex software mechanisms to manage the eventual consistency of data. Bembach (2014) implies the need for a thorough knowledge of data consistency theory as a prerequisite for work on such development solutions. Nevertheless, most software developers think in "transactional" terms, thanks to their education and to development trends that prevailed in the world until recently. Google Spanner's development team (Corbett et al., 2013), defining the rationale behind its solution, set the following thesis:

We believe it is better to have application programmers deal with performance problems due to overuse of transactions as bottlenecks arise, rather than always coding around the lack of transactions. (p. 8)

Developers have a particular problem in the absence of SQL, the standardized structured query language. Every NoSQL system has its implementation of nonSQL programming solutions to run queries on a database. Comparing these solutions with SQL databases, most relational databases are found to offer developers a much richer software interface than NoSQL databases that do not have SQL available. When evaluating usability, performance, and user-friendliness of various query-programming languages of databases, one usually asks questions such as:

- Does the language support aggregate functions?
- Does the language support windows functionality when working with huge amounts of data?

- Are analytic functions a part of the set of functionalities?
- Is there a functionality of temporary tables/documents required for execution of complex queries on a database?
- What is the load on the network by client-server-client communication running some typical queries?

Many of these questions received negative answers in the initial stage of development of NoSQL databases. Demands of the developer community were implemented over time by adding new functionalities. Not only have NoSQL systems evolved; relational systems also adopted the trend of implementing the features for which NoSQL systems gained popularity. Paradigms of both groups of databases have evolved on the basis of certain assumptions. As a matter of course, the need for a real system with particular properties necessitates using one in which they are inherent. A situation requiring the use of both types of the database is still an open issue, and it is the subject of this book.

The principles of these particular databases and ways to use them are clear and known to business-layer developers. The question is how to integrate the relational and NoSQL models. Many solutions of two general types are in practice.

A *native solution* involves the use of standard drivers and ways in which the business layer communicates with a particular database. Since a part of the data is in NoSQL, and the other part in the relational database, it is necessary to collate data. This is implemented in the business layer. When being extracted from a database, data are linked and converted into a format suitable for use in the user layer. When storing data in a database, the business layer is programmed to prepare data for storage and pass it on to the particular database.

A *hybrid solution* introduces an additional layer that provides SQL communication between the business layer and the data layer. Developers continue to use familiar SQL programming patterns in the business layer, and employ a new layer to translate these patterns to the NoSQL programming interface for communication with the NoSQL database.

In addition, vendors of NoSQL and relational systems make efforts to add the functionalities of the "counterpart" option, to convince the developer community that their solution is sufficient.

NATIVE SOLUTIONS

Every database management system (DBMS) has its own application programming interface (API) data management solution. In a relational environment, APIs are based on SQL standards, while the NoSQL world normally has its own, unstandardized solutions. One solution for integrating these two environments is to use APIs of the individual systems that need to be connected, leaving business-layer coding the task of linking and separating data in extraction and storage operations—not a practical solution at all, but one of the possibilities. In order to demonstrate the complexity of such a procedure in greater detail, concepts and examples of several individual systems from both worlds will be presented.

Relational Databases

RDBMS is a database management system based on Codd's relational model (Codd, 1970). It provides efficient support to applications that require persistence, consistency, and high availability of data. Its structure is simple and clear, and therefore easy to use. Data are stored in tables that consist of rows and columns. SQL is used to create tables, and to store and extract data. Complex queries over the simple structure are expressed in a declarative language based on everyday spoken language. Stonebraker and Cattel (2011) named these databases GPTRS (general purpose traditional row stores), with the following key properties:

- Disk-oriented storage.
- Tables stored row-by-row on disk—hence, a row store.
- B-trees as the indexing mechanism.
- Dynamic locking as the concurrency-control mechanism.
- A write-ahead log, or WAL, for crash recovery.
- SQL as the access language.
- A "row-oriented" query optimizer.

Relational tables strictly define the data model. The design of a table and related data types must be strictly observed. It is not possible to enter any data in a database until a table is created. A table consists of columns, and each column must be assigned the type of data being stored. This table definition is called a schema. A schema may also contain additional elements that more specifically define tables or facilitate their use. The primary key is a unique identifier of each record of a table. Indexes are data structures that allow faster and more efficient querying of tables by indexed columns. Relationships define logical connections between individual tables using relational keys. When building a relational model and database, it is assumed that the model and the associated physical structure are developed before developing the business layer. It is certainly possible to correct the model subsequently, but significant corrections usually require major corrections to the built business layer.

The goal of the relational model is to minimize data redundancy (Table 1). A JOIN clause links relational tables and provides the option of extracting a complex dataset with a relatively simple SQL query. Data integrity rules, implemented by establishing foreign keys and relational constraints, maintain consistency and integrity of the relational data model. They allow RDBMS internal mechanisms to ensure data integrity, regardless of business-layer coding.

The transaction, characterized by a set of properties called ACID, is the core of all operations in a relational database. A single transaction can consist of multiple individual insert, update, and delete operations. The transactional mechanism guarantees that all operations are successfully completed only if each and every one is successfully completed.

Data select, insert, update, and delete are basic operations of every DBMS. A relational DBMS uses SQL to perform these operations, regardless of the

Table 1. Relational tables

Vehicles							
Vin Number	License Plate	Manufacturer	MModel	First Registration	Fuel Type	PPower	Seats
JC1234567890A	A45O123	M01	T0101	01-APR-2016	Lpg	177	5
ZK28345AD4F0A	C25A555	M02	T0203	15-JUN-2016	Diesel	135	5
NN8730539648B	J54A854	M03	T0301	14-AUG-2016	Hybrid	155	5
Manufacturer		Model					
Code	Name	Manufacturer	Code	Name			
M01	Volkswagen	M01	T0101	Passat			
M02	Audi	M02	T0203	A6			
M03	Toyota	M03	T0301	RAV 4			

producer. Complex queries can be generated and data manipulated in often-complex relational models, using simple declarative language. Since relational models are normalized, such queries can be time-consuming. A table-join operation takes up resources and time of the RDBMS control mechanism, which extends the execution time. Still, producers of RDBMS systems provide various algorithms and optimization techniques to minimize this time. Table 2 lists several examples of SQL commands to perform various operations on the data from the Table 1.

NoSQL APIs

While the slogan *one size fits all* drove creators and proponents of RDBMS systems, the underlying philosophy on which various editions of NoSQL databases were built was *one size does not fit all*. Such an approach led to highly scalable products, not intended to solve all database-related problems of the developer community. Still, they are a nearly ideal solution for some problems, such as social networks or website analytics. The lack of transactions in the NoSQL concept will certainly not encourage developers of enterprise accounting software, for example, to use some versions of NoSQL databases. Using a combination of two database concepts separately, for the "transactional" part of the work and for saving documents, is no problem.

Regarding standardization, the problem with NoSQL databases is that each of them has a different data-storage model and different data-handling APIs. For this reason, applications and data are not portable, and the skills acquired while working with one database cannot be applied to another database. Furthermore, while the overview of APIs for the relational model

Table 2. SQL commands

Operation	SQL Statement
Insert a new vehicle record	insert into vehicles (vin, license_plate, make, model, registration_date, fuel_type, power, seats) values ('JC1234567890A','A45O123','M01','T0101','01-APR-2016','Petrol',177,5);
Update power data	update vehicles set power=185 where vin='JC1234567890A';
Select vehicles using fuel type Petrol	select vin, license_plate from vehicles where fuel='Petrol';
Select number of vehicles by manufacturer	select manufacturer, count(1) from vehicles group by manufacturer;
Count the number of Toyota vehicles	select count(1) from vehicles where manufacturer='M03';

only pertained to SQL, regardless of the vendor and version of the database, discussion of NoSQL models and APIs must be presented for individual databases or vendors. The models and APIs for HBase, MongoDB, and Oracle NoSQL will be briefly presented in the following text exactly in this order because it is the same historical order in which they appeared.

HBASE

HBase is the project the company Powerset presented in 2007, as a contribution to Hadoop. In simple terms, HBase is an open-source version of Google's Bigtable project. Google started developing the Bigtable data-storage system in 2004 and applied it in applications such as Google Earth, web indexing, Google Book Search, YouTube, and Gmail. Not until 2015 did Google offer a version of its product to the general public, as a service through Google Cloud Datastore. Meanwhile, HBase had transferred the same technology to a wide range of users in late 2007, with its first usable version 0.15.0. In May 2010, it became a top-level Apache project, and since then has not followed Hadoop versions, due to a much faster development cycle. At the time of this writing, the current version is 1.2.3.

The primary unit of an HBase database is a *column*. A *row* consists of multiple *columns* and is uniquely identified by a key (*row key*). A *table* is made up of a set of rows. When describing the structural elements of an HBase, it seems similar to a relational table. Still, new categories such as *cells*, *namespaces*, and *column families* introduce the primary differences in the internal structure of the observed data-organization models.

Each *column* can have multiple versions of stored data. These versions are observed as changes in column values over time. Individual values, or versions, are written in *cells*, and accompanied by information on the time at which they were entered. So, a column is made up of groups of cells, while several columns form a *column family*. Column families are usually formed based on semantics, or columns are linked together by another grouping rule defined independently by the user. The meaning of grouping is important because the HBase storage mechanism itself stores columns of the same family together, in files on storage systems. In an HBase system, the limit is 10 families, but there is absolutely no limit to the number of columns within a family or a table. Individual columns are referenced as family:qualifier pairs, and there is no limitation on the type or size of data stored. Tables and column families are static elements defined in advance, while columns are dynamic elements that can be added and removed while the database is being used.

At a higher level of data organization, *tables* are grouped into *namespaces*. Grouping is performed based on various criteria. For instance, tables can be grouped based on affiliation with a particular application, or on access rights related to data storage security.

HBase does not care what data the user stores in tables. There are no different types of data, but they are all considered to be of a single type of byte array.

The terminology of "table" and "columns" causes the model to be visualized as a classic spreadsheet, which is not correct. This concept is influenced by the legacy of a once totally dominant relational concept that many still keep in mind. It is much easier to present the model as a multidimensional map, in which components of the map are tags. The Example 1 illustrates the first line of the table Vehicles (Table 3) which using such a map.

Example 1

```
{
  "A0001": {
    "Identification": {
      "vin": {
        "Timestamp1": "JC1234567890A"
      }
    }"Registration": {
      "LicensePlate": {
```

Table 3. Vehicles

Row Key	Column Families		
	Identification	**Registration**	**CarType**
A0001	vin="JC1234567890A"	LicensePlate="A45O123" FirstRegistration="01-APR-2016"	Manufacturer="Volkswagen" Model="Passat" FuelType="Lpg" Power="177" Seats="5"
A0002	vin="ZK28345AD4F0A"	LicensePlate="C25A555" FirstRegistration="15-JUN-2016"	Manufacturer="Audi" Model="A6" FuelType="Diesel" Power="135" Seats="5"
A0003	vin="NN8730539648B"	LicensePlate="J54A854" FirstRegistration="14-AUG-2016"	Manufacturer="Toyota" Model="RAV4" FuelType="Hybrid" Power="155" Seats="5"

```
          "Timestamp1": "A450123"
      }"FirstRegistration": {
          "Timestamp1": "01-APR-2016"
      }
  }"CarType": {
      "Manufacturer": {
          "Timestamp1": "Volkswagen"
      }"Model": {
          "Timestamp1": "Passat"
      }"FuelType": {
          "Timestamp1": "Lpg""Timestamp2": "Petrol"
      }"Power": {
          "Timestamp1": "177"
      }"Seat": {
          "Timestamp1": "5"
      }
  }
  }
}
```

The functionality of data versioning within a column is certainly very remarkable feature. If the user does not specify time information, HBase itself writes the value of the original version of data at the time of its entry. This functionality can be user defined. Data within a column are arranged in descending order so that the most recent version is first and the oldest version is last. The data presented in Example 1 shows that the last fuel type was Lpg, and the previous one was Petrol. This is the logic adjusted to optimize data reading because the last version is always in the first place. The user decides the number of versions that HBase will store in individual columns. This decision is highly flexible because, in addition to the number of versions, it is also possible to specify a period of time. For example, HBase can be instructed to store only the versions of a column from the last month, regardless of the number of versions in a given period.

HBase API (Table 4) is available to the developer community to manipulate stored data using three primary methods: Get, Put, and Scan. The first two methods apply to a particular individual row, and therefore must be assigned a row key when called. The Scan method is related to a range of rows. Thus, it requires the start and end row key as parameters, and when they are excluded, the method scans the entire table.

Table 4. HBase API examples

Operation	API Statement
Insert a new vehicle record	put 'Vehicles',, 'Identification:vin', 'JC1234567890A' put 'Vehicles', 'A0001', Registration:LicensePlate', 'A45O123' put 'Vehicles', 'A0001', Registration:FirstRegistration, '01-APR-2016' put 'Vehicles', 'A0001',CarType:Manufacturer','Volkswagen' put 'Vehicles', 'A0001',CarType:Model',Passat' put 'Vehicles', 'A0001',CarType:FuelType',Lpg' put 'Vehicles', 'A0001',CarType:Power','177' put 'Vehicles', 'A0001',CarType:Seats','5'
Update power data	put 'Vehicles,' 'A0001', 'CarType: Power', '185'
Select vehicles using fuel type Petrol	scan ' Vehicles' , { COLUMNS => ['Identification:vin', 'Registration:LicensePlate'], FILTER =>"SingleColumnValueFilter('CarType' , 'FuelType', =, 'binary:Petrol')" }
Select number of vehicles by manufacturer	The solution is not available using native HBase API. Options like Apache Hive, HBase endpoint coprocessors or MapReduce jobs are available.
Count the number of Toyota vehicles	The solution is not available using native HBase API. Options like Apache Hive, HBase endpoint coprocessors or MapReduce jobs are available.

MongoDB

The 10gen company initially developed MongoDB in 2007 as a PaaS (platform as a service). In 2009, MongoDB Inc. launched the same-named database as an open-source project. The database initially attracted a large number of users, thanks to characteristics that made it highly suitable for the development of applications requiring simplicity and high-speed data processing. The database designers provided replication mechanisms that, in an incredibly simple way, replicated data across multiple servers that are not hardware intensive. A powerful, feature-rich API for data storage and extraction accompanied the high availability of data. MongoDB is a document-oriented database, in which a schema is defined by the code. In short, this database opened a new chapter for users previously burdened with the concept of tables, columns, rows, foreign keys, and transactions.

The main element of a MongoDB database is a collection. Comparing it with a relational database, the collection would be analogous to the table. While a table contains data rows, a collection consists of documents. There are several types of collection. A collection has a unique name within a database and can be unlimited or limited in size. The Example 2 illustrates the organization of data in a collection and accompanying documents for relational table Vehicles.

Example 2

```
{
    "Vin": "JC1234567890A",
    "LicensePlate": "A45O123",
    "Manufacturer": {
        "Code": "M01",
        "Name": "Volkswagen"
    },
    "Model": {
        "Code": "T0101",
        "Name": "Passat"
    },
    "FirstRegistration": "01-APR-2016",
    "FuelType": "Lpg",
    "Power": "177",
    "Seats": "5"
},
{
    "Vin": "ZK28345AD4F0A",
    "LicensePlate": "C25A555",
    "Manufacturer": {
        "Code": "M02",
        "Name": "Audi"
    },
    "Model": {
        "Code": "T0203",
        "Name": "A6"
    },
    "FirstRegistration": "15-JUN-2016",
    "FuelType": "Diesel",
    "Power": "135",
    "Seats": "5"
},
{
    "Vin": "NN8730539648B",
    "LicensePlate": "J54A854",
    "Manufacturer": {
        "Code": "M03",
        "Name": "Toyota"
    },
    "Model": {
        "Code": "T0301",
        "Name": "RAV4"
    },
```

```
    "FirstRegistration": "14-AUG-2016",
    "FuelType": "Hybrid",
    "Power": "155",
    "Seats": "5"
}
```

As already indicated, MongoDB is a document-oriented database, and it uses the BSON standard for organization and storage of data. BSON is open standard; the standard's web site (http://bsonspec.org/) emphasizes that it was intentionally designed to be lightweight, traversable, and efficient. The binary form of JSON provides easier data writing and indexing and traversing such records during data-extraction operations. BSON in use occupies slightly more space for data storage, but the performance of data extraction and storage is noticeably increased, compared to databases that use the pure JSON format. A BSON record is easy to translate into any native data format used by programming languages like PHP, C, or C #. A wide range of drivers for MongoDB translates the BSON format directly into the native form, without the intermediate step of converting to the JSON format.

BSON offers another important advantage over the JSON standard. While the JSON standard supports *key-value* pairs, where *value* can take a value of type string or number, BSON can store binary data or other specific types of data such as Timestamp, JavaScript code, Regular expression, or Object ID. So, BSON can store any JSON document. The opposite is not true; i.e., a BSON document that uses some specific data types is not necessarily a valid JSON document.

The flexibility and power of relational databases based on SQL is especially emphasized in the possibility of setting *dynamic queries* over a predefined data structure. MongoDB goes a step further, providing dynamic queries on a data structure that is not predefined. The *possibility of indexing data* is significant in this respect. And while MongoDB itself creates a unique index on the _id key, the user is able to form an index on any other key or combination of keys of a document. When forming an index, the user defines uniqueness as mandatory or optional. Indexing is provided on embedded documents as well, which offers an incredibly powerful mechanism for fast extraction of data on a given search criterion that includes the keys of embedded documents. Geospatial indexes are a special type that provides the user with various functionalities for extraction of location-based data. Obviously, the creators of the MongoDB database paid special attention to data indexing, along with the use of BSON and dynamic queries, in order to make the database extremely fast. If queries are still not as effective and fast as the user would like, there is a tool that records statistical information and a detailed plan for execution of each database query. MongoDB Profiler records this data in the db.system.profile collection and standard APIs provide extraction of the data, just as with any other collection within the database.

The *method of writing data* in memory structures on hard disks is based on the response speed.

MongoDB keeps and updates data in the memory, and writes them to the disk in specified time intervals. The time interval for recording depends on the settings defined by the user, and it is usual to perform writing once every second. Running an update operation hundreds or thousands of times a second can have various implications for a database. While running these operations in server memory increases the speed dramatically, the data may be lost due to an unexpected server failure. This is a compromise that MongoDB users are willing to make, bearing in mind that they do not use the database for transaction-oriented systems.

The database users regularly include storage and retrieval of binary-type data, like images or videos. This is another field where MongoDB performs extremely well using GridFS, which uses two collections within the database. GridFS stores metadata about the file in one collection, and in another the file itself, broken down into small pieces called *chunks*. In this way, neither the number of files nor their size is limited. In some cases, recording files in the database become much more efficient than keeping them in the server file system and may even make recording them possible at all. Similarly, it is easier to access specific parts of large files by extracting respective chunks, which again defines MongoDB as extremely fast in the field of storing and extracting data of any type.

Data replication in MongoDB is provided through the feature *replica sets*. When defining a replica set, one server is declared the primary server, and others are secondary servers. Only the primary server manages all data-writing operations and creates a log of these operations, which it propagates to all secondary servers. Each of them is responsible for writing the data in its database, ensuring replication of data. In the case of primary-server failure, one of the secondary servers becomes the primary server through the process of voting and takes over all data-recording privileges. It plays this role until the initially designated primary server starts functioning normally.

Sharding is the functionality of the MongoDB database that provides horizontal database scaling. In a situation where a single server cannot easily handle a huge amount of data, the data are distributed across multiple servers (called shards). Each of them is an independent server, and together they form a logical database. The user does not see these servers or communicate with them through the program interface; rather, the user communicates with a single database. The sharding mechanism ensures that each of the shard servers handles a small number operations and a small amount of data. In other words, each server is only responsible for the data assigned to it. Data are assigned to a particular shard server depending on the shard key and how the keys are distributed. A shard key represents one or more indexed fields that exist in each document of a collection. MongoDB divides data into chunks and distributes them across shard servers, according to a determined range of values, or using the hash function based on shard key values. This feature is yet another contribution to qualifying the MongoDB database as an extremely fast database for operating huge amounts of data.

Map and Reduce functions are available to users willing to take advantage of their mechanism, which is rather complicated and not highly efficient at processing data. For ad-hoc queries, analytics, and statistical analyses in real time, MongoDB has developed Aggregation Framework, a simple, flexible, and functional solution. The mechanism behind it is based on the aggregation pipeline. The process of aggregation is conducted through stages, where the result of each stage is the input to the next stage.

Table 5 shows the same simple data manipulation examples as those presented for SQL and HBase. MongoDB has a truly rich set of functions that operate at the level of either the entire document or a particular field. They are available for data insertion, updating and deletion, search in a database, and data aggregation. The strength of MongoDB is its simple, easy-to-learn syntax, and functionality.

Oracle NoSQL

In 2011, the first commercial producer of relational DBMS systems came out with its first version of NoSQL DBMS. The DBMS community leader realized the importance of the new data organization paradigm and named its product Oracle NoSQL Database. The product is part of its strategic response to modern-world issues related to the presence of extreme amounts of structured and unstructured data, originating from a huge number of data sources, and accompanied by the need for high processing speed. The Berkeley DB team developed it as a distributed database organized through nodes, programmable sets of components that receive, create, store, and send data. Oracle NoSQL Database is part of the key-value pair NoSQL databases. The

Table 5. MongoDB API examples

Operation	API Statement
Insert a new vehicle record	db.vehicles.insert({"Vin": "JC1234567890A", "LicensePlate": "A45O123", "Manufacturer":{"Code":"M01","Name":"Volkswagen"}, "Model": {"Code":"T0101", "Name":"Passat"}, "FirstRegistration": "01-APR-2016", "FuelType": "Lpg", "Power": "177", "Seats": "5"})
Update power data	db.vehicles.update({"Vin": "JC1234567890A"}, {$set: { "Power":"185" } })
Select vehicles using fuel type Petrol	db.vehicles.find({"FuelType": "Petrol"})
Select number of vehicles by manufacturer	db.vehicles.aggregate([{$group: {_id: "$Manufacturer.Name", count:{$sum:1}}}])
Count the number of Toyota vehicles	db.vehicles.find({"Manufacturer.Name":"Toyota"}).count()

key-value store is a structure that provides data storage, where a pair can be observed as a record in a relational database.

As its name suggests, the structure has two basic data-storage components: key and value. Key is the basic component for the organization of database records. The structural elements of a key that uniquely identifies a record in a database are major key and minor key. The major key is mandatory and can contain one or more keys. The structure of a key can use the minor key component, which can also consist of one or more keys. Database records are organized into clusters for scalability and data-access optimization purposes. The major key is the crucial component when organizing a cluster—i.e., all records that have the same value as this component are stored in the same cluster. An important characteristic of the Oracle NoSQL product is that it provides operation on data of the same major key component in a single atomic operation. Through clusters, data are further organized into shards, and these into nodes (physical servers). A database consists of a number of shards. The value of the major key component consequently defines the location in which the data is physically stored. Still, it is the database engine that takes care of the physical node for data storage; in this respect, the value of the key does not have a direct influence.

The value of a key component is a Java String, and as such can take any value desired by the user who plans to organize data. This creates a good opportunity to correlate logical and physical data organization. The value of a key is often organized using its analogy to file paths, delimiting different parts of a major key by a slash sign: "/". If the string also contains a minor key, the latter is separated from the major part by the combination of signs: "/-/". Thus, assuming the major key is the component VinNumber, the example of keys from Table 1 for the vehicle with VIN number *JC1234567890Abi* could be similar to those presented in Example 3.

Example 3

```
/JC1234567890A/-/LicensePlate
/JC1234567890A/-/Manufacturer
/JC1234567890A/-/Model
/JC1234567890A/-/FirstRegistration
/JC1234567890A/-/FuelType
/JC1234567890A/-/Power
/JC1234567890A/-/Seats
```

The key component is organized so that the minor key components denote particular features of a vehicle with a particular VIN number. If the logic of applications that will use the data requires reading the entire set of data associated with a VIN number, then this organization is not appropriate. For such an application request, it would be natural to organize an Avro record schema that would contain all elements of a VIN number, and data would be stored through one key-value pair. The corresponding Avro scheme, with the respective key /VinNumber/-/VehicleInfo, is presented in Example 4.

Example 4

```
{
    "type": "record",
    "namespace": "com.vehicles",
    "name": "VehicleInfo",
    "fields": [
      { "name": "LicensePlate", "type": "string" },
      { "name": "ManufacturerName", "type": "string" },
      { "name": "ModelName", "type": "string" },
      { "name": "FirstRegistration", "type": "string" },
      { "name": "FuelType", "type": "string" },
```

```
        { "name": "Power", "type": "float" },
        { "name": "Seats", "type": "float" }
    ]
}
```

In logical modeling, the user decides on the structure of data, guided essentially by the projection of what the application will demand from the DBMS system. It is possible to make a combination of the previous two organizations, which will store a part of the data into an Avro Schema and link it with the major key component, and model the other part of the data through the minor key component. For example, assume that searches by vehicle producer are frequent, and extract other vehicle data as well. All vehicle data would be organized through the Avro schema except the producer data, and this data would be set as the minor key component. The keys presented in Example 5 can be used.

Example 5

```
/VinNumber/-/VehicleInfo
/VinNumber/-/ManufacturerName.
```

Organizing data through various keys that differ in the minor key component ensures manipulation of a data set identified by the same major key through a single atomic operation. With this, Oracle provided full ACID functionality for record-update procedures. It also optimized data-reading processes in such a way that applications do not have to access data of large size (like images or videos) unless they expressly require it. This part of the process is also optimized between the application and DBMS through specially designed techniques and the Oracle NoSQL stream API interface.

Data in an Oracle NoSQL database can also be logically organized through a table-type structure. Use of SQL on tables is enabled for data extraction and update operations, as shown in Table 6. The table, with the related syntax for its creation, presented in Example 6 could define organization through key-value pairs.

Example 6

```
Create table Vehicles(
    VinNumber STRING,
    LicensePlate STRING,
```

Table 6. Oracle NoSQL API examples

Operation	SQL Statement
Insert a new vehicle record	insert into Vehicles (VinNumber,LicensePlate,ManufacturerName,ModelName, FirstRegistration,FuelType,Power,Seats) values ('JC1234567890A','A45O 123','Volkswagen','Passat','01-APR-2016','Petrol',177.5);
Update power data	update Vehicles set Power=185 where VinNumber='JC1234567890A';
Select vehicles using fuel type Petrol	select VinNumber, LicensePlate from Vehicles where FuelType='Petrol';
Select number of vehicles by manufacturer	select ManufacturerName, count(1) from Vehicles group by ManufacturerName;
Count the number of Toyota vehicles	select count(1) from Vehicles where ManufacturerName='Toyota';

```
ManufacturerName STRING,
ModelName STRING,
FirstRegistration STRING,
FuelType STRING,
Power FLOAT,
Seats FLOAT,
PRIMARY KEY (VinNumber)
)
```

The illustration of SQL features (Table 6) can be interesting from the viewpoint of users who have experience in the world of relational databases.

For users of the NoSQL world, the producer has provided API methods (put, get, delete) for data access and management, including multikey variations, and integration with MapReduce operations from the Hadoop environment. Client library APIs are developed for Java and C. Command line interface and JavaScript API are available to users as well. Complete mechanisms are also provided, in order to be able to carry out every transaction as a full ACID transaction or eventually consistent transaction, depending on the type of application and programming procedures implemented.

The latest version of Oracle NoSQL Database has introduced "time-to-live," the important feature in terms of support to the IoT world. The system now deals with automating outdated data by itself, either by deleting them or taking them off-line after the expiration of the specified time. Data search by various properties is provided through secondary indexes, which (together with SQL support) has brought the world of the NoSQL paradigm closer to the community of the relational data world. At the time of this writing,

Oracle has announced the forthcoming launch of the NoSQL Database Cloud service, with implemented export/import solutions for easy migration from existing solutions.

HYBRID SOLUTIONS

Software solutions that require using relational and NoSQL database concepts together find their biggest obstacle in the diversity of programming languages and interfaces for data manipulation on the NoSQL side. Development of the NoSQL market has resulted in a growing number of solutions that offer various data-organization models and data-management APIs. Nonportability of applications and data as a result of this heterogeneity has led to attempts to define common APIs for various NoSQL products. Other solutions introduce an overlay into the communication architecture, which reduces communication with various concepts to the SQL communication known to the majority of the programming community. Here are presented these efforts through the models for HBase (Vilaça, Cruz, Pereira & Oliveira, 2013) and F1 (Shute et al., 2012) databases. However, in terms of integrating the two concepts, the model that presents SQL as the universal solution seems to be powerful (Lawrence, 2014). All that lead to a decision that the Unity model can be used in testing hybrid solution.

Standardization Attempts

The concept of Bridge Query Language (BQL) is one of the attempts in interface standardization (Curé, Hecht, Le Duc & Lamolle, 2012). Proposed integration system is based on few premises. The first is that targeted data scheme should be based on a standard relational model in order to provide support for big SQL community. The second premise is that data could be managed either by a relational or NoSQL database of any type (column, document or key-value pairs). The third premise is that between the data source and the targeted scheme is meta layer with mapping language which takes into consideration denormalization nature of NoSQL database. Key integration element is BQL which translate SQL queries into vendor specific native API NoSQL requests. Curé et al. (2012) presented prototype which uses document (MongoDB) and column-family (Cassandra) database.

The other authors (Bugiotti, Cabibbo, Atzeni & Torlone, 2014) were trying to standardize NoSQL database design regardless of vendor. Their efforts were based on NoAM (NoSQL Abstract Model) model considering the fact that different NoSQL models share some common modeling features. Their goal was to define unique data presentation model independent of NoSQL vendor respecting principles of scalability, consistency, and performance. The main emphasis was put on aggregates, mutually related groups of application data, with the intention to present them as atomic units of data suitable for vendor specific ways of aggregate data.

One of the attempts to define a common API for interface standardization resulted in "the SOS platform" (Atzeni, Bugiotti & Rossi, 2014). Interestingly, the name of the platform (SOS - Save Our Systems) is indicative of the whole aspiration of the programming community to overcome the problems inherent in the NoSQL environment. The authors start from the assumption that modern systems, like social networks, require web-size scalability and flexibility in the data structure. In this connection, operations on data are extremely simple and do not require a strict form of consistency. Atzeni et al. define SOS as "a programming environment where non-relational databases can be uniformly defined, queried and accessed by an application program" (Atzeni, Bugiotti & Rossi, 2014, p.2). In implementing this concept, the platform applies two layers between the application and NoSQL databases: Meta-layer and Common Interface (Figure 1).

The Meta-layer generalizes data structures by relativizing concepts of any of the underlying NoSQL DBMS systems. The example includes the Redis, MongoDB, and HBase databases, not precluding the use of any other relational or NoSQL database. The generalization is based on the theoretical possibility of representing any data model through a collection of structures, a set of constraints, and a set of operations that can be executed on them. This concept is applied to three different data-organization types. *The key-value* organization is specific to Redis. In this data organization, each key is connected to a unique value from the collection. Different types of data and a set of basic operations on them are supported. Based on the *document* organization, MongoDB stores data in JSON-like structures, and has a strong set of operations for manipulation at the document level or the level of individual fields. HBase, also previously described, is based on a flexible organization of *records*, making it possible for tables to have unlimited numbers of columns that can be organized into column families.

Figure 1. The SOS platform
Atzeni et al., 2014.

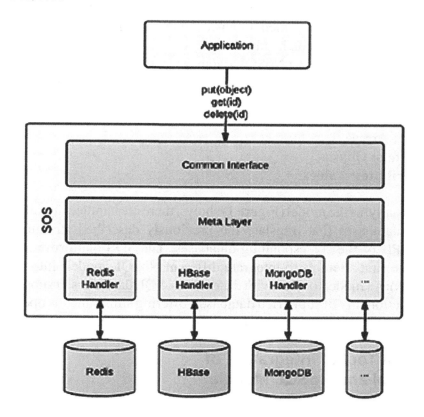

SOS uses three elements to generalize the heterogeneity of the specified data models: Struct, Set, and Attribute. Combining these elements provides an abstraction of a collection of objects characterized by the nested structure.

Set is an instance of any NoSQL database, and the instance itself can be represented as a *Set* collection. Every collection consists of one or more objects uniquely identified by a key within a collection. For example, an instance of the database is represented by Set in the observed HBase database. Since the database consists of tables, each table represents a *Set*. Key-value pairs or table columns are represented by attributes. Column families are represented by *Structs*. A similar structure applies to MongoDB at the level of the database, and collections that are equivalent to tables in HBase. The *set* represents documents, and *Attributes* represent key-value pairs.

The Common Interface part of the platform is represented by Java API. Its primary class is NonRelationalManager that supports the put, get, set, and delete methods for management of basic operations on data of the supported databases. These methods handle Java objects and are responsible for their serialization into the target NoSQL database, and the entire process is based on meta-layer structures. The meta-layer is implemented in JSON through the following mapping:

- **Sets:** Arrays.
- **Structs:** Objects.
- **Attributes:** Values.

Eventually, as the model (Figure 1) shows, there are handlers for individual NoSQL databases that translate the previously described structures into native APIs of the corresponding databases. The SOS platform represents one of the first attempts to integrate different NoSQL models into a single programmer's model to work with different NoSQL databases. It supports the basic functionality of supported databases, offering simultaneous operability of multiple databases, acknowledging all the specifics of their data models.

SQL as a Tool of Integration of Relational and NoSQL Models

Data extraction and manipulation of all relational database systems are based on the unique standard of the structured query language SQL. Its implementations vary slightly among RDBMS producers. Acceptance of the standard by producers allowed integration of various databases and brought the developer community to a situation that it is almost the same which relational database product they will use. Countless numbers of software projects are built on this proposition. Limitations of relational databases resulted in the appearance of the NoSQL system, which does not have a standard such as SQL offers. Interaction with databases is reduced to the use of specific APIs for each database. This reduces the portability of NoSQL systems and requires highly complex coding.

Most NoSQL systems never supported SQL, even in their basic functionality. SQL is highly valuable for a number of reasons. Primarily, it provides data portability between various relational databases. In its core, it consists of simple English sentences that make understandable structures for data definition, manipulation, and control. The base of experts and users of SQL is huge. NoSQL system evaluation processes have recognized its importance, so some producers have introduced some of its segments in their data-management processors. Certain attempts are made to standardize data view and to build common APIs for access to various NoSQL databases, on the basis of standardization ideas established by SQL. Still, SQL offers itself as a universal solution to ensure a single interface for access to and integration of the relational and NoSQL worlds. Some of the attempts of developer and scientific communities to offer solutions for integration through SQL are:

- Distributed Query Language (DQE)
- F1
- Unity

Distributed Query Language

Vilaça et al. (2012) consider a situation where NoSQL databases are becoming increasingly interesting for implementations in various types of applications already developed based on RDBMS, or yet to be developed. In their paper, Vilaça et al. (2012) present the *DQE-distributed query engine* as a platform to execute SQL queries on NoSQL databases, while keeping their data-model scalability and flexibility. DQE represents a strong concept that will combine scalability and flexibility of NoSQL schemas with the expressiveness of SQL. Further, they show how simple key-value operations and the associated data model can be mapped into SQL structures, and describe a full implementation of the model on the HBase database using Apache Derby's query engine. Figure 2 shows the DQE architecture.

Building the concept of the platform, the authors start from the internal RDBMS architecture. They divide it into two blocks at the highest level: *query processor block* and *storage manager block*. Their intention is to keep and use the existing components and add new ones that would cover the specifics of NoSQL databases. Query processor takes over SQL requests from applications, compiles them, translates them into a code understandable to database storage, and sends them for execution. The part of components taken over from Apache Derby's query engine remains unchanged. JDBC driver, as the component that provides interaction with the application at the highest level with the database, does not change. Connection handler manages connections established between the application and DQE, and it

Figure 2. Distributed query engine architecture
Vilaça et al., 2012.

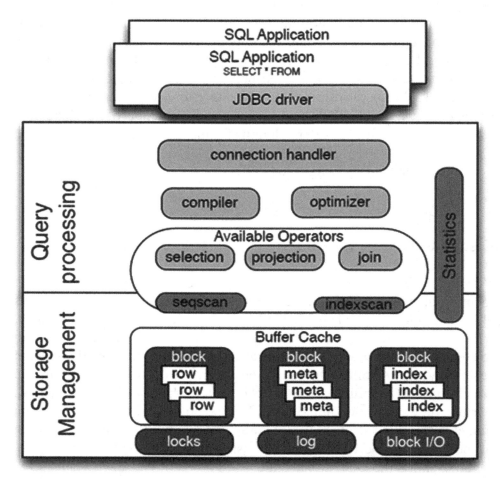

is also used in the original form. Compiler and optimizer also remain the same, as does the logic for implementation of generic relational operators of selection, projection, and join. This ensures a unique and unchanged interface for programmers of the intermediate layer, regardless of the addition of the NoSQL database in the business layer on which DQE rests.

Two groups of components are changed in the original Derby's Apache engine. The first is responsible for mapping the relational model into the NoSQL model, and the other for implementation of sequential and index-scan operators. DQE uses simple mapping of relational components into HBase tables. The relational primary key is mapped to HBase row's key. All relational columns are mapped into one column family of the HBase table, and each individual, relational column is mapped to a column of the HBase table. All columns of the HBase table have a corresponding column of the relational table. The absence of a column in a row of the HBase table is assumed as a NULL value of the corresponding column in the relational table. Additional HBase tables represent unique and nonunique secondary indexes.

Two new operators are added for implementation of sequential and index-scan operators in Derby's set of generic relational operators. They are based on the index and filter functionalities of the HBase database, and they minimize aggregate data-extraction processes and amount of data that is processed per corresponding SQL request. Join and aggregation operators, normally unsupported by the basic HBase architecture, are thus implemented through the DQE architecture. In order to provide this functionality in the HBase database, the authors had to implement the data order native to the natural data type in the relational database. Here, natural data type means (for example) the date or number data type. Data are naturally arranged in descending or ascending order, in accordance with the data type in the relational data model. Data types are unknown to the NoSQL model of the HBase database. A key column of the HBase database is a plain byte array, and it does not know anything about data order. SQE finds the solution to the problem in mapping the natural data order into plain byte values of HBase table keys, by implementing the mapping for integer, decimal, char, varchar, and date data types. If a key consisting of several columns is involved, concatenating the corresponding plain byte values carries out implementation.

The proposed DQE model architecture provides NoSQL model scalability. All DML operations are performed without interdependence of DQE instances. At the same time, all the options of the SQL philosophy and the related relational data model are available through conversion of user queries into simple put, get, scan, and delete operations at the level of HBase.

F1

Google's response to the demands of modern web applications is realized through the project F1. This hybrid database emerged as a solution to the problems with MySQL database, which, with the expansion of the AdWords business, became a functional bottleneck. The project team (Shute et al., 2012) defined the following development assumptions:

- **Scalability:** The system must be scalable in a way that simple expansion is achieved only by adding new resources.
- **Availability:** F1 must be available at all times, and downtimes of the system are not allowable because it drives Google's core business.
- **Consistency:** F1 must offer ACID properties characteristic of the relational paradigm.
- **Usability:** F1 must provide full SQL functionality.

The assumptions are only seemingly mutually exclusive, integrating the best properties of the relational and NoSQL models. The Internet giant does not recognize this exclusiveness of set development objectives and, in 2012, put the F1 database into production, using it for the Internet marketing business. The hybrid database product integrates the best aspects of the two paradigms on the basis of Spanner (Corbett et al., 2012). Spanner is yet another database developed in the Google kitchen. It features a high degree of scalability, global distribution, and strict consistency, along with synchronous data replication. Google's development team added to the F1 system a number of new features, creating the environment that serves hundreds of applications with hundreds of thousands of requests per second, on data hundreds of TB in size.

The global architecture (Figure 3) places *F1 Client library* as the communication entry point. It receives requests for actions on data and forwards them to *Load Balancer*. Since this is a distributed database, this component decides which server it will address. It will certainly look first for the closest server; in case that server is inactive or overloaded, it sends the request to the next available server. The task of the balancer is a quick and regular assignment of requests, to minimize extended response time such that the user would not significantly notice. An individual Engine of the F1 server organizes realization of data read and write requests by communicating with the Spanner database of the corresponding server or sending the request to another server in the distribution chain. Each of the Spanner servers communicates exclusively with its Colossus File System (CFS). *Slave Pool* and *Master* components support distributed SQL queries. Slave Pool consists of processes responsible for the execution of the distributed part of the SQL query, while monitoring and management of these processes are the task of Master. Master communicates with individual F1 servers, providing the list of available Slaves. For efficient processing of large MapReduce requests, direct communication of individual Slave processes with the Spanner database is enabled as well.

Figure 3. F1 architecture
Shute et al., 2012.

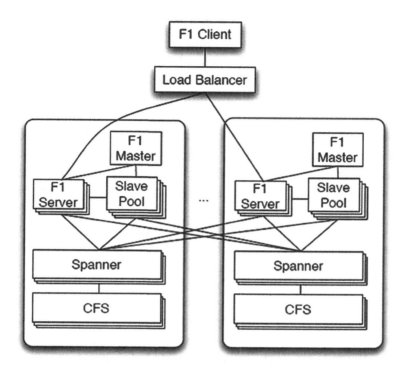

Scalability of this architecture is clearly recognizable by the independence of individual components. F1 Server does not have data; therefore it is possible to add new servers to increase the throughput of the system. The situation is the same with the Slave Pool organization, which can be expanded to provide an increase in the number of processes for the realization of distributed SQL queries and MapReduce requests. Since Spanner is responsible for keeping data, adding a new server provides data redistribution without compromising the existing processes of the entire system. Redistribution is transparent to F1 Servers, and thereby to F1 Clients as well.

Synchronous replication to data centers that are geographically dispersed causes a relatively high latency period in relation to standards of relational databases. Google solves this problem by defining new behavioral patterns on the client side in interaction with the database. It introduces an entirely new set of APIs through which it promotes the use of a parallel and asynchronous approach to data reading, and all this is provided by a new data-organization concept. NoSQL and SQL interfaces are available to Google's developer community for appropriate use. Standard SQL structures are expanded by additional functionalities, aimed at supporting new data organization. An excellent thing is a possibility of joining Spanner's data with external data like BigTable or CSV sources. Given all this, it can be concluded that the powerful Google has provided its own solution, assuming the right to take over the desired functionalities from two different worlds and add a number of innovative solutions that will ensure implementation.

The F1 data model is similar to the classic relational data organization. A view of the basic structure of the model (Figure 4) shows expansion of the initial model through an explicit hierarchy of tables, and the introduction of the Protocol Buffer data type. The relational tables in the same-named data organization have a separate physical implementation, and substantial resources are used just to connect them when extracting data and storing, while checking referential integrity rules. To simplify these operations, the F1 model introduces a *cluster* structure in which it physically stores related data. The logic behind the creation of clusters is very simple. *A cluster* contains rows from various tables that are in a direct relation. Each cluster consists of one *root* row and rows that are in a direct relation with it. The example taken over from Shute et al. (2012) presents a cluster with the root row from the Customer table, as well as rows from the Campaign table and AdGroup tables subordinated to it. Each child row is right below its parent record, while all records are arranged by the primary key order. It is important that data of one cluster be located in the Spanner directory structure that is physically located on a single Spanner server.

Figure 4. Example of the F1 model compared to relational model
Shute et al., 2012.

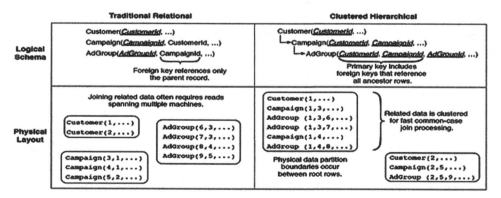

Another important feature of the model is the Protocol Buffer data type. Clusters solve the issue of allocation of related data at the table level. Protocol Buffer allows storage of structured data types within an individual table column, but also nesting of Protocol Buffers themselves. Its application allows the use of *repeated fields* structures. This feature reduces the need for multiple child tables and increases the performance of the F1 engine in data-extraction processes. On the Spanner side, Protocol Buffer represents a physical unit for data storage, implemented through a blob structure. The same structure can be used on the client side, where the user sees it as a separate atomic business object. This structure provides the user with the abstraction of the business world, programmed without a need to connect a series of tables that will represent the same object in the relational world.

UNITY

Lawrence (2014) considered DQE-like solutions to connect the relational and NoSQL worlds and found a solution in SQL, which provided a theoretical foundation for the system called Unity. Unity is a generalizable integration and virtualization system based on SQL interface. According to Lawrence, the key features of the system are (Lawrence, 2014):

- Unity uses a SQL query processor and optimizer that include support for push-down filters and cross-source hash joins.
- Unity has a SQL dialect translator that brings different SQL dialects of relational-database vendors to the same form.
- Unity has a SQL-form to NoSQL APIs translator, and operators not supported by native NoSQL database APIs are performed using the Unity virtualization engine.
- Unity offers a mapping of SQL functions into appropriate forms supported by various vendors of relational and NoSQL databases.
- Unity provides data virtualization allowing queries and joins across relational and NoSQL data sources.

Lawrence (2014) refers to previous research and papers in this field, mentioning among others the previously described *SOS Platform*, which provided integration of various NoSQL systems with a single system of APIs. He emphasizes that the deficit of these solutions is their orientation on a single data architecture. In this respect, Unity represents a good concept for the developer community and SQL-based solutions. It offers compatibility with existing SQL solutions and new ones being developed by the developer community, based on the SQL standard. At the same time, it offers the possibility of using the appropriate data-organization philosophy that meets the needs and requirements that applications bring to developer teams. Unity provides an answer to growing needs of web applications for simultaneous use of NoSQL and relational systems.

The concept on which Unity is based is intriguing. In terms of portability, it opens the possibility of switching between various NoSQL systems in a way that only relational systems could. The declarative syntax of the SQL language keeps the logic of relational systems, hiding the logics of various data-organization methods of corresponding NoSQL solutions. All knowledge and experience developed on countless SQL-based projects are now usable. It is possible to extract certain parts of these projects for which the relational paradigm was inappropriate, and place them into NoSQL solutions. Unity also offers a kind of extension of the NoSQL system, by implementing unsupported operators through its virtualization engine. It seems that this architecture allows the use of the best of the two philosophies, using the interface most appropriate for most of the developer community.

At the time of this writing, Unity (Unity, 2017) as a commercial product is available on the market of JDBC drivers. It supports Oracle, MySQL, SQL Server, and any relational JDBC data source. On the NoSQL side, it supports the MongoDB database. Unity features support for the Quandl (Quandl, 2017) marketplace for financial and economic data, ServiceNow (ServiceNow, 2017), and the Splunk (Splunk, 2017) platform for real-time operational intelligence. JDBC API interface is at the highest level of the architecture (Figure 5). It communicates with *Parser* and *Translator* in the next layers, passing to them the SQL query passed from Java application code. The *parser* supports the SQL sentence syntax based on the SQL-92 standard. It generates a parse tree that Translator converts into a relational operator tree while validating relational data source (relational schema). The NoSQL part is passed to the NoSQL engine without this validation. Schema Generator generates a schema for the corresponding NoSQL model and keeps it in the NoSQL database. *Query Optimizer* passes the execution to the database layer while maximizing the use of corresponding database engines. Special techniques are developed for the needs of joins across the two data concepts, and they proved efficient in benchmark tests. The operation of the optimizer is based on the idea of sending parts of the requested query's execution logic

Figure 5. Unity architecture
Lawrence, 2014.

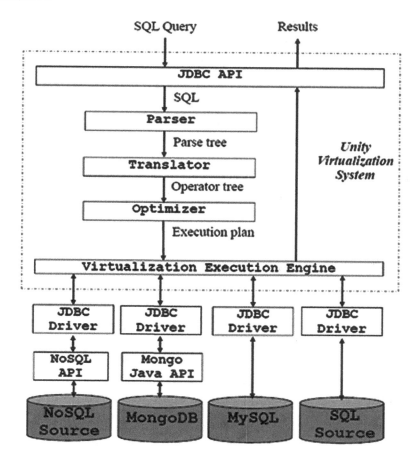

to the source database, if it supports execution through its native functionality. Other parts of the logic are executed in the system's virtualization engine. Execution Engine has implementations of the execution logic of all relational operators, in case the data spans different sources. *JDBC MongoDB driver* converts SQL queries to the native API of this database. Another important feature of the entire architecture is *Function and Dialect Translator*, whose role is to map function calls and SQL dialects, reducing their use to a unified syntax. Mapping rules are stored in the virtualization engine database. The absence of mapping in the database for a function or a part of SQL structure means that the particular functionality is not implemented in Unity.

REDUCING TO ONE OPTION: RELATIONAL OR NoSQL

Efforts of producers of DBMS systems to satisfy the developer community and market demands have resulted in the recent real expansion of functionalities that have brought the two separated worlds considerably close together. One big difference that identified the paradigms (SQL and NoSQL) is overcome by adding the SQL interface in the standard set of functionalities in many NoSQL DBMSs. ACID and BASE concepts come close together. NoSQL databases add the ACID functionality, while SQL databases provide tuning of the consistency functionality by implementing greater scalability. Shifts in data modeling are obvious in previous examples. Thus, particular NoSQL systems support tabular organization, and SQL databases support document-like organization. Entire application sets in various industries are migrated from RDBMS to NoSQL DBMS on these technical grounds (Table 7). Possibilities offered to the developer community (Hill, 2016) lead to the conclusion that the question is no longer which of the two worlds to select (because boundaries between them gradually disappear), but rather which data organization to choose in terms of application requirements. The selection should offer the best performance and ensure data quality.

Considering the conclusion that the physical database design boils down to the requirement for best performance, Hill (2016) specifies *scalability, indexing, and correctness* as the key factors in reaching desired performance. The scalability issue requires selecting an appropriate trade-off between the

Table 7. Examples of migration of RDBMS to MongoDB (taken from RDBMS to MongoDB Migration Guide, 2016)

Organization	Migrated From	Application
eHarmony	Oracle and Postgres	Customer Data Management and Analytics
Shutterfly	Oracle	Web and Mobile Services
Cisco	Multiple RDBMS	Analytics, Social Networking
Craigslist	MySQL	Archive
Under Armour	Microsoft SQL Server	eCommerce
Foursquare	PostgreSQL	Social, Mobile Networking Platforms
MTV Networks	Multiple RDBMS	Centralized Content Management
Buzzfeed	MySQL	Real-Time Analytics
Verizon	Oracle	Single View, Employee Systems
The Weather Channel	Oracle and MySQL	Mobile Networking Platform

ACID and BASE concepts, respecting database dimensioning (data quantity and number of users), and using the CAP theorem as a guide. Indexing features of a database engine should offer the possibility of indexing on all fields on which search conditions would be set while allowing for resources required by the indexes. *Correctness* concerns the stage of logical modeling of the data model and its correctness, in order for the appropriate implementation to provide quick responses, but also simple modification or expansion of the data structure without affecting system performance. Assumptions of the translation of a RDBMS model to a NoSQL model using MongoDB, as well as the functionalities that Oracle has built into its RDBMS to support the functionalities of the NoSQL world, are presented below.

RDBMS to MongoDB

In June 2016, the MongoDB community issued a white paper that presented assumptions and best practices for migration of a relational data organization onto their database. It requires making a number of decisions and designing many solutions specific to each application or data model. Furthermore, all stakeholders must be involved, beginning with architects of the data model and applications at the lowest level, and ending with product owners at the highest business level. The complex migration procedure is divided into three stages: the first concerns data schema design, followed by application integration, and finally the data migration itself.

The most important stage of the migration procedure is *data modeling*. The task is to transfer the model implemented through relational tables into a document-based model. As described in the section that briefly presented features of the MongoDB database, tables of the relational model are represented by collections, and table rows are represented by documents. The NoSQL paradigm replaces table normalization and complex JOIN actions with embedded documents or document references. Of course, it would be possible to make a simple mapping of tables into collections and rows into documents, but this would practically negate all the advantages that the document-based NoSQL database offers. A relational model could be implemented in many ways, but it should be noted that design should be based primarily on application requirements. The relational model that the developer community largely used in past decades is often complex in practice and contains dozens of relational tables for the simplest problems. The document model simplifies this organization and gives it a much more natural and intuitive form. The model from Table 1 is expanded by the data on vehicle registrations and technical controls and simplified for purposes of presentation.

The relational model (Figure 6) contains five tables. In the derived model, the entire structure is placed in a single document (Vehicle) with associated embedded documents (Vehicle.Registration and Vehicle.Registration. TechnicalControl). The focus is on a vehicle with its registration data, and every registration is accompanied by data on conducted technical controls. It is evident from this data organization that a single read operation can access the entire document, and the document itself is stored in a single object in the storage system. The entire object is part of a single physical node, which ensures horizontal data scalability or data distribution across multiple nodes. Full denormalization in the above example is not always the appropriate transformation model. For example, analytical applications require data aggregation, and a normalized model is appropriate.

Figure 6. Relational and document data model

RELATIONAL MODEL

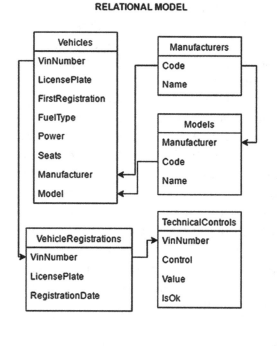

DOCUMENT MODEL

Similar to the relational model, normalization is conducted by splitting collections, and referencing is conducted by using the *id* attribute. MongoDB advises referencing in the following cases (MongoDB, 2017):

- When embedding does not offer satisfactory performance when reading data implicated in data duplication.
- When an object is referenced by different objects.
- When it is necessary to model complex many-to-many relationships or large hierarchical data sets.

The Aggregation Framework through pipeline processes and the $lookup functionality connect referenced data and perform data aggregation, thereby offering the relational-model users functionalities similar to those they had, admittedly much easier to obtain by SQL queries in the first place. For data extraction, MongoDB developed indexing options at a similar level to relational products. The following indexing functionalities are supported (MongoDB, 2017):

- **Compound Indexes:** Query engine performs database search using a combination of several indexes, depending on the values of attributes that define the filter.
- **Unique indexes:** Through the use of these indexes, MongoDB controls uniqueness of records in collections.
- **Array Indexes:** Columns containing arrays can be indexed. This is a powerful mechanism for querying such data, which significantly improves database search performance.
- **Time to Live Indexes:** These indexes are responsible for document lifetime, and ensure removal of expired data from the database.
- **Geospatial Indexes:** These indexes provide fast and efficient querying of two-dimensional space when storing geolocations within a database. With associated functions of MongoDB APIs that rely on stored geospatial data, they optimize queries related to locations.
- **Sparse Indexes:** This index type is used on fields that are attributes of only a certain number of documents in a collection, or that are not part of all documents. These indexes support and optimize querying of documents by these attributes.
- **Partial Indexes:** In addition to the attribute indexed, these indexes can be additionally restricted to a certain number of documents that satisfy a given criterion, defined when creating the index.

The second stage of migration is related to *application integration*. In the relational model, SQL is the integration element between the application and the database. The NoSQL world communicates through APIs or methods implemented in various programming languages. MongoDB's ecosystem supports a number of drivers for more than 30 of today's most popular programming languages. The previous sections presented some hybrid solutions that offer SQL as the connection between the program and the database layer, or as the base well known to the developer community from the relational world. MongoDB has provided BI Connector as a connection with a number of BI tools that have been traditionally used with relational database products. A number of producers of BI solutions have also developed connectors for MongoDB, and allowed the possibility of extracting data from this NoSQL database, providing analytical and predictive possibilities on semi-structured and unstructured data.

Still, in terms of programming, important relational-database functionalities responsible for the scenario of migration to the NoSQL world relate to the transactional data integrity observed through the ACID principle, and provision of data validations and constraints. MongoDB has offered solutions for the transactional model of system behavior. At the level of individual documents, write operations fully satisfy the ACID principle, and appropriate ways to handle multi-document transactions are also available. At the level of the primary server, MongoDB provides strong consistency; at the level of replications, it provides eventual consistency. In most cases, data validation is conducted at the level of the relational DBMS product's engine, which ensures easy maintenance of data quality without special programming. MongoDB provides validation at the database level through several internal mechanisms. The feature Document Validation provides the administrator the possibility of ensuring checks at the levels of document structure, data type, ranges of the date component of data, and mandatory data. Previously mentioned indexing possibilities can also be used to set a part of validation rules on data and provide transfer of these controls from the program code to the database level.

The last stage, *data migration*, can be performed for simple cases by transforming the relational dataset into the JSON format and then importing the JSON data using the *mongoimport* tool. More complex application and database systems require more complex migration procedures. They cannot be performed easily and at one time. These are mostly the cases involving multiple application systems on a relational database, and not all of them are transferred to versions that support the NoSQL paradigm; or cases where only some new functionalities involve the use of the NoSQL database. Such situations require incremental migrations, securing both data worlds until the full transformation of the application part of the system migrated from the relational to the NoSQL world. There are a number of ETL tools from independent producers that support such migrations.

Examining the approach and functionalities that MongoDB offers makes much easier the relational developer community's decision to migrate and use the NoSQL functionalities that today's application world requires.

NoSQL and Oracle RDBMS

As of Version 12c, Oracle RDBMS has added to the database engine full support for work with the JSON data notation. JSON stores textual data in the form of key-value pairs, and was originally developed for JavaScript. Today, it is supported in almost all major programming languages for development of web applications and is usually used as the communication model between the application business layer and REST web services. It is important to note that support for JSON is integrated into all other functionalities of the ORACLE RDBMS engine, such as SQL and Analytics. The functionality made available to the developer community is briefly presented through:

- Creation of tables that store JSON data.
- Data extraction.
- Identification of columns.
- Dot notation query transformation.

JSON documents are stored within VARCHAR2, CLOB, or BLOB columns. An example is the relational table Vehicles. The syntax for creating a table that will store this JSON document structure is presented in Example 7.

Example 7

```
CREATE TABLE vehicle_documents
(
  id    RAW(16) NOT NULL,
  data  CLOB,
  CONSTRAINT vehicle_documents_pk PRIMARY KEY (id),
  CONSTRAINT vehicle_documents_is_json_ok CHECK (data IS JSON)
);
```

Table records are uniquely identified by the primary key *id*. The content of the table (JSON documents) is stored in the CLOB column *data*. A check constraint that verifies the validity of JSON document structure on every insert and update operation is set at the table level. Insert of data is provided by a combination of the known DML syntax and JSON notation (Example 8).

Example 8

```
INSERT INTO vehicle_documents (id, data)
VALUES
(
  SYS_GUID(),
'{
"Vin": "JC1234567890A",
"LicensePlate": "A450123",
  "Manufacturer": {
"Code": "M01",
  "Name": "Volkswagen"
  },
"Model": {
    "Code": "T0101",
"Name": "Passat"
},
  "FirstRegistration": "01-APR-2016",
"FuelType": "Lpg",
  "Power": "177",
"Seats": "5"
}'
);
```

JSON data are available through SQL queries using the dot notation syntax. In Example 9 is presented such simple query.

Example 9

```
SELECT d.data.Vin "VIN Number",
       d.data.LicensePlate "License Plate",
       d.data.Manufacturer.Name "Manufacturer",
       d.data.Model.Name "Model",
       d.data.FirstRegistration "First Registration"
  FROM vehicle_documents d
 WHERE d.data.Vin = 'JC1234567890A';
```

Conditional operators are used within SQL for verification of JSON content. The operator *IS JSON* is used within the specified syntax to create a table that is not mandatory if the formed CLOB column will not contain JSON documents anyway. In such a case, this condition could be used to select rows that contain or do not contain JSON documents, and thus perform desired operations on them. There are two more JSON conditions: *JSON_EXISTS* and *JSON_TEXTCONTAINS*. The first returns the logical value true if there is a JSON path within the document; the second returns the same value if the queried text string is found in JSON property values.

For complex extraction of JSON data from a relational table, ORACLE RDBMS offers the functions *JSON_VALUE, JSON_QUERY,* and *JSON_TABLE. JSON_QUERY* finds value in a JSON document and returns only scalar values as strings. For the case of attempted extraction of complex structures (e.g., an array), execution of this SQL engine function will return an error. The Example 10 illustrates the use of JSON_VALUE functions.

Example 10

```
SELECT
  JSON_VALUE(d.data,'$.Vin') "VIN Number",
  JSON_VALUE(d.data,'$.LicensePlate')"License Plate",
  JSON_VALUE(d.data,'$.Manufacturer.Name') "Manufacturer",
  JSON_VALUE(d.data,'$.Model.Name') "Model",
  JSON_VALUE(d.data,'$.FirstRegistration') "First Registration"
 FROM vehicle_documents d
 WHERE d.data.Vin = 'JC1234567890A';
```

The JSON_QUERY function returns a complete segment of a JSON document that can consist of one or more values. Thus, in the Example 11 is presented a query that would return VIN number and producer data for the requested vehicle.

Example 11

```
SELECT JSON_VALUE(d.data,'$.Vin') "VIN Number",
  JSON_QUERY(d.data,'$.Manufacturer') "Manufacturer"
FROM vehicle_documents d
WHERE d.data.Vin = 'JC1234567890A';
```

The JSON_TABLE function is interesting and comprises the functionalities of the previously described functions. It can be used to present JSON document structure in the form of a relational table, and facilitate queries. Thus, for the table vehicle_documents, it would be possible to create a view that would allow easy formation of queries without knowing the JSON structure of the document (Example 12).

Example 12

```
CREATE VIEW v_vehicle_documents AS
SELECT d.vin_number,
       d.license_plate,
       d.manufacturer_code,
       d.manufacturer_name,
       d.model_code,
       d.model_name,
       to_date(d.first-reg,'dd-mon-yyyy'),
       d.fuel_type
       d.power,
       d.seats
FROM   vehicle_documents,
       JSON_TABLE(data, '$'
           COLUMNS (vin     VARCHAR2(50 CHAR) PATH '$.Vin',
license_plate       VARCHAR2(50 CHAR) PATH '$.LicensePlate',
manufacturer_code VARCHAR2(50 CHAR) PATH '$.Manufacturer.Code',
manufacturer_name VARCHAR2(100 CHAR) PATH '$.Manufacturer.
Name',
model_codeVARCHAR2(50 CHAR) PATH '$.Model.Code',
model_nameVARCHAR2(100 CHAR) PATH '$.Model.Name',
first_regVARCHAR2(50 CHAR) PATH '$.FirstRegistration',
fuel_typeVARCHAR2(50 CHAR) PATH '$.FuelType',
powerVARCHAR2(50 CHAR) PATH '$.Power',
seatsVARCHAR2(50 CHAR) PATH '$.Seats') d;
```

Table 8.

Vin Number	Manufacturer
JC1234567890A	{"Code": "M01","Name": "Volkswagen"}

Oracle provided support to efficient and fast queries through indexing JSON data. Users can use Function-base, B*Tree, Bitmap, and JSON Search indexes. Maintaining indexes is a very demanding database function, and any decision on creation of indexes should be carefully considered. If the resource cost in maintaining an index is much higher than the help it provides in executing queries, then its existence is not justified. There are a number of factors to be taken into account, including (Oracle_JSON, 2017):

- Experience shows most indexes on JSON data are function-based indexes. The resource cost of their maintenance is much higher than in conventional B*Tree indexes.
- JSON document size plays an important role. Larger documents require more resources for maintenance of indexes.
- Full-text indexes and bitmap indexes in their primary functionality are highly resource intensive. As such, these indexes are not intended for frequently changing JSON data.

Having analyzed only part of the functionalities in Oracle's main database product that bring the relational world closer to the NoSQL world, the relational world seems to provide good and fast answers to NoSQL challenges. Arguments that the relational world is dying away seem groundless. The world of relational data is adapting to the challenges of the time and the requirements of modern applications. It is expanding its basic functionality with a rich set of functionalities that help Oracle to remain a leader in the database market.

REFERENCES

Atzeni, P., Bugiotti, F., & Rossi, L. (2014). *Uniform access to non-relational database systems: The SOS platform.* Paper presented at the 24th International Conference, CAiSE 2012, Gdansk, Poland. Retrieved February 20 from http://www.inf.uniroma3.it/~atzeni/psfiles/CAiSE2012Atzeni.pdf

Bembach, D. (2014). *Benchmarking eventually consistent distributed storage systems.* KIT Scientific Publishing. Retrieved February 20 from https://books.google.ba/books?id=7rQVBAAAQBAJ

BSON. (2017). Retrieved July 15, 2017 from http://bsonspec.org/

Bugiotti, F., Cabibbo, L., Atzeni, P., & Torlone, R. (2014). *Database design for NoSQL systems* (Technical Report). Universita degli studi Roma.

Codd, E. F. (1970). A relational model of data for large shared data banks. *Commun. ACM, 13*(6), 377-387. DOI:10.1145/362384.362685

Corbett, J. C., Dean, J., Epstein, M., Fikes, A., Frost, C., Furman, J. J., & Hsieh, W. (2013). Spanner: Googles globally distributed database. *ACM Transactions on Computer Systems, 31*(3), 8. doi:10.1145/2518037.2491245

Curé, O., Hecht, R., Le Duc, C., & Lamolle, M. (2011). Data integration over NoSQL stores using access path based mappings. In Lecture Notes in Computer Science: Vol. 6860. DEXA 2012 (pp. 481-495). Berlin: Springer. doi:10.1007/978-3-642-23088-2_36

Hills, T. (2016). *NoSQL and SQL data modeling – Bringing together data, semantics, and software* (1ˢᵗ ed.). Technics Publications.

Lawrence, R. (2014). Integration and virtualization of relational SQL and NoSQL systems including MySQL and MongoDB. *International Conference on Computational Science and Computational Intelligence*, 285-290. doi:10.1109/CSCI.2014.56

MongoDB. (2017). *MongoDB manual 3.4.* Retrieved June 23, 2017 from https://docs.mongodb.com/manual/meta/pdfs/

Oracle_JSON. (2017). *JSON in Oracle database.* Retrieved February 5, 2017 from http://docs.oracle.com/database/122/ADJSN/json-in-oracle-database. htm#ADXDB6246)

Quandl. (2017). Retrieved July 22, 2017 from www.quandl.com

ServiceNow. (2017). Retrieved July 22, 2017 from www.servicenow.com

Shute, J., Oancea, M., Ellner, S., Handy, B., Rollins, E., Samwel, B., & Tong, P. et al. (2012). F1- The fault-tolerant distributed RDBMS supporting Google's ad business. In *Proceedings of the 2012 ACM SIGMOD International Conference on Management of Data* (pp. 777–778). ACM. doi:10.1145/2213836.2213954

Splunk. (2017). Retrieved July 22, 2017 from www.splunk.com

Stonebraker, M., & Cattell, R. (2011). Ten rules for scalable performance in 'simple operation' datastores. *Commun. ACM*, 72–80. Retrieved January 12, 2017 from https://pdfs.semanticscholar.org/19fa/d669f413027d816857f2600f8040255152ce.pdf

Unity. (2017). *Unity JDBC*. Retrieved July 22, 2017 from www.unityjdbc.com

Vilaça, R., Cruz, F., Pereira, J., & Oliveira, R. (2013). *An effective scalable SQL engine for NoSQL databases*. HASLab - High-Assurance Software Laboratory, INESC TEC and Universidade do Minho Braga. doi: 10.1007/978-3-642-38541-4_12

Chapter 7

Bridging Relational and NoSQL Worlds:
Case Study

ABSTRACT

The chapter presents a real case study of the integration of relational and NoSQL databases. The example of a real project related to vehicle registration, particularly to testing vehicles for compliance with environmental standards, explains how those two worlds can be integrated. Oracle database is used as a relational database, while MongoDB is used as NoSQL database. The chapter sustains that the COMN notation can be successfully used in the process of modeling both relational and nonrelational data. All three ways of integration of relational and NoSQL databases are tested. The native solution was tested by using of native drivers for communication with Oracle and MongoDB databases. The hybrid solution used a Unity product. The reducing-to-one option, in this case, SQL, was tested on Oracle database. The capabilities of Oracle 12c database to work both with relational and nonrelational data by using SQL were tested.

INTRODUCTION

NoSQL databases proved to be ideal support to the requirements of Big Data applications for storing large amounts of unstructured data. Relational databases proved their functionality and efficiency by providing all the

DOI: 10.4018/978-1-5225-3385-6.ch007

necessary conditions for functioning of transactional systems that require data consistency. Every NoSQL system has its own API and does not support SQL and the JDBC standard. Practice often leads to situations requiring a mixture of the two systems. Their integration and building of software solutions based on the integration require taking a special approach and making an extra effort. This chapter presents a case study of a real-world solution that imposed a mix of the two data organization concepts on the set requirements. This is the case of software that supports the procedures of testing vehicles for compliance with the requirements defined by environmental standards. Data modeling and analysis of user requirements confirm the situation that requires simultaneous use of relational and NoSQL databases. Methods of connecting the two conceptually different databases were analyzed in order to obtain a single programming interface. Analysis of the case, data modeling and an example of a method aimed at connecting the two database worlds are presented below.

CASE STUDY: VEHICLE REGISTRATION

Testing vehicles for compliance with environmental standards is a usual procedure within the vehicle registration process in Bosnia and Herzegovina. Until 1 January 2017, this part of vehicle inspection was not adjusted with international standards. However, since the beginning of 2017 new rules and tests have been introduced in order to harmonize the so-called vehicle environmental tests with new legal regulations, in accordance with international standards in this field. The main purpose of the eco-testing procedure is to create preconditions on the car market to make a selection of cars that can operate in road traffic, based on specified environmental standards. One of the tasks in the process of adjusting the existing environmental tests with international, primarily European, standards was to develop the appropriate software (i.e., EcoTest software). At the beginning, the client of the software design project defined specific guidelines for its development. Some of these guidelines were used in this case study:

- EcoTest is separate software that will record all data of an environmental testing procedure.

- EcoTest needs to be designed in Web technology with development of a data model on appropriate databases, assuming that the software will use cloud-based infrastructure.
- The software should be flexible and provide a simple extension of the designed data model with structured and unstructured data.
- The software must communicate with other programs which are used in the overall vehicle registrations process, where data on the financial component of the process and final result of testing are very important.
- Based on the vehicle type, age, engine type and maximum speed, the software determines whether a vehicle needs to undergo the eco-test at all.
- The software must support communication with all measuring devices which are certified for vehicle eco-testing procedures.
- Testing of measurement results and provision of the environmental testing assessment should be carried out based on the stored limit values which the producer of the tested car provides.
- If the test produces negative results, the software should generate a recommendation to the vehicle owner to remedy these defects.
- EcoTest needs to provide the functionality of fast and simple database search by all elements of the data model and fast availability of all multimedia records related to the vehicle testing procedure.

The very process of testing vehicles for compliance with specified environmental standards is a part of the roadworthiness control when registering a motor vehicle. The procedure is conducted by specialized organizations, the so-called technical inspection stations (STPs). The procedure is initiated by a vehicle owner by bringing the car to the STP. He or she demands the procedure of technical inspection of the vehicle to be carried out. The teams who are specialized in performing these tasks identify the owner by personal documents and identify the vehicle using the vehicle identification number (VIN) tag and license plate. After the owner and the vehicle are successfully identified, the process of testing the vehicle roadworthiness and its compliance with the environmental standards of the category to which the vehicle belongs are carried out. The resulting data are recorded by the software and a bill for the services provided is issued. The STP information system analyzes the test data and, based on them, establishes roadworthiness and environmental condition of the vehicle. The test results, together with financial indicators of the transaction, are forwarded to the Agency for Identification Documents, Registers, and Data Exchange of Bosnia and Herzegovina (IDDEEA). The

IDDEEA is a data source to other state services conducting the motor vehicle registration process, but also to some other organizations that are active participants in this process (e.g. insurance companies).

The user has defined the matters that are important for the system and relevant data. The process requires a wide range of data, but, in order to simplify the presentation of the case study, it will be reduced, focused on the eco-test, and adjusted to the needs of the book. The definition of the process implies that the entities are: the vehicle owner, the vehicle, and the site where the testing is conducted. The vehicle owner is identified by using personal documents to determine single common identifier numbers (JMBG), name, family name, town, address, and home number. In addition, the vehicle owner has to provide his/her mail address and telephone. The vehicle data consist of the mentioned VIN tag, its registration mark (if the vehicle is not registered for the first time), and data on the characteristics of the vehicle and the engine (i.e., brand, model, type, production year, emission standard, fuel type). The testing site contains data on the STP: the owner's name, address, and location. Data on the environmental testing of a vehicle consist of data on testing time, vehicle, vehicle owner, STP, and test result. Financial elements of the conducted test are contained in the bill, that consists of a test identifier, bill date, bill items, and final result of the test.

CASE STUDY: DATA MODELING

The described user requirements are the basis for data modeling. Since the case study is aimed at using a concrete example to illustrate the possibility of connecting the two worlds of relational and NoSQL, COMN notation is selected for data modeling. Namely, as Chapter 3 has already illustrated, COMN notation allows to recognize real-world entities and concepts, logical modeling, and physical modeling for both relational and NoSQL databases.

Logical Data Modeling

The analysis of the real world from the perspective of the user of future software identified the real-world entities. The vehicle owner, the vehicle, and the STP are real-world objects, while the eco-test and the invoice are concepts (Figure 1). The vehicle owner demands the vehicle testing to be conducted. Therefore, the verb *demand* describes the relationship between

Figure 1. Real-world entity types in COMN EcoTest

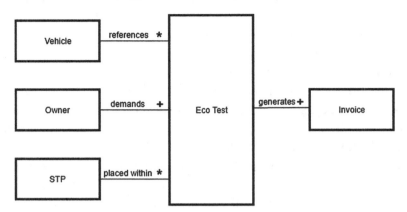

these entities. The vehicle is the subject of the testing, so this relationship is defined by the expression *be tested*. The STP conducts the vehicle testing, so the verb *conduct* is used to describe the relationship between the entities STP and eco-test. Upon a conducted testing, the STP issues an invoice for the provided services, and the verb *issue* is used for the relationship between the entities STP and invoice.

The vehicle owner can demand the eco-test to be conducted for multiple vehicles he/she owns, and multiple times during one or more calendar years. The vehicle owner appears in the system only with his/her first appearance and demands for a vehicle testing to be conducted. This is the reason why the sign + is shown on the line marking the relationship between *Owner* and *Eco-Test*. On a daily basis, following owners' demands, STPs perform their activity on vehicles which they inspect for roadworthiness and compliance with environmental standards. An individual STP can receive multiple demands to conduct environmental tests at different times. Similarly, an individual STP can exist also by not performing a single environmental testing procedure (facilities in preparation, facilities waiting for operation permit, etc.). That is why the sign * is placed on the line of the relationship *Eco-Test - STP*, specifically on the side of the *Eco-Test* entity. An individual vehicle can be subject to testing on multiple occasions, just as the description for the vehicle owner relationship indicates, but can also be within a category for which eco-testing is not conducted at all (e.g., electric drive cars). These statements imply cardinality *1 or more* on the side of the entity eco-test and

1 or 0 on the opposite side, so the relationship is marked with an asterisk on the side of *Eco-Test*.

An invoice is generated for a conducted eco-test, thereby establishing a 1:1 relationship between the two entities. Still, this relationship is reduced to 1:N for the reasons that characterize the real world in which the modeled process takes place. Namely, human error may occur while generating an invoice, then resulting invalid. After establishing a fault, it is necessary to cancel such an invoice and issue a new one. Such a simple example implies the existence of one or more invoices for a conducted eco-test, and it is also necessary to account for possible corrections of rules that would establish generation of more than one invoice for a single eco-test.

The beneficiary accepted the proposed global model with three real entities and two concepts. The next step was logical design of data needed for storage in an appropriate RDBMS. Each entity was analyzed separately and a data set was defined for each of them. Initially, each of the entities was mapped into

Figure 2. EcoTest COMN logical model

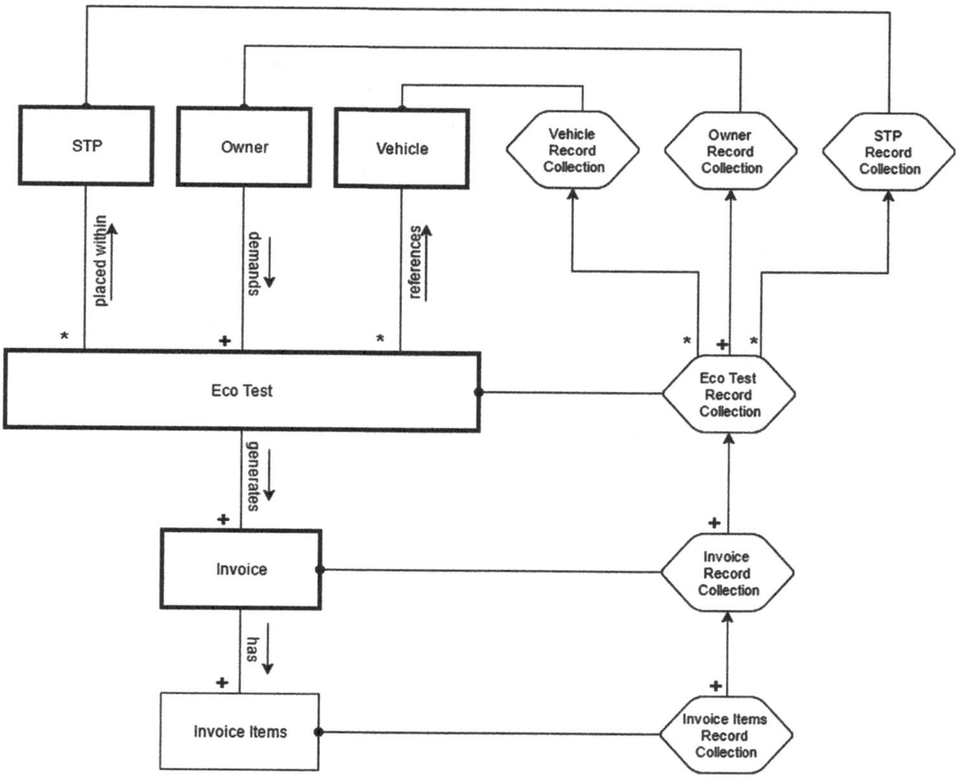

a record collection (Figure 2). This analysis established an additional entity: *Invoice Items*. The initial idea of the beneficiary was an invoice that covers all costs of an eco-test in a single amount, without additional analytics. Still, in subsequent analysis it was decided to differentiate individual elements that make up financial cost for the vehicle owner, as in the usual practice, after all. Thus, each *Entity* of the initial model (Figure 1) was mapped to *Entity Record Collection* (Figure 2).

A part of the logical data modeling procedure is to define identifiers of individual data collections. Thus, it is necessary to define data that will uniquely identify an instance of each of the collections or, more specifically, to create keys that differentiate a record of a collection from all others. Using keys, one data collection will reference another data collection.

This is still a logical interpretation of the data model, which is independent of RDBMS and the paradigm that will be used in physical modeling and storage of data. The term key, or reference, is universal and is syntax of the real world that surrounds us and that is tried to be modeled. In the next step of modeling, the presentation of real-world entities was removed from the diagram, and the presentation of record collections was left in order to more clearly define record components and mutual references (Figure 3).

Each record collection was assigned a unique identifier. The term is known from the relational theory as a *primary key*. The mark PK was placed next to this component on the diagram. The real world knows the so-called composite keys. They are characteristic of composite data types and are made up of more than one component. Since the past practice in development has shown many difficulties when using this type of key as the primary key, it was decided not to use it in modeling. The usual practice of the teams with whom the developer collaborated was to use the so-called surrogate keys, while possible composite keys were used to define *unique keys*. An example of this kind of key is the unique identifier of *Eco-Test*. An eco-test is uniquely identified by a STP identifier and an integer sequence. Still, the decision is to use a simple surrogate identifier ID whose realization would be dictated by the RDBMS chosen for data storage.

The elaboration of each individual record collection indicated additional elements of the model, noting that this is a simplified model for the purposes of this book. Vehicles are categorized primarily into predefined groups. Therefore, the type of vehicle *category* was introduced. It has three possible values: car, bus, and truck.

The next feature of the *Vehicle Record Collection* is the vehicle version according to the producer's classification. Every producer of cars defines

Figure 3. EcoTest data types with components

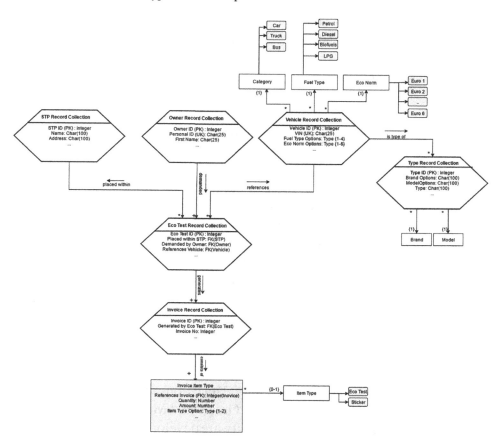

models and vehicles types within them. The new record collection *Type* is introduced, and two data types *Brand* and *Model* are defined for it.

When *Invoice Item Type* was defined, it was assumed that the owner can be billed for the testing procedure and for a sticker indicating the environmental standard and compliance with it, as proven by the test. The feature *Item Type* was added, with two possible values: *Eco Test* and *Sticker*.

Relationships between collections were established using foreign keys. They are defined by a verb that describes the relationship between collections and the sign FK. So, for example, the Eco Test collection contains the following foreign keys:

- Placed within STP: identifies the STP in which the vehicle testing is conducted.

- Demanded by Owner: identifies the owner who initiated the testing process with his/her vehicle.
- References Vehicle: identifies the vehicle being tested.

Physical Data Modeling

The analysis of the requirements raised the question on which paradigm to use when choosing the appropriate database. The relational model imposes strict limitations, defined by table design and data types. The NoSQL model provides high flexibility in the design and expansion of the data model and in the storage of binary data, such as photos, audio, and video records or specific records from measurement instruments. Data on cars are mainly standardized, but from type to type also contain rather specific data that are not simple to place in relational tables. Technological progress brings a number of new vehicle characteristics for which the structure of data model needs to be changed fairly frequently. On the other hand, information on the financial transaction of payment for the test service and data on the testing itself are clear, standardized, and explicit and, as such, convenient for the relational data model. It is on these data that further progress of the vehicle registration procedure depends, and so they require integrity and consistency based on the ACID transactional model.

The short analysis shows that a part of data belongs to the relational world and the other part to the NoSQL world. Oracle and MongoDB databases are chosen as specific DBMS systems for software development. Oracle database will be responsible for transactional data related to the financial transaction that the vehicle owner or user pays upon completion of a test and for the test result, which affects other vehicle registration processes. MongoDB database will store all other data related to the testing procedure. They include the organization conducting the testing, the vehicle, the vehicle owner, and test results.

The initial data model (Figure 4), on which tests were conducted, includes two components. The first involves the MongoDB collection with data on the conducted testing. The second component, the Oracle relational component, has tables for the storage of financial transactions and data on the validity of the conducted tests.

Tables 1 and 2 show examples of data written in notations typical of relational and document data models.

Figure 4. EcoTest physical model

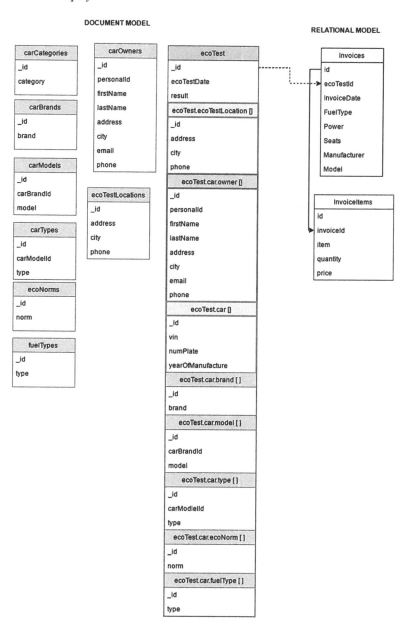

Table 1. MongoDB collections

Collection	Document Example

carCategories	{
	"_id": "5881d672a7ae131b90e6c34c",
	"category": "Truck"
	}

carBrands	{
	"_id": "5880d8d7a7ae131b90ff547e",
	"brand": "Mercedes Benz"
	}

carModels	{
	"_id": "5881d803a7ae131b9005d684",
	"carBrandId": "5880d8d7a7ae131b90ff547e",
	"model": "190E"
	}

carTypes	{
	"_id": "5881dc1ba7ae131b9061eb10",
	"carModelId": "5881d803a7ae131b9005d684",
	"type": "A1"
	}

ecoNorms	{
	"_id": "5881f2fda7ae131b90ff6b4c",
	"norm": "EURO 1"
	}

fuelTypes	{
	"_id": "5881f48ca7ae131b90ff6b4f",
	"type": "DIESEL"
	}

ecoTestLocations	{
	"_id": "5881f52da7ae131b903e3cc5",
	"name": "STP Apro Mehanizacija",
	"city": "Mostar",
	"address": "Bisce polje 15",
	"phone": "+38736555888"
	}

carOwners	{
	"_id": "5881db0ba7ae131b9061eb0f",
	"personalId": "2312983150011",
	"firstName": "Tihomir",
	"lastName": "Krtalic",
	"city": "Mostar",
	"adress":
	"Franjevacka 16a",
	"email": "tihomir.krtalic@hera.ba",
	"phone": "+38763475393"
	}

continued on following page

Table 1. Continued

Collection	Document Example

ecoTest	{
	"_id": "5888aa33a7ae1325e8453b3c",
	"ecoTestDate": ISODate("2017-01-25T08:50:19.287Z"),
	"car": {
	"_id": "5881f6b6a7ae131b90ff584a",
	"brand":
	{ "_id": "5880d8d7a7ae131b90ff547e",
	"brand": "Mercedes Benz"
	},
	"model":
	{ "_id": "5881d803a7ae131b9005d684",
	"carBrandId": "5880d8d7a7ae131b90ff547e",
	"model": "190E"
	},
	"type":
	{ "_id": "5881dc1ba7ae131b9061eb10",
	"carModelId": "5881d803a7ae131b9005d684",
	"type": "XYZ"
	},
	"vin": "WV1236546546564",
	"numPlate": "E25J123",
	"yearOfManufacture": 2006,
	"ecoNorm":
	{ "_id": "5881f2fda7ae131b90ff6b4c",
	"norm": "EURO 1"
	},
	"fuelType":
	{ "_id": "5881f48ca7ae131b90ff6b4f",
	"type": "DIESEL"
	},
	"owner":
	{ "_id": "5881db0ba7ae131b9061eb0f",
	"personalId": "2312983150011",
	"firstName": "Tihomir",
	"lastName": "Krtalc",
	"city": "Mostar",
	"adress": "Franjevacka 16a",
	"email": "tihomir.krtalic@hera.ba",
	"phone": "+38763475393"
	}
	},
	"ecoTestLocation":
	{ "_id": "5881f52da7ae131b903e3cc5",
	"name": "STP Apro Mehanizacija",
	"city": "Mostar",
	"address": "Bisce polje bb",
	"phone": "+38736555888"
	},
	"result": "PASSED"
	}

293

CASE STUDY: BRIDGING RELATIONAL AND NoSQL WORLDS

The adoption of two databases that use different data organization paradigms is a big challenge by itself. Relational databases use structured data language to define and manipulate data. In the relational world, this language is universal and powerful, with a huge developer community. The languages of the NoSQL world are vendor-specific and focused on internal data organization, in the case of this case study on a document collection. SQL is an excellent choice for complex queries, and the very concept of relational database gives them a basis for this functionality. Queries in NoSQL databases by themselves are not as powerful as those in relational databases are. A decision to use two databases of different concepts implies combining respective language variants in the construction of a software backend component or reducing to one language variant by using an appropriate integration mechanism.

In order to test the model and different solutions integrating the two data worlds, specific examples that the software needs to solve are defined. The first task (Figure 5) is to insert data of the conducted testing into MongoDB database, while simultaneously entering data on the financial transaction and passing of the test in the relational database.

The second task (Figure 6) is to generate a report on success in passing the test and financial elements of conducted tests by different vehicle types.

Native Solution

The *native solution* involves the use of native drivers for communication with Oracle and MongoDB databases. In the action of storing data into a database, the business layer prepares data and passes them to the respective database

Table 2. Oracle relational tables

Table	Invoice		
ID	INVOICE_NUMBER	INVOICE_DATE	EKO_TEST_ID
1	1	24/1/2017/ 12:23:57	5888aa33a7ae1325e8453b3c
Table	Invoice_items		
ID	INVOICE_ID	ITEM_DESCRIPTION	QTY	PRICE
1	1	Eko test	1	32.00

in the form and dialect which it natively understands. The integration of the data which are retrieved from both sources is carried out also in the business layer. Upon extraction, the data are linked and transformed into a suitable form for the user layer.

For the project design and the development of the testing, REST Web services, the Java programming language, and the Java EE 7 framework were used. It is common to use JPA (Java Persistence API) for work with relational data when using this technology. JPA offers the functionality of object-relational mapping of data from relational sources. The specificity of the task is manifested in the use of multiple data sources, and their linking is not planned by the JPA specification. Therefore, it was not possible to use JPA. The lack of the functionality was overcome by organizing access to the Oracle database through the JDBC (Java Database Connectivity) driver, while the Java MongoDB driver was used to access the MongoDB database. It is not possible to map the results of queries from the MongoDB database

Figure 5. Insert in NoSQL and relational database

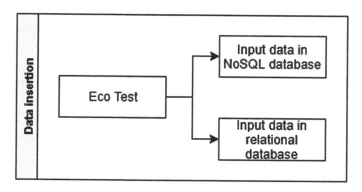

Figure 6. Retrieval of data from NoSQL and relational databases

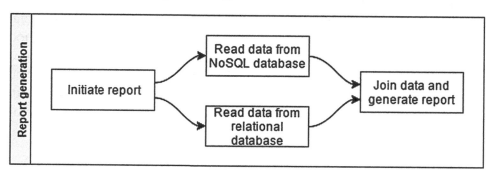

with Java objects directly, so the researchers decided to use the open-source library Gson. This Java library performs conversion in two directions: It can be used to convert Java objects into their JSON representation or JSON string to an equivalent Java object.

Data Insertion

The first task in testing the native model is the data manipulation operation of inserting data. A set of data on the vehicle, the vehicle owner, and measurement results is collected through the eco-testing procedure. Upon completion of the testing (Figure 5), the collected data have to be stored in the NoSQL database. The method *addEcoTest(EcoTest ecoTest)* implements this functionality (Example 1). The native MongoDB driver for Java is used as a database connector and the mentioned Gson library is adopted for conversion of a Java object into a JSON string.

Example 1

```
public void addEcoTest(EcoTest ecoTest) {
    MongoCollection collection = mongoClientProvider.
getMongoCollection("ecoTest");
    GsonBuilder gsonBuilder = new GsonBuilder();
    gsonBuilder.registerTypeAdapter(Date.class, ser);
    gsonBuilder.registerTypeAdapter(Date.class, deser);
    Gson gson = gsonBuilder.create();
    String json = gson.toJson(ecoTest);
    Document doc = Document.parse(json);
    String id = new ObjectId().toHexString();
    doc.append("_id", id);
    collection.insertOne(doc);
}
```

A technical inspection station charges the vehicle owner for the service of the conducted testing. The owner is issued an invoice. Data on the financial transaction, or on the bill, are stored in the relational database. The method *addNew(Invoice invoice)* implements this functionality by creating a record in the relational table *Invoice* (Example 2). The formed record contains the column EKO_TEST_ID, a link to the conducted eco-test, and data written in the NoSQL database. The JDBC driver for Oracle was used as the connector to the relational database.

Example 2

```
public void addNew(Invoice invoice) throws SQLException {
    Connection conn = null;
    PreparedStatement preparedStatement = null;
    String insertSQL = "INSERT INTO INVOICE(ID,INVOICE_NUMBER,
INVOICE_DATE, EKO_TEST_ID) values(?,?,?,?)";
    try {
        conn = dataSource.getConnection();
        preparedStatement = conn.prepareStatement(insertSQL);
        preparedStatement.setBigDecimal(1, invoice.getId());
        preparedStatement.setInt(2, invoice.
getInvoiceNumber());
        preparedStatement.setDate(3, new java.sql.Date(invoice.
getDate().getTime()));
        preparedStatement.setString(4, invoice.getEkoTestId());
        preparedStatement.executeUpdate();
    } finally {
        if (conn != null) {
            conn.close();
        }
        if (preparedStatement != null) {
            preparedStatement.close();
        }
    }
}
```

Analytics of a financial transaction consists of one or more components. Individual components are written into the relational database Inivoice_items. The method *addNew(InvoiceItems invoiceItem)* with the type parameter *invoiceItem* uses the JDBC driver for Oracle (Example 3), like the previous method.

Example 3

```
    public void addNew(InvoiceItems invoiceItem) throws
SQLException {
        Connection conn = null;
        PreparedStatement preparedStatement = null;
        String insertSQL = "INSERT INTO INVOICE_
ITEMS(ID,INVOICE_ID, ITEM_DESCRIPTION, QTY, PRICE)
values(?,?,?,?,?)";
        try {
            conn = dataSource.getConnection();
            preparedStatement = conn.
prepareStatement(insertSQL);
```

```
            preparedStatement.setBigDecimal(1, invoiceItem.
getId());
            preparedStatement.setBigDecimal(2, invoiceItem.
getInvoiceId());
            preparedStatement.setString(3, invoiceItem.
getItemDescription());
            preparedStatement.setBigDecimal(4, invoiceItem.
getQty());
            preparedStatement.setBigDecimal(5, invoiceItem.
getPrice());
            preparedStatement.executeUpdate();
        } catch (SQLException ex) {
            int a = 1;
        } finally {
            if (conn != null) {
                conn.close();
            }
            if (preparedStatement != null) {
                preparedStatement.close();
            }
        }
    }
```

For DML update and delete operations, it is necessary to previously retrieve data from the database in which they are located. Therefore, it is necessary to provide the business layer with data retrieval methods. The method *List<EcoTest> getAll()* is created for retrieval of all eco-tests from the MongoDB (Example 4). It uses the native MongoDB driver in communication with the MongoDB database. Since the use of drivers provides results in the JSON format, the conversion of JSON strings to an equivalent Java object is ensured by the use of Gson methods.

Example 4

```
public List<EcoTest> getAll() {
    MongoCollection collection = mongoClientProvider.
getMongoCollection("ecoTest");
    MongoCursor<Document> cursor = collection.find().
iterator();
    if (cursor != null) {
        String cursorString = util.cursorToString(cursor);
        GsonBuilder gsonBuilder = new GsonBuilder();
        gsonBuilder.registerTypeAdapter(Date.class, ser);
        gsonBuilder.registerTypeAdapter(Date.class, deser);
        Gson gson = gsonBuilder.create();
```

```
        List<EcoTest> list = gson.fromJson(cursorString, new
TypeToken<List<EcoTest>>() {
        }.getType());
        return list;
    } else {
        return null;
    }
}
```

A user request for the retrieval of a specific document occurs much more often than for the retrieval of all records of a collection. Each document is uniquely identified by the value of the *_id* attribute. The method *EcoTest get(String id)* receives exactly this identifier as the parameter and requests the desired document from the database (Example 5). The MongoDB returns a response with the specified document in a JSON string, which Gson then converts into a Java object.

Example 5

```
public EcoTest get(String id) {
    MongoCollection collection = mongoClientProvider.
getMongoCollection("ecoTest");
    Bson filter = eq("_id", id);
    Document document = (Document) collection.find(filter).
first();
    if (document != null) {
        String json = document.toJson();
        Gson gson = new Gson();
        EcoTest ecoTest = gson.fromJson(json, new
TypeToken<EcoTest>() {
        }.getType());
        return ecoTest;
    } else {
        return null;
    }
}
```

The retrieval of data on invoices is realized similarly to the presented method of the retrieval of eco-tests, whether it is about all tests or an individual test. These data are in the relational database, and the extraction of these data takes place by the Oracle JDBC driver. The methods *List<Invoice> getAll()* (Example 6) and *BigDecimal getValueByEcoTestId(String ecoTestId)* (Example 7) represent the ways in which it is possible to retrieve all data on invoices and the invoice sum for a particular eco-test.

Example 6

```
public List<Invoice> getAll() throws SQLException {
    Connection conn = null;
    PreparedStatement preparedStatement = null;
    String selectSQL = "SELECT ID,INVOICE_NUMBER, INVOICE_DATE,
EKO_TEST_ID FROM INVOICE";
    List<Invoice> invoiceList = null;
    try {
        conn = dataSource.getConnection();
        preparedStatement = conn.prepareStatement(selectSQL);
        ResultSet rs = preparedStatement.executeQuery();
        invoiceList = new ArrayList<>();
        while (rs.next()) {
            Invoice invoice = new Invoice();
            invoice.setId(rs.getBigDecimal("ID"));
            invoice.setInvoiceNumber(rs.getInt("INVOICE_
NUMBER"));
            invoice.setDate(rs.getDate("INVOICE_DATE"));
            invoice.setEkoTestId(rs.getString("EKO_TEST_ID"));
            invoiceList.add(invoice);
        }
    } catch (SQLException ex) {
    } finally {
        if (conn != null) {
            conn.close();
        }
        if (preparedStatement != null) {
            preparedStatement.close();
        }
    }
    return invoiceList;
}
```

Example 7

```
public BigDecimal getValueByEcoTestId(String ecoTestId) throws
SQLException {
    Connection conn = null;
    PreparedStatement preparedStatement = null;
    String selectSQL = "SELECT SUM(QTY*PRICE) VALUE FROM
INVOICE I, INVOICE_ITEMS IT WHERE I.EKO_TEST_ID=? AND  I.ID=IT.
INVOICE_ID";
    BigDecimal value = null;
    try {
        conn = dataSource.getConnection();
```

```
            preparedStatement = conn.prepareStatement(selectSQL);
            preparedStatement.setString(1, ecoTestId);
            ResultSet rs = preparedStatement.executeQuery();
            while (rs.next()) {
                value = rs.getBigDecimal(1);
            }
        } finally {
            if (conn != null) {
                conn.close();
            }
            if (preparedStatement != null) {
                preparedStatement.close();
            }
        }
        return value;
    }
```

Generating Reports

The completion of the first task by using a native solution presented the methods that operated on an individual database, which was either relational or NoSQL. None of the examples involved simultaneous work with both databases, while the nature of the second test involves exactly such a task. It defines the retrieval of data on the financial value of eco-tests conducted per vehicle model. Relational tables of invoices and MongoDB collections of eco-tests need to be linked in order to get the required data. A native driver, as its name suggests, is the connector for an individual database. Therefore, its use eliminates the possibility to make queries that would be performed on Oracle and MongoDB databases at the same time. The problem of linking databases and extracting the data is solved in several steps. All completed eco-tests are retrieved by the method *List<EcoTest> getAll()* (Example 4). The method *public BigDecimal getValueByEcoTestId(String ecoTestId)* returns the value of an invoice for a submitted *ecoTestId* (Example 7). Upon retrieval, the data are linked by a key. Linking results in an object of the class *ReportModel*. It contains data on a vehicle model and the total value of invoices for the vehicle model. Thus, the result of the method is a Java object that is passed to the report engine that uses it to generate the expected report (Example 8).

Example 8

```java
public List<ReportModel> getValueByCarModel() throws
SQLException {
    List<EcoTest> ecoTestList = ecoTestBean.getAll();
    HashMap<String, ReportModel> h = new HashMap<>();
    for (EcoTest ecoTest : ecoTestList) {
        ReportModel reportModel = h.get(ecoTest.getCar().
getModel().getId());
        if (reportModel == null) {
            reportModel = new ReportModel();
            reportModel.setValue(new BigDecimal(0));
            reportModel.setCarBrend(ecoTest.getCar().
getBrand());
            h.put(ecoTest.getCar().getModel().getId(),
reportModel);
        }
        BigDecimal value = invoiceBean.
getValueByEcoTestId(ecoTest.getId());
        if (value != null) {
            BigDecimal newValue = reportModel.getValue().
add(value);
            reportModel.setValue(newValue);
        }
    }
    return new ArrayList<>(h.values());
}
```

Hybrid Solutions

As Chapter 6 outlined, the biggest obstacle in the realization of program solutions that require simultaneous use of relational and NoSQL database is in the diversity of programming interfaces for manipulating data on the side of NoSQL. The heterogeneity of these solutions is increased by the rapid development of the NoSQL market and the amount of different solutions from the standpoint of the data organization model and associated APIs. Efforts to overcome this situation resulted in attempts to define common APIs for a variety of NoSQL products. However, a more logical solution, from the point of critical mass of development community knowledge, introduces an overlay into the communication architecture, thus reducing different communication concepts to SQL communication, which is known to the majority of programming communities. The *hybrid solution*, therefore, introduces an additional layer which provides communication between the business layer and the data layer on the SQL standard. Accordingly, it is not relevant whether the source data are from the relational or the NoSQL world of data organization. The concept seems acceptable, considering the known and widely used SQL standard. The use of clear and well-known SQL patterns of programming on the business layer, with the adoption of a new layer that would translate it into the NoSQL programming interface for communication with the NoSQL database, seems to be a good solution. In order to present this solution for the completion of given tasks, the Unity model has been chosen (Lawrence, 2014).

In the product vision (Unity, 2017), the authors of UnityJDBC stand out as their main objective is *to make processing data simple*. The basic properties of the MongoDB drivers of this product are:

- Access to MongoDB collections using SQL including WHERE filters and ORDER BY clause.
- Data manipulation using standard SQL functions that are not natively supported in the MongoDB.
- Use of JOIN clause between MongoDB collections and relational tables of databases that are supported by Unity.
- Full support for nested documents and strings including functionalities of filters and regular expressions (RegEx).

The above description allows to conclude that the Unity is primarily a tool to support reporting software. Example 9 shows how data from relational and NoSQL databases can be combined in order to come up with a solution to their simultaneous use.

Example 9

```
public List<ReportModel> getValueByCarModel() throws
UnsupportedEncodingException {
        List<ReportModel> reportModelList =new ArrayList();
        Connection con =null;
        Statement stmt =null;
        ResultSet rst;
        String url ="jdbc:unity://"+ getWebInfPath()+"/
EcoTestSources.xml";
```

```
try{
            Class.forName("unity.jdbc.UnityDriver");
            con = DriverManager.getConnection(url);
            stmt = con.createStatement();
            String sql ="select e.car.brand, sum(it.qty*it.
price) from MongoEcoTest.\"ecoTest\" e, OracleInvoices.IVICA.
INVOICE i, OracleInvoices.IVICA.INVOICE_ITEMS it\n"
+"where e._id=i.eko_test_id and it.invoice_id=i.id\n"
+"group by e.car.brand";
            rst = stmt.executeQuery(sql);
while(rst.next()){
                System.out.print(rst.getObject(1));
                Gson gson =new Gson();
                CarBrands carBrand = gson.fromJson(rst.
getObject(1).toString(), CarBrands.class);
                ReportModel reportModel =new ReportModel();
                reportModel.setCarBrend(carBrand);
                reportModel.setValue(new
BigDecimal((BigInteger) rst.getObject(2)));
                reportModelList.add(reportModel);
                System.out.print(rst.getObject(2));
                System.out.println();
}
}catch(Exception ex){
            System.out.println("Exception: "+ ex);
}finally{
if(con !=null){
try{
                con.close();
}catch(SQLException ex){
                System.out.println("SQLException: "+ ex);
}
}
}
return reportModelList;
```

The task anticipates the generation of a report on the realized financial transactions by the type of vehicle in the process of eco testing. The created method List <ReportModel> getValueByCarModel () retrieves data using a unique SQL query (Example 10).

Example 10

```
select
  e.car.brand, sum(it.qty*it.price)
from
  MongoEcoTest.\"ecoTest\" e,
```

```
  OracleInvoices.IVICA.INVOICE i,
  OracleInvoices.IVICA.INVOICE_ITEMS it\n
where
      e._id=i.eko_test_id
  and it.invoice_id=i.id\n
group by
  e.car.brand
```

The query is executed on two data sources: MongoEcoTest and OracleInvoices. These sources are described in the UnityJDBC configuration file EcoTestSources.xml. The Where clause of a SQL query reveals the possibility of linking data from different sources. The query result is a Java object that can be forwarded to the report engine for the formatting and presentation of the retrieved data.

Reducing to One Option: SQL

The creators of RDBMS systems have made significant efforts. During recent years, they have developed functionalities that were closer to NoSQL world and the characteristics that made it desirable in the modern market. On the other side, the greatest difference between two paradigms prevailing by adding SQL interface to a standard set of functionalities. ACID and BASE concepts become much closer. NoSQL vendors add ACID option as standard functionality. On the other hand, the SQL database, through tuning of the consistency functionality, implements greater opportunities for scaling. Progress is evident also in the field of data modeling. NoSQL systems, too, increasingly support the organization of tabular data, while SQL database implements the data organization analogue to documents and key-value pairs. Table 7 in Chapter 6 presented the migration of some of the most famous applications from RDBMS to NoSQL DBMS, which are based partly on the described functionality. The boundaries between these worlds slowly disappear. Selecting the right model storage should offer the best performances and ensure data quality.

Inserting Data

Oracle 12c RDBMS has been selected to test the solution provided by this concept. Through this version, Oracle has provided users with an engine base with full support for working with JSON notation of data. The support for

JSON is incorporated in all the functionalities of Oracle RDBMS engine, such as SQL and Analytics. JSON documents are stored in the VARCHAR2, CLOB or BLOB columns. While creating corresponding column, the check constraint that controls the validity of the content and JSON format of records are being defined. In order to store data on the conducted eco-test, a relational table ECO_TEST has been created (Example 11). Unique identifier of the record in the table is the column *id*, and a JSON structure with information about the test is placed in a CLOB column *doc*. The constraint *valid_json* controls the contents of the column *doc* while data are entered or updated.

Example 11

```
CREATE TABLE ECO_TEST
(
idNUMBER,
    doc    CLOB,
CONSTRAINT valid_json CHECK(doc ISJSON),
CONSTRAINT id_pk PRIMARYKEY(id)
);
```

The method *List <Ecotest> Getall ()* retrieves all eco-tests from the table *Eco_test* (Example 12). As with the native solution, the method uses the JDBC driver for Oracle and accepts the content from the database columns *id* and *doc*. The column *doc* is necessary to parse into the Java object *doc*, which is part of the object *Ecotest*. As in the previous examples, the Gson library has been used to convert a JSON string to a Java object. The method *Ecotest get (BigDecimal id)* is based on the same logic, and its result is a Java object of an eco-test given through parameter *id* (Example 13).

Example 12

```
public List<EcoTest> getAll() throws SQLException {
        Connection conn =null;
        PreparedStatement preparedStatement =null;
        String selectSQL ="SELECT I.ID, I.doc FROM ECO_TEST I";
        List<EcoTest> ecoTestList =null;
try{
            conn = dataSource.getConnection();
            preparedStatement = conn.
prepareStatement(selectSQL);
```

```
                ResultSet rs = preparedStatement.executeQuery();
                ecoTestList =new ArrayList<>();
while(rs.next()){
                EcoTest ecoTest =new EcoTest();
                ecoTest.setId(rs.getBigDecimal(1).toString());
                String ecoTestString = rs.getString(2);
                Doc doc =new Gson().fromJson(ecoTestString,
Doc.class);
                ecoTest.setDoc(doc);
                ecoTestList.add(ecoTest);
}
}finally{
if(conn !=null){
                conn.close();
}
if(preparedStatement !=null){
                preparedStatement.close();
}
}
return ecoTestList;
}
```

Example 13

```
public EcoTest get(BigDecimal id)throws SQLException {
        Connection conn =null;
        PreparedStatement preparedStatement =null;
        String selectSQL ="SELECT I.ID, I.doc FROM ECO_TEST I
WHERE I.ID=?";
        EcoTest ecoTest =new EcoTest();
try{
                conn = dataSource.getConnection();
                preparedStatement = conn.
prepareStatement(selectSQL);
                preparedStatement.setBigDecimal(1, id);
                ResultSet rs = preparedStatement.executeQuery();
                rs.next();
                ecoTest.setId(rs.getBigDecimal(1).toString());
                String ecoTestString = rs.getString(2);
                Doc doc =new Gson().fromJson(ecoTestString, Doc.
class);
                ecoTest.setDoc(doc);
}finally{
if(conn !=null){
                conn.close();
```

```
}
if(preparedStatement !=null){
                preparedStatement.close();
}
}
return ecoTest;
}
```

A similar logic is also used for the DML operation of inserting a new record into the table of eco-tests. The input parameter of the class *addEcoTest (Ecotest Ecotest)* is a Java object that contains data on the conducted testing (Example 14). The methods of the Gson library convert it to a JSON format suitable for import into the column *doc* of the relational table *Eco_test*.

Example 14

```
Public void addEcoTest(EcoTest ecoTest)throws SQLException {
        GsonBuilder gsonBuilder =new GsonBuilder();
        Gson gson = gsonBuilder.create();
        String json = gson.toJson(ecoTest);
        Connection conn =null;
        PreparedStatement preparedStatement =null;
        String insertSQL ="INSERT INTO ECO_TEST(ID, DOC)
values(?,?)";
try{
        conn = dataSource.getConnection();
        Clob docClob = conn.createClob();
        docClob.setString(1, json);
        preparedStatement = conn.
prepareStatement(insertSQL);
        preparedStatement.setBigDecimal(1,new
BigDecimal(1));
        preparedStatement.setClob(2, docClob);
        preparedStatement.executeUpdate();
}finally{
if(conn !=null){
                conn.close();
}
if(preparedStatement !=null){
                preparedStatement.close();
}
}
}
```

Report Generation

The report which was defined by the task presents the aggregate data on financial transactions by vehicle models. In this concept of data storage, the required information is provided in three tables: *eco_test, invoice,* and *invoice_items.* The method *List <ReportModel> getValueByCarModel ()* connects tables and retrieves the requested data (Example 15). An interesting fact about the query is that it does not reach a complete JSON record, which is contained in the column *eco_test.doc*, but only the component of JSON *eco_test.doc.car.model.* The result of the method is the object reportList, that can be forwarded to the report engine for formatting and display in the desired format.

Example 15

```
publicList<ReportModel> getValueByCarModel()throws SQLException
{
        Connection conn =null;
        PreparedStatement preparedStatement =null;
        String selectSQL ="select e.doc.car.model, sum(S.QTY*S.
PRICE)\n"
+"from eco_test e, invoice i, invoice_items s\n"
+"where e.id=I.EKO_TEST_ID and i.id=S.INVOICE_ID\n"
+"group by e.doc.car.model";
        List<ReportModel> reportList =null;
try{
            conn = dataSource.getConnection();
            preparedStatement = conn.
prepareStatement(selectSQL);
            ResultSet rs = preparedStatement.executeQuery();
            reportList =new ArrayList<>();
while(rs.next()){
                ReportModel report =new ReportModel();
                String carBrandString = rs.getString(1);
                CarBrands carBrand =new Gson().
fromJson(carBrandString, CarBrands.class);
                report.setCarBrend(carBrand);
                report.setValue(rs.getBigDecimal(2));
                reportList.add(report);
}
}finally{
if(conn !=null){
                conn.close();
}
```

```
if(preparedStatement !=null){
                preparedStatement.close();
}
}
return reportList;
}
```

These examples demonstrate the functionality of Oracle 12c database to use the JDBC driver and a standard SQL record, and to read the information on the eco-test from the relational table in which it is possible to put JSON objects. The features of indexing data stored in this way and their combination with the other columns of relational tables are particularly interesting.

REFERENCES

Lawrence, R. (2014). Integration and virtualization of relational SQL and NoSQL systems including MySQL and MongoDB. *International Conference on Computational Science and Computational Intelligence*, 285-290. doi:10.1109/CSCI.2014.56

Unity. (2017). *UnityJDBC vision*. Retrieved July 22, 2017 http://www.unityjdbc.com/about.php

Chapter 8
Which Way to Go for the Future:
The Next Generation of Databases

ABSTRACT

The chapter presents how relational databases answer to typical NoSQL features, and, vice versa, how NoSQL databases answer to typical relational features. Open issues related to the integration of relational and NoSQL databases, as well as next database generation features are discussed. The big relational database vendors have continuously worked to incorporate NoSQL features into their databases, as well as NoSQL vendors are trying to make their products more like relational databases. The convergence of these two groups of databases has been a driving force in the evolution of database market, in establishing a new level of focus to resolving big data requirements, and in enabling users to fully use data potential, wherever data is stored, in relational or NoSQL databases. In turn, the database of choice in the future will likely be one that provides the best of both worlds: flexible data model, high availability, and enterprise reliability.

INTRODUCTION

The last 10 years of database development were extremely dynamic: the huge number of new, primarily NoSQL databases emerged, new database languages and application programming interfaces (APIs) were developed,

DOI: 10.4018/978-1-5225-3385-6.ch008

and new features related to distribution and high availability were added. At the beginning of this period, the differences between NoSQL and relational databases seemed clear and unambiguous and included the ACID/BASE approach, CAP theorem, high availability, distribution, work with unstructured data, and the like. But after 10 years of database development, all those who were expecting that two big clearly separated groups of databases—relational and NoSQL—would be established, today must admit they were wrong. Namely, during the last 10 years, the differences between relational and NoSQL databases continuously shrunk. The big relational database vendors (Oracle, Microsoft, and IBM) have continuously worked to incorporate NoSQL features into their databases, and NoSQL vendors tried to make their products more like relational databases (see Chapter 5). The convergence of these two groups of databases has been a driving force in the evolution of the database market; in establishing a new level of focus for resolving Big Data requirements; and in enabling users to fully use data potential, wherever data is stored, in relational or NoSQL databases. In turn, the database of choice in the future will likely be one that provides the best of both worlds: a flexible data model, high availability, and enterprise reliability.

NoSQL VS. RELATIONAL DATABASES

The comparison between relational and NoSQL databases can be discussed concerning different features such as work with different data formats, use of data schema, joins, consistency, scalability, high availability, and so on. But, considering the process of convergence of these two groups of databases, questions related to the point of comparison can be issued. However, the differences between these two groups of databases still exist, although they are not so clear as they were 10 years ago. Here, two approaches are used to explain the differences and similarities between relational and NoSQL databases:

- Relational database answers to typical NoSQL features.
- NoSQL database answers to typical relational features.

Table 1 presents the typical NoSQL features (described in detail in Chapter 2) and how the three biggest vendors of relational databases (Oracle, Microsoft, and IBM) answer them.

Table 1. Relational database answers to typical NoSQL features

NoSQL Feature	Relational Answer
Based on the nonrelational model (denormalized and redundant structure), storing different structures like JSON, XML, etc.	Oracle, Microsoft, and IBM enable support for both JSON and XML. Oracle database enabled JSON support in two ways: by API through a family of simple Oracle document access (SODA) and natively as part of SQL and PL/SQL commands. Microsoft SQL Server enabled built-in JSON support as part of T-SQL. IBM DB2 provides three ways to support JSON: by API, JSON command-line interface (CLI), and JSON wire listener.
Distributed and cluster oriented	Oracle supports distribution and clusters by Oracle RAC, Data Guard, GoldenGate, Recovery manager (RMAN), etc. Microsoft's distributed availability groups make the base for data distribution. Distributed Transaction Coordinator (DTC) provides support for distributed transactions. Microsoft availability groups enable MS SQL Server to rely on the Windows server failover clustering. IBM supports distribution and clusters by Platform Cluster (PCM) and IBM Cloudant (DBaaS).
Schema-free/schemaless (no need to define the database structure to store and manage data)	Oracle SODA API is designed for schemaless application development. Microsoft SQL Server 2016 Azure SQL Database introduced a hybrid approach to support schemaless use. IBM features for work with JSON enable schemaless application development.
Use CAP and BASE approach	Oracle supports ACID transactions, even for distributed transactions where two-phase commit is used. For resolving in-doubt distributed transactions, Oracle offers, together with an automatic, manual approach. The Oracle Maximum Availability Architecture offers a selection of architecture patterns for resolving CAP issues. Microsoft supports ACID transactions, even for distributed transactions where two-phase commit is used. The high availability of SQL Server is closely related to Microsoft Azure SQL Database. Also, support for high availability uses MS AlwaysOn basic availability groups, group Managed Service Accounts (gMSAs), database mirroring, database-level failover, etc. The last version of SQL Server enables implementation of the distributed transaction support when a new availability group is created. IBM supports ACID transactions. The CICS (customer information control system) transaction server is the base for distributed transaction processing. CICS enables transactions to run under various conditions, including ACID. High availability in DB2 is supported by different solutions, including IBM Data Engine for Hadoop and Spark, IBM Spectrum Scale file system, IBM Spectrum Conductor for Spark, IBM Spectrum Symphony, IBM Platform Cluster Manager, and IBM Cloudant.

continued on following page

Table 1. Continued

NoSQL Feature	Relational Answer
Support Big Data	Oracle developed Big Data SQL to enable unified query of distributed data stored in different Big Data storage (HDFS, Hive, HBase, Oracle NoSQL, etc.). It enables analysis of these data in a way as they all are stored in the Oracle database. Microsoft developed PolyBase, an interface for Microsoft analytics platform systems. The latest versions of MS SQL Server can work with PolyBase and query data stored in HDFS, Hadoop, or Azure Blob Storage and combine the results with relational data stored in SQL Server. IBM developed a data engine for Hadoop and Spark with integrated cluster management as well as IBM Spectrum Conductor for Spark as a multitenant solution.
Open source	Oracle offers Oracle Berkeley DB as a family of open-source, embeddable databases. Microsoft announced SQL Server on Linux and provided the running of open-source services in Azure. IBM offers the IBM Open Platform with Spectrum Scale file system, an open-source alternative to the Hadoop file system.
Horizontally scalable	Oracle enabled horizontal scalability by using sharding, where shards can run on single-instance or Oracle RAC databases. Oracle still has limited sharding up to 1,000 shards. Microsoft also uses sharding to enable horizontal scalability. It offers two approaches to using sharding: writing of custom code and use of MS Azure SQL Database elastic features. IBM DB2 horizontal scalability is based on z/OS Parallel Sysplex cluster technology.

Table 2 presents the typical relational features (described in detail in Chapter 1) and how NoSQL databases answer them. Because of a large number of different NoSQL databases, the analysis is based on the solutions offered by typical representatives for each category of NoSQL databases already described in previous chapters.

As presented in Tables 1 and 2, the differences between relational and NoSQL databases related to core features are unclear. The Gartner Report (Heudecker, Feinberg, Adrian, Palanca, & Greenwald, 2016) highlighted the high level of convergence between these two databases by explaining why they stopped using the term *NoSQL* to imply nonrelationality:

NoSQL formerly implied alternative data types and scaling strategies from relational DBMSs. However, relational DBMSs have added, or are adding, features from NoSQL, while NoSQL DBMSs have added, or are in the process of adding, features from relational DBMSs. Therefore, the term "NoSQL" is no longer useful as a product distinction. (Heudecker et al., 2016, p. 28)

Table 2. NoSQL database answers to typical relational features

Relational Feature	NoSQL Answer
Join	Graph stores support joins, but graph joins are small by nature, unlike RDBMS joins.
SQL	Column-family stores use SQL-like query languages, including Hive Query Language (HQL) used on Hadoop with HDFS or HBase data storage, and Cassandra Query Language (CQL) used by Cassandra column store. Document Couchbase store uses N1QL query language developed for querying the JSON data. Graph Neo4J store uses the Cypher query language to query and update the graph.
ACID transactions	Document MarkLogic Server store enables ACID transactions. Graph Neo4j store is ACID compliant.
Consistency	Key-value Oracle NoSQL database provides different consistency policies, from strict to weak. Document MongoDB in a single-server configuration provides strict consistency. Also, MongoDB allows configuration of consistency by using the isolation operator, although an isolated write operation does not guarantee all-or-nothing atomicity. Where a sequence of write operations in MongoDB is to be executed as a single transaction, a two-phase commit can be implemented in the application. The two-phase commit allows a variation where the query predicate includes the application identifier as well as the expected state of data in the write operation. MongoDB allows clients to see the results of writes before the writes are durable. Column-family HBase store provides strict consistency for individual rows. Graph Neo4j store in single-server configuration is strictly consistent (ACID compliant). If Neo4j uses a cluster configuration, then write to the master is eventually synchronized to the slaves, while slaves are always available for reads.

The Gartner Report concludes that "the operational database management systems (OPDBMS) market has shifted from a phase of rapid innovation to a phase of maturing products and capabilities" (Heudecker et al., 2016, p. 26). After 10 years, NoSQL databases are becoming mature, but the market is still flooded with a large number of diverse NoSQL databases. While the first relational databases have been on the market more than 30 years, most NoSQL databases have just 10 years on the stage with many important features still unimplemented.

The problem with the NoSQL database world is a lack of standardization. As explained, NoSQL is an umbrella term for many diverse products. The design, data stores, query languages, and other features of NoSQL databases vary considerably among different NoSQL products, which is not the case with traditional SQL databases. The consequence is that the learning curve for NoSQL databases is slower, since a developer who is familiar with one type of NoSQL database is not always prepared to work with a different one. This is a serious barrier to wider NoSQL adoption.

The main driving force of NoSQL development was the demands of Web 2.0 applications, meaning that NoSQL databases were created to resolve those demands. The result is that when application requirements extend beyond the "insert-read-update-delete" cycle of typical Web applications, NoSQL databases have little to offer to business intelligence and analytic tools.

One of the open issues with NoSQL databases is vendor support on a global scale. NoSQL databases tend to be open source, with just a few firms handling support, so they lack the credibility that the established RDBMS vendors like Oracle, IBM, and Microsoft enjoy (Richards, 2015).

INTEGRATION OF RELATIONAL AND NoSQL DATABASES: OPEN ISSUES

Chapter 6 described two approaches related to the integration of relational and NoSQL databases—native and hybrid—plus an additional approach based on reduction to one database, either relational or NoSQL. The practical implementation of these approaches, based on a case study of vehicle registration, was explained in Chapter 7. The task was the integration of two databases, Oracle as relational and MongoDB as NoSQL. During work on the implementation of native, hybrid, and solution based on reduction to relational databases, developers were faced with different, sometimes unexpected, difficulties. Those difficulties are summarized as follows:

- Native solution:
  - The data integration required an additional "quantity" of program code.
  - Extensive manual work on program code for optimization was necessary in order to obtain optimal performance, especially when work with the database is in question.
  - It is necessary to have developers with different knowledge—that is, developers with knowledge about SQL and JDBC as well as developers with knowledge about NoSQL drivers and MongoDB query syntax.

- Hybrid solution:
  - Database communication was reduced on JDBC, but the additional configuration for access to different databases was necessary.
  - Data manipulation (insert, update, delete) was complex and hard to implement.
  - Based on third-party vendors tools, the consequence is that overall capabilities are lower in comparison to capabilities that offer original database vendors.
- Reduction to a relational database:
  - Vendor specific—that is, dependent on features offered by a particular database vendor, in this case, Oracle.
  - Loss of specific characteristics of NoSQL databases.

Generally, it can be concluded that, in the case of integration of relational and NoSQL databases, there are the following open issues:

- The responsibility of developers (programmers) for the optimization of database work is considerably increased, which means that additional programming and time is necessary for completing this task.
- It is vital that the developing team has developers with different knowledge, although the communication among these developers sometimes can be difficult because they usually come from completely different worlds (relational and NoSQL). Although it is not always easy to find developers with good knowledge of NoSQL databases, finding developers with knowledge of both worlds, relational and NoSQL, is equal to winning the jackpot.
- The market is full of many different drivers and tools offered by third-party vendors, but finding appropriate drivers or tools for particular problems is a time-consuming and exhaustive process.

Considering these open issues, it is not accidental that big database vendors (Oracle, Microsoft, and IBM) are going in the direction of convergence toward NoSQL databases, with the main task to offer to their users the best from both worlds in one database management system.

Nevertheless, the main question is: Is there any point in the integration of relational and NoSQL databases when these two database types converge on each other? However, taking into account the fact that convergence is a process and that even in an ideal case it will take some time (and time is something that organizations are constantly short of), it means that organizations will not have a choice but to use integration if they want to analyze relational and NoSQL data together.

In addition, to make work, especially configuration and maintenance, with their database easier for users, all three big vendors offer cloud solutions—that is, database as a service (DBaaS). In this model, users are free of database administration and maintenance because those activities become the responsibility of the database vendor (i.e., service providers). Users' focus can change from technology issues to data issues—that is, they can fully concentrate on gaining valuable insights from stored data.

FEATURES OF THE NEXT GENERATION OF DATABASES

Since the year 2000, the main drivers for database development have been Web 2.0 technologies, global e-commerce, Big Data, social networks, cloud computing, and the Internet of Things (IoT). They each demand and reflect significant changes in application architectures to which databases must respond. How databases responded to these challenges was explained in the first seven chapters of this book. The overall conclusion is that at the end of the stage is the process of convergence between relational and NoSQL databases. As explained, the reason for this convergence lies in the demanding requests of modern businesses related to the ability to deploy applications with global scope and with mobile and social context. Generally, users are not deeply interested in technological issues; they do not want to know the details of data storage (relational or NoSQL), data formats, or data distribution. But they are extremely interested in the high availability of their data, ease of access, and ease of use of different analytic (business intelligence) tools in order to make better decisions. When the development of databases is questioned, users expect existing and future databases to answer the call to the challenges of modern businesses.

Although the forecasts are a thankless task, especially related to the development of technology, the next generation of database features is based on predictions of emerging technology requirements in the next few years.

Summarized here are different predictions (Ferguson, 2017; Gutierrez, 2016; Marr, 2016; Mayo, 2017; Press, 2016; Shacklet, 2016; Smith, 2016; Tableau, 2016; van Rijmenam, 2016) about technologies that will shape the database management systems in the near future.

- **Blockchain:** This refers to a shared, immutable ledger for recording the history of transactions (IBM BC, 2017). Blockchain technology enables distribution of digital information, not copying, creating the backbone of a new type of Internet. The platform for the development of blockchain technologies is open and programmable, with huge potential for countless new applications such as the digital currency Bitcoin, which is currently the most famous one. Blockchain allows literally anyone (individuals, public or private organizations, Web sites, etc.) to send anything of value (birth and death certificates, marriage licenses, educational degrees, financial accounts, contracts, medical records, insurance claims, votes, etc.) that can be coded anywhere in the world where the blockchain file can be accessed. This ledger represents the truth because mass collaboration constantly reconciles it. Humans will not need to trust one another in the traditional sense because the new platform ensures integrity (Tapscott & Tapscott, 2015). Since each chain is just a distributed database, blockchain technology will potentially have a big impact on furthering database development, especially database distribution capabilities.

- **Artificial Intelligence (AI):** This is a branch of computer science dealing with the simulation of intelligent behavior in computers (Merriam-Webster, 2017) worthy of the development of many of today's core technologies, including neural networks, machine learning, natural language processing, intelligent agents, and the like. The present development of AI has shown that quality data is key to its success, especially related to predictive and learning AI capabilities. Deep learning, a subfield of machine leaning inspired by neural networks, is fostering further development of artificial general intelligence. Today, deep learning is becoming a buzzword because the two main preconditions were fulfilled: vast computer power and Big Data. They enable the creation of artificial neural networks to find patterns in vast amounts of data. Deep-learning algorithms do not need humans to train them. Rather, they use massive data sets, numerous videos/images/articles, and so on, to figure out for themselves how to recognize different objects, sentences, images, and the like (van Rijmenam, 2016). Without a large quantity of quality data, deep-learning algorithms cannot accomplish their tasks.

- **Internet of Things (IoT):** This is a system of interrelated computing devices, mechanical and digital machines, objects, animals, or people that are provided with unique identifiers and the ability to transfer data over a network without requiring human-to-human or human-to-computer interaction (TechTarget, 2017). IoT is a new and still immature domain. However, it continues to grow, and in 2016, about 6.5 billion devices were connected to the Internet, which is expected to grow to 50 billion devices in 2020 (van Rijmenam, 2016). In the near future is expecting that IoT and related technologies will have a huge impact on organizations, affecting their business strategies, risk management, and different technical issues such as architecture, network design, and security. IoT provides the collection of vast amounts of data from different devices. The result will be a dramatic increase of data to be stored and analyzed that will put additional burdens on database technology. Before IoT, the IT approach to data analytics has been to collect and store data and then to analyze it. IoT needs a different approach because there are too much data to store, so analysis of data streams must be conducted on the fly. In addition, data filtering and analysis are sometimes distributed in gateways at the edge of the network or in the "things" themselves to minimize communication over slow networks (Jones, 2016).
- **Mixed Reality:** This refers to the merging of the virtual and real worlds by devices like Microsoft Hololens. Mixed reality potentially offers organizations better performance for the tasks at hand as well as better understanding of organizational data. The manufacturing industry already uses some forms of mixed reality to enable better repairs, faster product development, and improved inventory management. Additionally, mixed reality could help decision makers to understand complex data sets and to make better decisions.
- **Cloud:** The cloud is used as a metaphor for *the Internet*, so the phrase *cloud computing* means a type of Internet-based computing, where different services, including servers, storage, and applications, are delivered to an organization through the Internet (Beal, 2014). In recent years, cloud computing has attracted the attention of many organizations because it enables organizations to access and share computing resources (servers, applications, databases) through the Internet in a secure and scalable manner. By moving data and data analytics to the cloud, organizations try to accelerate the adoption of

the latest database and analytical tools' capabilities to turn data into action and to cut costs in ongoing maintenance and operations.

- **Dark Data Usage:** Gartner (2017) defines *dark data* as the information assets organizations collect, process, and store during regular business activities but generally fail to use for other purposes such as analytics, business relationships, and direct monetizing. Similar to dark matter in physics, dark data often comprise most organizations' universe of information assets. Thus, organizations often retain dark data for compliance purposes only. Storing and securing data typically incurs more expense (and sometimes greater risk) than the value (Gartner, 2017). The Big Data explosion forced organizations to turn huge volumes of Big Data that are not being used (dark data) into useable and valuable data by using different data analytic tools.

- **Database as a Service (DBaaS):** DBaaS is a cloud-computing service model that provides users with some form of access to a database without the need for setting up physical hardware, installing software, or configuring for performance. In this model, the service provider is responsible for and takes care of the administrative tasks and maintenance. In this case, the users of DBaaS are fully focused on gaining valuable insights from stored data (Techopedia, 2017). As explained in Chapter 5, all three leading database vendors—Oracle, Microsoft, and IBM—offer DBaaS.

- **Predictive Analytics:** This is the branch of advanced analytics used to make predictions about unknown future events. Many techniques, including statistics, data mining, modeling, and machine learning, are used in predictive analytics with the aim to analyze data to make predictions. These techniques allow business users to create predictive intelligence by uncovering patterns and relationships in both the structured and the unstructured data (PredictiveAnalytics, 2017). But the shortage of good data is the most common barrier to organizations in employing predictive analytics, meaning that the main precondition for its use is the vast amount of quality data. It is a point where predictive analytics meets database management systems and vice versa.

The driving force behind the development of all these technologies is not only to help organizations to deal with Big Data but also to empower them to efficiently and effectively respond to today's and the future's business challenges. Described technologies can bring the changes and lead to new business solutions only if organizations become fully aware of the value of the data they collect and find ways to use that data to enhance everyday business. It means that organizations must empower their employees by using the right data because, in the today's business environment, the employees are becoming the frontline decision makers. They face the customers, sell the products and services, and build the products in the factory. To be successful in their regular activities, employees need full insights into their customers, and they need to make the right decisions and to offer to customers what they want. Combining internal and external data, as well as structured and unstructured data, is crucial in gaining valuable insights. This is still the main driving force in database development because the main task of databases should be to ensure all data that business users need to be successful in performing their tasks.

This book has shown that data vendors (at least the biggest) are aware of their responsibilities, not only in ensuring storage of vast amounts of quality data but also in providing a solid data foundation crucial for development and successful implementation of many other technologies (IoT, AI, predictive analytics, cloud, DBaaS, blockchain, etc.).

Bridging the gap between relational and NoSQL databases could lead to database evolution in the sense that they will provide support for different and often opposite user requirements by enabling combinations of both approaches and tunable and configurable capabilities that will give users the possibility to use databases in the way that best suits their needs.

As explained in "NoSQL vs. Relational Databases," the process of convergence between relational and NoSQL databases is already on the stage. The result of this process will be the development of the next generation of databases with new features. Taking into consideration current solutions and the announcements related to new database releases, the main feature of the next database generation should be configurability. Rather than offering dozens of incompatible technologies that involve significant compromises, it would be better to offer a coherent database architecture that offers as configurable behaviors the features that best meet application requirements (Harrison, 2015).

The success of the convergence process will be crucial for enabling database configurability. Figure 1 presents the trends that are focused on the processes of convergence related to database consistency, schema usage, and SQL—that is, database languages.

Tables 1 and 2 described the two-way process of convergence: from relational to NoSQL and vice versa, from NoSQL to relational. Figure 1 shows three of what may be the most visible areas of convergence.

Figure 1. Convergence between relational and NoSQL databases

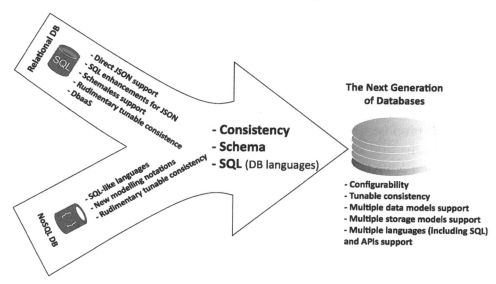

- **Consistency:** As explained in Table 1, relational databases are still committed to strict consistency, even for distributed transactions. However, there are some signs of change, as some vendors offer the possibilities of running transactions under various conditions, including ACID (IBM's CICS). The changes are visible on the sides of NoSQL databases that primarily offer eventual consistency. Today, most also offer strict consistency, at least at the level of the single-object transaction. Some NoSQL databases, like MongoDB and Cassandra, offer a tunable consistency model that allows the administrator or developer to choose a level of consistency based on application requirements. This approach is something that other database vendors, especially relational, should take into consideration. Namely, the main reason for "giving up" strict consistency lies in need of distributed databases to survive network partitioning. Although implementing multi-row transactions within an eventually consistent, network partition-tolerant database is a significant engineering challenge (Harrison, 2015, p. 195), the potential benefits are worth such effort.
- **Schema:** Giving up data modeling in the process of NoSQL database development proved to be very dangerous in the long run. NoSQL databases emerged as support for Web applications, and in that context, they proved to be successful. But the weaknesses of NoSQL databases

came to light in the context of support for business intelligence applications. The business user requirements related to data analysis through BI tools showed that the need for a comprehensible and unambiguous data model that can be used for business intelligence is even more important in the world of Big Data than it was in the relational era (Harrison, 2015, p. 197). It is not strange that each day, there are more advocates of data modeling in the NoSQL world, where some propose new modeling notations for presenting everything from the real-world objects and concepts to a functional database running either a NoSQL or SQL database (see Chapter 3). Table 1 shows that both relational and NoSQL databases offer support for JSON, meaning that hybrid solutions, in the context of the schema, are already at that stage.

- **SQL (Database Languages):** As Table 2 presented, most NoSQL databases already have some kind of SQL-like languages such as HQL, CQL, N1QL, and Cypher. It is clear that most NoSQL vendors recognized the necessity to provide support for SQL in order to attract more experienced developers and users to enhance usability and programmer efficiency and to provide easier integration with business intelligence and analytic tools. This trend of SQL adoption in the NoSQL world proved that the term *NoSQL* is unfortunate because of it, at first glance, implies a complete rejection of the SQL language. As explained in Chapter 2, it is generally accepted today that "No" stands for "not only" and that it emphasizes that NoSQL databases emerged with the aim to overcome the technical limitations of relational databases rather than to abandon SQL. According to Harrison (2015, p. 198), "the emerging challenge to unify databases is not so much to provide SQL access to nonrelational systems as to allow non-SQL access to relational systems," because SQL is not an ideal language for all problems (e.g., graph traversal operations). Relational database vendors are already working to resolve such issues. Oracle developed Big Data SQL (see Chapter 5)—data virtualization that makes it possible to search nonrelational data stored in different Big Data storages like Apache Hive, HDFS, Oracle NoSQL Database, Apache HBase, and other NoSQL databases. It enables unified query for distributed data as well as the possibility to view and analyze data from disparate data stores in a way as if all were stored in the Oracle database. Microsoft offers PolyBase to access data stores in

HDFS, Hadoop, or Azure Blob Storage and combines the results with relational data stored in SQL Server (see Chapter 5), while IBM offers Cloudant (DBaaS) for handling a broad range of data types like JSON, full text, and geospatial (see Chapter 5).

Figure 1 shows the results of the explained convergences in consistency, schema, and database language (SQL) and the possible characteristics of the next database management system, as follows (Harrison, 2015):

- Configurability,
- Tunable consistency,
- Multiple data models support,
- Multiple storage models support,
- Multiple languages (including SQL) and APIs support.

Configurability should be one of the most powerful features of the next database management system because, within single DBMS, it should be possible to support different application requirements through pluggable features or configuration options.

Tunable consistency refers to the capability of DBMS to allow administrators and/or developers to choose different levels of consistency, from strict (ACID) to weak.

In an ideal case, the next database architecture should support multiple data models, both relational and nonrelational. With new data modeling notations like COMN at our disposal, data modeling should be the most important part of database development again.

Multiple storage models support refers to the capability of DBMS to allows different physical data storage, row or columnar oriented, in order to efficiently support data distribution and high availability.

SQL should remain the primary database access language for most developers and users, but the next database management system should ensure support for some specific requests related to graphs, document-style queries, MapReduce processing, or other DAG algorithms (Harrison, 2015).

The described features of the next database management systems are the result of the analysis of existing relational and NoSQL database capabilities presented in previous chapters of this book and analysis of different predictions related to emerging technologies that could be dominant in the next few years.

But this does not mean that some new disruptive technologies will not arise in the very near future and expose databases to new challenges. However, what is known is that the next databases must offer full support for different business user requirements and enable organizations to use databases as tools for empowering their employees with better data insights, and consequently, better decision making at all organizational levels.

REFERENCES

Beal, V. (2014). *Cloud computing explained.* Retrieved February 17, 2017 from http://www.webopedia.com/quick_ref/cloud_computing.asp

Ferguson, S. (2017). *Big data, analytics market to hit $203 billion in 2020.* Retrieved February 17, 2017 from http://www.informationweek.com/bigdata/bigdataanalyticsmarkettohit$203 billionin2020/d/did/1327092

Gartner. (2017). *IT glossary: Dark data.* Retrieved February 17, 2017 from http://www.gartner.com/it-glossary/dark-data/

Gutierrez, D. (2016). *Big data industry predictions for 2017.* Retrieved February 17, 2017 from http://insidebigdata.com/2016/12/21/bigdataindustrypredictions2017/

Harrison, G. (2015). *Next generation databases: NoSQL, NewSQL, and big data. Apress.* doi:10.1007/978-1-4842-1329-2

Heudecker, N., Feinberg, D., Adrian, M., Palanca, T., & Greenwald, R. (2016). *Magic quadrant for operational database management systems.* Retrieved February 17, 2017 from https://www.gartner.com/doc/reprints?id=1-3JD7HF0&ct=161005&st=sb

IBM BC. (2017). *Understand the fundamentals of IBM Blockchain.* Retrieved February 17, 2017 from https://www.ibm.com/blockchain/what-is-blockchain.html

Intelligence, A. (2017). In *Merriam-Webster.* Retrieved February 16, 2017 from https://www.merriam-webster.com/dictionary/artificial%20intelligence

Jones, N. (2016). *Top 10 IoT technologies for 2017 and 2018.* Retrieved February 16, 2017 from http://www.gartner.com/newsroom/id/3221818

Marr, B. (2016). *17 predictions about the future of big data everyone should read*. Retrieved February 17, 2017 from https://www.forbes.com/sites/bern ardmarr/2016/03/15/17predictionsaboutthe futureofbigdataeveryoneshould read/#524f24a41a32

Mayo, M. (2017). *Big data: Main developments in 2016 and key trends in 2017*. Retrieved February 17, 2017 from http://www.kdnuggets.com/2016/12/ bigdatamaindevelopments2016keytrends2017.html

PredictiveAnalytics. (2017). *What is predictive analytics?*. Retrieved February 17, 2017 from http://www.predictiveanalyticstoday.com/what-is-predictive-analytics/

Press, G. (2016). *2017 predictions for AI, big data, IoT, cybersecurity, and jobs from senior tech executives*. Retrieved February 17, 2017 from https:// www.forbes.com/sites/gilpress/2016/12/12/2017predictionsforaibigdataiotc ybersecurityandjo bsfromseniortechexecutives/print/

Richards, J. (2015). *Advantages and disadvantages of NoSQL databases – What you should know*. Retrieved March 1, 2017 from http://www. hadoop360.datasciencecentral.com/blog/advantages-and-disadvantages-of-nosql-databases-what-you-should-k

Shacklett, M. (2016). *6 big data trends to watch in 2017*. Retrieved February 17, 2017 from http://www.techrepublic.com/article/6bigdatatrendstowatch in2017/

Smith, T. (2016). *10 big data trends for 2017*. Retrieved February 17, 2017 from https://dzone.com/articles/10bigdatatrendsfor2017

Tableu. (2016). *Top ten big data trends for 2017*. Retrieved February 17, 2017 from https://www.tableau.com/sites/default/files/media/Whitepapers/ whitepaper_top_10_big_data_trends_2017.pdf

Tapscott, D., & Tapscott, A. (2015). *SXSW preview: What's the next generation internet? Surprise: It's all about the Blockchain!*. Retrieved March 3, 2017 from http://dontapscott.com/2015/03/sxsw-preview-whats-the-next-generation-internet-surprise-its-all-about-the-blockchain/

Techopedia. (2017). *Database as a service (DBaaS)*. Retrieved February 17, 2017 from https://www.techopedia.com/definition/29431/database-as-a-service-dbaas

TechTarget. (2017). *Internet of things (IoT)*. Retrieved February 16, 2017 from http://internetofthingsagenda.techtarget.com/definition/Internet-of-Things-IoT

van Rijmenam, M. (2016). *The top 7 big data trends for 2017*. Retrieved February 17, 2017 from https://datafloq.com/read/the-top-7-big-data-trends-for-2017/2493

Glossary

ACID Transactions: ACID is acronym for the main properties of the relational database transaction: atomicity, consistency, isolation, and durability, with emphasis on strict consistency of transaction.

Ambari: A web-based tool for provisioning, managing, and monitoring Apache Hadoop clusters.

Artificial Intelligence: A branch of computer science dealing with the simulation of intelligent behavior in computers worthy of the development of many of core technologies, including neural networks, machine learning, natural language processing, intelligent agents, and the like.

Avro: A data serialization system which provides operation with rich data structures (binary data format; JSON format, a container file to store persistent data; remote procedure call) and simple integration with dynamic languages.

BASE Approach: BASE is acronym for basically-available, soft state, eventually consistent properties of NoSQL database transactions, with emphasis on eventual consistency of transaction.

Big Data: A phenomenon explained by 6Vs (volume, velocity, variety, veracity, variability and visibility) of data, or through its purpose to gain hindsight (metadata patterns from historical data), insight (a deep understanding of issues or problems), and foresight (more accurate predictions in the near future) in a cost-effective manner.

Big Table: A nonrelational database system using the GFS for storage.

Blockchain: A shared, immutable ledger for recording the history of transactions, open and programmable technology that enables distribution of digital information, not copying, and creating the backbone of a new type of Internet.

BQL: Acronym for Bridge Query Language, an integration system that translates SQL queries into vendor specific native API NoSQL requests.

BSON: Acronym for binary JavaScript Object Notation that is a binary-encoded serialization of JSON-like documents, which supports the embedding of documents and arrays within other documents and arrays.

CAP Theorem: It states that any networked shared-data system can have at most two of three desirable properties: consistency (C), high availability (A) and tolerance to network partitions (P).

Cassandra: A column-family, a scalable multi-master store without specialized master nodes.

Causal Consistency: Type of consistency where a read operation may not return the most recent value but will not return an out of sequence value either.

Chukwa: A data collection system for managing large distributed systems, built on top of the HDFS and MapReduce framework.

Cloud: A type of Internet-based computing, where different services, including servers, storage, and applications, are delivered to an organization through the Internet._

Cluster: A collection of commodity components to provide scalability and availability at a low cost.

Column-Family: A type of NoSQL databases that are column-oriented, i.e., with data stored in columns.

COMN: Acronym for concept and object modeling notation that is designed to enable data modeling in both relational and NoSQL databases. It enables integration of real objects, data, and implementation, and allows operations and functions, from user requests to logical models, to functional databases, to be represented in a single model, regardless of whether it is executed in a relational or NoSQL database management system.

DAG: Acronym for directed acyclic graph, which is a directed graph that contains no cycles, i.e., it is related to modelling situations in which, in some sense, going forward is sometimes possible but going backward is definitely not.

Dark Data: The information assets organizations collect, process, and store during regular business activities but generally fail to use for other purposes such as analytics, business relationships, and direct monetizing.

DBaaS: Acronym for database as a service that is a cloud-computing service model that provides users with some form of access to a database without the need for setting up physical hardware, installing software, or configuring for performance because the service provider is responsible for and takes care of the administrative tasks and maintenance.

Distributed Database: A logically interrelated collection of shared data and their description, physically distributed over a computer network.

Document Store: A type of NoSQL databases designed to store and manage documents encoded in standard data exchange formats (XML, JSON, BSON).

DQE: Acronym for distributed query engine as a platform to execute SQL queries on NoSQL databases, while keeping their data-model scalability and flexibility.

Eventual Consistency: Type of consistency where the system may be inconsistent at any point in time, but all individual operations will eventually be consistently applied, i.e. if all updates are stopped, then the system will reach a consistent state.

GFS: Acronym for Google File System, a distributed cluster file system allowing all disks within the Google data center to be accessed as one massive, distributed, redundant file system.

Graph Store: A type of NoSQL databases that excel at dealing with highly interconnected data focusing on relationships, rather than data.

Hadoop: An open-source software framework for storing data and running applications on clusters of commodity hardware and standard solution for storage and processing huge amounts of unstructured data.

HBase: A column-family store, which uses Hadoop HDFS in order to support structured data storage for large tables.

HDFS: Acronym for Hadoop Distributed File System that is the primary storage system used by Hadoop applications.

High Availability: Refers to a system or component that is continuously operational for a desirably long length of time.

Hive: An open-source and SQL-based language used on Hadoop, often called SQL for Hadoop.

Horizontal Scalability: The ability to increase capacity by connecting multiple hardware or software entities so that they work as a single logical unit.

Hybrid Solution: Introduction of an additional layer, which provides SQL communication between the business layer and the data layer.

IoT: Acronym for Internet of Things, a system of interrelated computing devices, mechanical and digital machines, objects, animals, or people that are provided with unique identifiers and the ability to transfer data over a network without requiring human-to-human or human-to-computer interaction.

JSON: Acronym for JavaScript Object Notation that is a minimal, readable format for structuring data, primarily used to transmit data between a server and web application.

Key-Value: A type of NoSQL databases that uses a key to locate a value (traditional data, BLOBs – Binary Large OBjects, files) in simple, standalone tables, known as hash tables.

Mahout: A scalable machine learning and data mining library for Hadoop.

MapReduce: A distributed processing framework for parallelizing algorithms across large numbers of potentially unreliable servers and capable of dealing with massive datasets.

Mixed Reality: The merging of the virtual and real worlds by using special devices.

Monotonic Consistency: Type of consistency where a session will never see a piece of data reverted to an earlier point in time, that is, once a data is read, it is not possible to see an earlier value of the data.

N1QL: Acronym for non-first normal form query language that is query language developed for querying the JSON data in Couchbase store.

Native Solution: The use of standard drivers and ways in which the business layer communicates with a particular database.

NoAM: Acronym for NoSQL Abstract Model that define unique data presentation model independent of NoSQL vendor respecting principles of scalability, consistency, and performance.

NoSQL Database: Nonrelational, distributed, open-source, and horizontal scalable data stores.

Pig: A part of the Hadoop ecosystem providing execution framework for parallel computation and support for the procedural, high-level data flow language Pig Latin.

Predictive Analytics: A branch of advanced analytics used to make predictions about unknown future events by using many techniques, including statistics, data mining, modeling, and machine learning.

RDF: Acronym for Resource Description Format, a general framework for how to describe any Internet resource such as a Web site and its content.

Relational Database: A collection of data organized as a set of formally-described tables from which data can be accessed or reassembled in many different ways without having to reorganize the database tables; based on three pillars: relational model, ACID transactions, and SQL language.

Relational Model: Database model based on two-dimensional tables, called relations, a row of a table called tuple, a column header called an attribute, and a domain, which is a set of possible values that can appear in each column.

Schemaless: One of the main NoSQL features, meaning that there is no need to define database structure to store and manage data.

Sharding: Partitioning the data across multiple databases based on a key attribute.

SOS Platform: Acronym for Save Our Systems, which is a programming environment where non-relational databases can be uniformly defined, queried and accessed by an application program.

Spark: An in-memory, distributed, fault-tolerant, fast, and general compute engine for Hadoop data.

Strict Consistency: Type of consistency where a read operation always returns the most up-to-date value of data.

SQL: Acronym for SQL Structured Query Language, the standard language for relational database management systems.

Tez: A generalized data flow programming framework, built on Hadoop YARN, which provides a powerful and flexible engine to execute an arbitrary DAG of tasks to process data for both batch and interactive use-cases.

UDM: Acronym for Unified Data Modeling, techniques that support features like document schema of NoSQL databases, reverse engineering of data from an existing database, and visual refactoring of existing databases.

URIs: Acronym for Uniform Resource Identifiers, explicit identifiers for each node that does not need to point at any actual website or web page, but must be globally consistent throughout the web.

W3C: Acronym for World Wide Web Consortium, an international community where member organizations, a full-time staff, and the public work together to develop web standards.

Weak Consistency: Type of consistency where the system does not make any guarantee that it will ever become consistent – namely, if a server fails, then an update may be lost.

YARN: Acronym for yet another resource negotiator, a framework for job scheduling and cluster resource management.

ZooKeeper: A high-performance coordination service for distributed applications, which provides coordination and synchronization of services within a cluster.

Index

Recommended Reference Books

ISBN: 978-1-4666-9834-5
© 2016; 314 pp.
List Price: $195

ISBN: 978-1-4666-9770-6
© 2016; 485 pp.
List Price: $200

ISBN: 978-1-4666-6539-2
© 2015; 2,388 pp.
List Price: $2,435

ISBN: 978-1-4666-9466-8
© 2016; 2,418 pp.
List Price: $2,300

ISBN: 978-1-4666-9572-6
© 2016; 854 pp.
List Price: $465

ISBN: 978-1-5225-0058-2
© 2016; 1,015 pp.
List Price: $465

Stay Current on the Latest Emerging Research Developments

Become an IGI Global Reviewer for Authored Book Projects

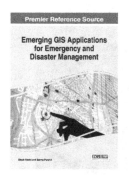

Premier Reference Source

Emerging GIS Applications for Emergency and Disaster Management

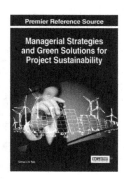

Premier Reference Source

Managerial Strategies and Green Solutions for Project Sustainability

Premier Reference Source

Comparative Approaches to Using R and Python for Statistical Data Analysis

Premier Reference Source

Solutions for High-Touch Communications in a High-Tech World

The overall success of an authored book project is dependent on quality and timely reviews.

In this competitive age of scholarly publishing, constructive and timely feedback significantly decreases the turnaround time of manuscripts from submission to acceptance, allowing the publication and discovery of progressive research at a much more expeditious rate. Several IGI Global authored book projects are currently seeking highly qualified experts in the field to fill vacancies on their respective editorial review boards:

Applications may be sent to:
development@igi-global.com

Applicants must have a doctorate (or an equivalent degree) as well as publishing and reviewing experience. Reviewers are asked to write reviews in a timely, collegial, and constructive manner. All reviewers will begin their role on an ad-hoc basis for a period of one year, and upon successful completion of this term can be considered for full editorial review board status, with the potential for a subsequent promotion to Associate Editor.

If you have a colleague that may be interested in this opportunity, we encourage you to share this information with them.

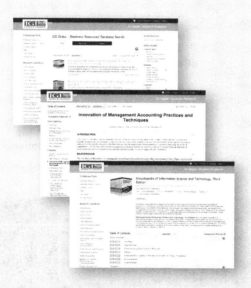

Printed in the United States
By Bookmasters